Deliver First Class Web Sites:
101 Essential Checklists

S81 S21 S23

the last date stamped below.

Deliver First Class Web Sites: 101 Essential Checklists

by Shirley Kaiser

Copyright © 2006 SitePoint Pty. Ltd.

Technical Reviewer: Ian Lloyd   **Editor**: Georgina Laidlaw
Managing Editor: Simon Mackie   **Index Editor**: Nigel d'Auvergne
Technical Editor: Priya Singh   **Cover Design**: Jess Bentley
Technical Director: Kevin Yank   **Cover Layout**: Alex Walker
Printing History:
   First Edition: July 2006

Published by SitePoint Pty. Ltd.

424 Smith Street Collingwood
VIC Australia 3066.
Web: www.sitepoint.com
Email: business@sitepoint.com

ISBN 0-9758419-0-4
Printed and bound in the United States of America

About the Author

Shirley Kaiser created SKDesigns[1] in 1996 to focus on creating visually appealing web sites that are based on web standards and universal accessibility, and are optimized for speed and search engines. You'll find her designs featured as best practice examples in major publications and textbooks, such as *JavaScript + CSS + DOM Magic*[2] and *The Complete Guide to Using and Understanding the Internet*.[3] Shirley also helps to promote web standards as a Web Standards Project (WaSP) Steering Committee member.

In addition to authoring this book, Shirley is a contributing author to *Creating Web Pages with HTML and Dynamic HTML*. She's also written dozens of articles and tutorials for WebReference.com, Digital Web Magazine, WebsiteTips.com, and her weblog, Brainstorms & Raves.[4]

Aside from her web work, Shirley is a professional musician with Bachelor of Arts (B.A.) and Master of Arts (M.A.) degrees in Piano Performance. She's also a devoted mom who cherishes time with friends, spoils her dogs, and enjoys photography, reading, movies, growing flowers, and cooking and eating tasty food all over the world.

Shirley lives in central California's Sacramento area (Carmichael) with her family, not far from where she grew up.

About the Expert Reviewer

Ian Lloyd is a web designer and developer who believes passionately in the importance of web standards. He is a member of the Web Standards Project[5] and has spoken at several high profile web conferences, including South By Southwest in Austin, Texas and @Media in London.

Unlike many of his peers, Ian does not run his own company but remains a "salary man", working for Nationwide Building Society in the UK (where he constantly harps on about web standards, accessibility and usability to anyone with a sympathetic ear!).

Ian lives in Swindon, UK, a town that is known only for two things: the famous "magic roundabout"—a mega roundabout that comprises five individual but joined roundabouts, and for being that place off television show *The Office* (thus making it second in dullness only to Slough). That said, Ian does his best to get out of Swindon in his treasured air-cooled VW Camper van[6] when he's not glued to the laptop for one reason or another.

---

[1] http://skdesigns.com/
[2] Makiko Itoh, *JavaScript + CSS + DOM Magic* (Indianapolis, New Riders Press, May, 2002).
[3] Linda Bird, *The Complete Guide to Using and Understanding the Internet* (Englewood Cliffs, NJ: Prentice-Hall, 2004).
[4] http://brainstormsandraves.com/
[5] http://webstandards.org/
[6] http://vwkombi.com/

Ian is married to Manda who really doesn't get all this techy stuff—or, for that matter, the Volkswagen fascination—but puts up with it regardless.

About the Technical Director

As Technical Director for SitePoint, Kevin Yank oversees all of its technical publications—books, articles, newsletters, and blogs. He has written over 50 articles for SitePoint, but is best known for his book, *Build Your Own Database Driven Website Using PHP & MySQL*. Kevin lives in Melbourne, Australia, and enjoys performing improvised comedy theatre and flying light aircraft.

About SitePoint

SitePoint specializes in publishing fun, practical, and easy-to-understand content for web professionals. Visit http://www.sitepoint.com/ to access our books, newsletters, articles, and community forums.

To my son Chris and my
daughter Heidi, who are truly
and forever my sunshine.

Table of Contents

Preface

There are literally thousands of books, and millions of articles and tutorials, covering just about every aspect of creating web sites. So, why write another book? Why write this particular book? And why should you buy it?

I've been in the business of designing, developing, and maintaining web sites for an entire decade now. While I've seen plenty of well planned, well executed, and wonderfully maintained web sites and web projects, I've also seen or fixed the problems that result when people ignore, skip, or aren't even aware of important issues, best-practice approaches, or critical steps in the web site development process.

In addition, I've known incredibly talented programmers who can practically program in their sleep, but, for instance, don't know much about the appropriate use of color to help the visually impaired use web sites. I've met plenty of amazingly talented designers who don't know much about best practice approaches to CSS, or how to optimize a web site for search engines. There is indeed a lot to know about creating and maintaining truly effective, efficient, successful web sites that are easy to maintain.

So, as I planned this book, I thought about how helpful it would be to have a single source of solid information on best practices for everything from planning, designing, developing, and testing, to launching a web site and maintaining it in the long term. By compiling all this information into checklists, we've turned a vast wealth of detail into convenient, easy-to-scan, simple-to-use chunks organized by topic. Using the checklists in this book will help you to make sure that you cover all the bases for every web site project you undertake. And, while the checklists draw on my ten years of experience creating and maintaining web sites and managing web projects, I also reference plenty of experts. The references included here are also fabulous resources for learning more about particular topics.

How should you use these checklists? I consider them guidelines, not definite requirements set in stone. At the same time, each individual checklist item is included in this book for a good reason. If you understand a particular checklist item's purpose, you'll be able to make an educated decision about whether or not to include it for a specific web project. To help with that, you'll find reasonably detailed explanations for nearly all of the individual checklists, along with helpful references and real-world examples.

Who Should Read this Book?

This book is ideal for anyone who's responsible for delivering high-quality web sites. If you're a web developer, designer, or project manager, by using these checklists you can be assured that you've delivered a site that follows accepted best practices and is of the highest standards. If you're responsible for commissioning or specifying a web site, you can use these checklists as a basis for your specification, and to ensure that the web site is right the first time. No detailed technical knowledge is assumed or required to use the checklists contained in this book.

What's in this Book?

This book contains 16 chapters that are designed to parallel your progress through a web project's development, launch, and subsequent ongoing maintenance. As such, you can apply any of these chapters as they relate to the work you have at hand, and jump around between chapters and checklists as you need to. On the other hand, for an overall view of the process—perhaps in developing your first site, or first commercial site—the procedural, chapter-by-chapter approach might be the best path to take.

Chapter 1: Let's Get Started ... but How?

So, you're going to develop a web site? Great! ... But where do you begin? This chapter explains the key starting points for any web project, beginning with a checklist to help you start project planning. We also consider a checklist to help you complete valuable research so that you can make educated decisions, and outline the key considerations as you begin to develop a web site style guide. Finally, we provide a checklist of tips to help you work with others in the project team.

Chapter 2: What to Find Out: Initial Questions to Answer

In this chapter, we look at the site- and client-specific questions you'll need to answer as you begin the project. The first checklist will help you define the site's target audiences; the second will help you determine the site's objectives among those users. Next, we look in depth at the budgetary considerations of the project, with checklists that will help you ascertain the costs of hosting, marketing, expert advice, ecommerce, hardware and software, and more.

Chapter 3: Preparing Web Site Content

Sometimes, content can be the most overwhelming aspect of a web project, but this chapter aims to make the job easy! We kick off with a basic checklist for gathering and itemizing content, which should put you in good stead to complete a full content inventory a little later on. We then address the questions of providing accessible web content, before reviewing checklists that will help you prepare web copy and images for use within the site.

Chapter 4: Managing all the Content

This chapter begins with a checklist that explains how to undertake a full content inventory as part of a content assessment. Once you've done so, you'll be able to assess your content management needs, and compare content editing and management tools on a range of important points, using the detailed checklists provided.

Chapter 5: Web Site Usability: Focusing on the User

In focusing on the user, our first step in Chapter 5 is to create a user-friendly index page. From there, we expand our view with checklists designed to ensure that the site focuses on users. These checklists will help you ensure that the site's pages load quickly; that the site caters to users with a range of abilities, disabilities, and access devices; that the site's creators follow established conventions and best practices; and that the site presents user-friendly error messages to visitors.

Chapter 6: Color

It may sound extreme, but the colors you choose can make or break a web site! Before you can really begin to work with color, you need to set up your work area and computer so that colors are displayed accurately—the topic of the first checklist in this chapter. Next, we discuss checklists that will help you choose an effective, attractive, and usable color scheme for the site, and see how we can use color to enhance the site's functionality and readability.

Chapter 7: Information Architecture

This chapter introduces the basic concepts behind information architecture before providing checklists that will guide you in improving the findability of content on your site. Next, we take a close look at the common organization schemes and structures, before exploring in detail the considerations involved in planning the architecture of key page types and directories. The final checklists in this chapter provide advice on creating user- and search engine-friendly URLs for all the files on your site.

Chapter 8: Navigation

Navigation is a critical element of your site's design, so this chapter looks at the topic at its most basic—the Golden Rules of navigation—before delving into the various levels of navigation. Checklists in this chapter explain the details of creating usable and functional global, sectional, in-page, and supplemental navigation systems. We also discuss the intricacies of providing useful site indexes and search tools in separate, highly focused checklists.

Chapter 9: Best Coding Practice: W3C Standards and Recommendations

The separation of content from presentation is an accepted best practice, and key among the foundations on which this chapter is based. The detailed checklists here will help you to create HTML, XHTML, and CSS markup that is standards-compliant, bug-free, and that functions successfully—or degrades gracefully—on as many browsers and alternative devices as possible.

Chapter 10: Creating Accessible Web Sites

Having explored the bare bones of creating an accessible site—including markup and navigation accessibility considerations—first up in this chapter, we move on to look at the ways in which color, images, multimedia files, forms, and tables can be used to enhance—or destroy—a user's experience of your web site. The tips and advice provided in these checklists will help you to hone your site so that most users (if not all!) are able to access the information it contains easily and without hassle.

Chapter 11: Web Site Optimization

Optimizing your web site starts at code level, which is why this chapter's first checklists explore the ways in which you can clean up your markup: by minimizing URLs and optimizing CSS and JavaScript. Later checklists explain the optimization of image, multimedia, and alternative file formats.

Chapter 12: Search Engine Optimization

After a quick primer on SEO success, this chapter jumps straight into checklists that will help you work with keywords and phrases, make your site search engine-friendly, and avoid offending, or being blacklisted by, search engines. Substantial checklists are provided to help you streamline your efforts to list the site in search engines, and create ongoing links and SEO maintenance campaigns that will see your search rankings rise, rather than decline over time.

Chapter 13: Design

Whole books can—and have—been written on web design, but this chapter aims to encapsulate the key considerations in a series of checklists that begin with basic principles. We then move on to explore the specifics of working with typography, discuss brainstorming techniques, and address that most challenging of tasks: finalizing the site's design!

Chapter 14: Testing

The Getting Started checklist in this chapter will help you establish your site's testing requirements and protocols, and identify the hardware and software that will be needed during the testing phase. After a quick review of the constituents of good testing practice, the chapter steps through checklists that explain general testing procedures, as well as guidelines for accessibility and usability testing. By the chapter's end, you'll have the know-how and confidence to complete the tests and ensure that your site is ready to launch!

Chapter 15: Preparing for Launch

These checklists will prove invaluable to you time and time again. Pre-launch can be a stressful time, and the checklists in this chapter have been designed to take the pressure off and let you focus on the bigger issues in those final days before the site is launched to the world. Final checks, including templates, markup, layouts, content, functionality, and server-side requirements are covered, before we discuss the processes of soft launch, launch, and site handover.

Chapter 16: Post-launch Follow-up

A post-launch review is a great way to ensure that the site launch has been completed, the client is happy, and the project team has learned all they can from the process. Checklists are provided to help you conduct the review and complete those niggling post-launch tasks before you tackle the bigger jobs—orienting new staff to the site, and promoting the site—for which detailed checklists are also provided. Finally, this chapter breaks down the responsibilities involved in managing and completing ongoing maintenance tasks into a series of checklists that will help save your sanity in the months to come!

Appendix A: Ecommerce Checklists

This appendix, provided specially for those working with ecommerce projects, contains two compact but valuable additional checklists. The first will help you to assess your needs for ecommerce content usage and management, while the second highlights the kinds of features you should seek in an ecommerce package. Together, these checklists should help you to assess the various tools on the market and choose those that will meet the specific needs of the project you have at hand.

This Book's Web Site

Located at http://www.sitepoint.com/books/checklists1/, the web site supporting this book will give you access to the following facilities.

Updates and Errata

The Corrections and Typos page on the book's web site, at http://www.sitepoint.com/books/checklists1/errata.php, will always have the latest information about known typographical and code errors, and necessary updates for changes to technologies.

The SitePoint Forums

While I've made every attempt to anticipate any questions you may have, and to answer them in this book, there is no way that any book could cover everything there is to know. If you have a question about anything in this book, the best place to go for a quick answer is http://www.sitepoint.com/forums/—SitePoint's vibrant and knowledgeable community.

The SitePoint Newsletters

In addition to books like this one, SitePoint offers free email newsletters. The *SitePoint Tech Times* covers the latest news, product releases, trends, tips, and techniques for all technical aspects of web development. The long-running *SitePoint Tribune* is a biweekly digest of the business and moneymaking aspects of the Web. Whether you're a freelance developer looking for tips to score that dream contract, or a marketing major striving to keep abreast of changes to the major search engines, this is the newsletter for you. The *SitePoint Design View* is a monthly compilation of the best in web design. From new CSS layout methods to subtle Photoshop techniques, SitePoint's chief designer shares his years of experience in its pages. Browse the archives or sign up to any of SitePoint's free newsletters at http://www.sitepoint.com/newsletter/.

Your Feedback

If you can't find your answer through the forums, or you wish to contact me for any other reason, the best place to write is books@sitepoint.com. We have a well-manned email support system set up to track your inquiries, and if our support staff is unable to answer your question, they send it straight to me. Suggestions for improvement as well as notices of any mistakes you may find are especially welcome.

Acknowledgements

I wish to thank everyone at SitePoint for making this book possible, especially Priya Singh, the technical editor, and Georgina Laidlaw. Special thanks go to Simon Mackie, my tireless, incredibly helpful, and exceptionally kind editor, who was always full of encouragement and provided invaluable insight throughout this entire process. I agreed to write this book because Simon would be my editor.

In addition, big thanks go to Ian Lloyd, my expert reviewer, who packed his helpful advice with humor that made me laugh throughout the comments he made on every single chapter.

Thanks also to Dan Thies and Jill Whalen for so kindly taking the time to answer my SEO questions for the checklists on SEO.

I also appreciate all the support and understanding I received from my family and friends throughout this book's development, especially my daughter, Heidi. I couldn't have written this book without Heidi taking care of so much for me while I lost myself to writing at my computer.

Lastly, I couldn't have written this book without my two cocker spaniels nudging me to take a break and go play when I needed it the most, and keeping me company during all those long hours of writing when everyone else was sound asleep.

Let's Get Started ... but How?

Perhaps you've thought about building your dream home—the spacious rooms with spectacular views from every window, the colorful flowers in the garden, and the dinner parties you'll throw for your friends. You might have a folder with photos of homes that inspire you, and brochures on cabinets and floor treatments stashed away for future reference. Maybe you've even sketched out a few floor plans when the urge has struck you in the middle of the night.

On the other hand, maybe you've never really given your home much thought, but now it's time to build. Perhaps you don't know where or how to start, or even what questions to ask.

Building a new web site, or revamping an existing one, is not unlike working on that dream home, in that in both projects, careful planning is essential. When you plan well, you'll save time, money, and undoubtedly avoid many sleepless nights. This chapter will provide helpful checklists to get your web site project off to a good start—they'll help you plan your site, and prepare for the creation of a web site style guide.

Planning to Stay on Schedule and Within Budget

While I can not promise the same for your dream home, it *is* possible to launch a web site on schedule and stick to your budget without losing sleep or suffering excessive stress. The secret is to spend some time planning the project carefully right from the start. Establish a realistic schedule, then follow it through by including all the specific details and tasks in your plan. Before you can plan your site, though, you need to know how to plan effectively so that you can optimize the time and budget you have available.

Effective Pre-planning

If you look closely at professional, successful web sites that serve their users well, such as Amazon.com, you'll find that the details of these sites' offerings, functionality, audiences, and so on have been considered and addressed, and that the sites work flawlessly. In fact, Amazon.com works so well that visitors don't even think about it. Instead, they're free to focus on the reason why they're there in the first place—to shop for products or research a potential purchase before they buy.

Making time to undertake effective planning, ensuring rock-solid organization, and providing continuous attention to detail are vital steps if you're to create and maintain a successful web site that allows visitors to focus on the real reason for their visit, rather than petty frustrations over the workings of your site.

Deciding how to go about your web project is the first step towards its effective planning. The following checklist outlines the steps you will need to take to get started.

Checklist 1.1

☑ **Choose a focus, and keep it simple.**

The team behind the web site project may have a multitude of terrific ideas about content, features, and functionality that should be included on the site. But the truth is that the site will be far more effective if you select a single focus and achieve it well. Choosing a focus will also help you to identify bottom-line profitability goals for your web site, and to set priorities accordingly.

Keeping your energies focused on a single goal can help you to achieve short- and long-term goals. For example, if you were producing a Teacher's Aid web site, a short-term goal may be to launch the site by June 1, in order to sell teaching aids online as teachers prepare for the next school year. Your long-term goals for the site may include the development and publication of helpful online articles as a public service to teachers, while promoting your business and expanding your product lines.

Delegate decision-making tasks.

I can still see my mom shooing us out of the kitchen, emphatically telling us, "Too many cooks spoil the broth." She always had a smile on her face, but she also didn't want us children turning the heat up or down, or adding ingredients to her cooking without her permission. It was her kitchen, after all, and she was the final decision-maker in that environment.

Just as too many cooks can ruin dinner, too many decision-makers can spoil a web site project. Let me tell you a couple of true stories about my clients, and you'll see what I mean.

One of my recent clients had three decision-makers trying to manage a small web application project. They each had drastically different ideas about the visual appearance and navigational functions for the graphic design of their new web application. And, though one person was my main contact for the project, each decision-maker wanted me to create his or her respective and unique design concept, which stifled my role as their designer. The result of this approach was that the project costs increased by almost 10%, and the job took more than a week longer to complete than we'd originally planned.

Too Many Cooks...

The lesson here is that having too many top-level decision-makers involved in a web project can cause that project to go over-budget, miss important deadlines, result in blurred job roles, and frustrate project staff.

In contrast, another client of mine—a large textbook publisher—has a highly efficient decision-making approach that I've always admired. One project team member is responsible for web site-related decisions. She communicates well with the team, getting helpful feedback and keeping team members informed of the site's progress. She and I communicate frequently and work closely together as I design and develop the web site.

We always get her company's projects completed on time or ahead of schedule, and we stay within budget. Over the years, I've worked with several of this publisher's web site project team members, all of whom have had similar approaches to managing the site's evolution. Together, we've completed dozens of successful web site and CD-ROM projects.

Delight in Delegation

Delegating responsibilities and decision-making power can help to keep projects on schedule and within budget, and is often a positive experience that boosts staff morale. Make the most of the opportunity to delegate where you can!

☑ Plan ahead.

Do your best to forecast your requirements for additional help, skills, or technologies that you might need as the site grows. You can save money in the long run if you eliminate costly redesigns and the need to rework certain parts of the site, so planning for growth is important.

Let's consider our house-building analogy again. If your initial house design allows for the future addition of extra rooms, you'll build the house's foundations and framing accordingly, ensuring that you have plenty of space—and the structural capabilities—to add rooms later. This approach is far less costly and more efficient than building the house without foresight, moving the entire house to new property, and tearing out parts of the existing house to accommodate the new rooms.

In the online world, forward thinking might lead you to build your site using technologies like Cascading Style Sheets (CSS), which allow you to change the look of an entire site with comparatively little hassle, or server-side includes, which can help ease the maintenance burden of the more commonly used sections of your site. See Chapter 9 and Chapter 11 for information about these particular techniques.

You should allow for growth and changes within the site's design from the very beginning. After all, one of the many exciting benefits of a well-planned web site is that it makes the tasks of updating content, making changes, and expanding online communications easy.

Imagine, for example, that you start a floristry web site with plans to sell flowers online. Then, around Valentine's Day, you decide to sell stuffed toys too, and at Christmas you want to expand this offering to include gifts and hampers. Later still, you may decide to specialize in balloon bouquets and party planning. If you haven't designed your site to allow for this kind of growth, including these extra categories and subcategories will become frustratingly difficult. If the expansion is executed inefficiently, the additional content could dramatically increase your site's load times, or even stop it from working correctly.

As you can see, while you may not have a clear idea about where your site will be in one or two years' time, it's important to realize that *it will change over time*. As such, you should plan the site with future expansion in mind, selecting a design approach, development technologies, and other tools and methodologies that will allow you to expand as easily as possible when the time comes.

Just about any site element or content item can require alterations over time, but here are some of the pages and elements that tend to change and grow the most:

- ❑ homepage content

- ❑ section navigation, internal page navigation

- ❑ new articles, press releases, newsletters

- ❑ new sections

- ❑ new or updated products and services

- ❑ pages that contain user comments

- ❑ advertising

While, at first, you might want to generate revenue by publishing advertisements on your web site, you may also receive inquiries from companies who want to advertise their products or services through your site. When that time comes, the job of including ads will be much easier if you've planned for it right from the start.

☑ **Allow plenty of time to plan and develop your new web site.**

Begin planning as soon as possible to ensure that you meet—or even beat—the site launch deadline.

Doing your Homework and Making Educated Decisions

Knowledge is power! Gaining a solid understanding of the Web and how sites succeed will allow you to make well-informed decisions about creating and maintaining one of your own. Web-related technology frequently changes and improves, so allow yourself time to stay up to date, so you can keep your web site at its best.

Checklist 1.2

☑ **Learn about and understand the common types of web site features and content.**

If you need a jump-start, see Chapter 3.

☑ **Read case studies about how businesses that are different from, and similar to, your own have created their sites.**

Case studies can provide valuable insights and tips about goal setting, focus, problems and solutions, usability issues, market analysis, and other related details of the web site creation and management processes. They may also include candid comments about mistakes that were made, their consequences, and the steps the companies in question took to resolve them. You can develop a better web site by learning from these real-world examples.

Two excellent online web site case studies[1] are Gerry Gaffney and Phillip Pagendarm's *Website Redesign—a Case Study*,[2] and *Website Case Study*, by Royal Borough of Windsor and Maidenhead.[3]

☑ **Visit other web sites.**

Visiting and researching other web sites can provide tremendous insight as you plan your own. Compile a list of the sites you visit, and make plenty of detailed notes—in conjunction with your browser's bookmarks—for future reference.

---

[1] See also Kelly Braun, et al., *Usability: The Site Speaks for Itself* (Berkeley: Apress, 2003); Malmsten, Ernst, et al., *Boo Hoo: A Dot Com Story* London: Random House Business Books, 2002).
[2] http://www.infodesign.com.au/usabilityresources/general/redesigncasestudy.asp
[3] http://www.windsor.gov.uk/education/case_study.htm

What should you make notes about? Good question! Pay special attention to what those other sites offer, how they're organized, how the navigation is laid out, and whether or not you find it easy to use. Take note of what works and what doesn't, functionality-wise, how colors and graphics impact your impression of the sites, which features are intuitive, and which design elements are easy to use. Be sure also to note the problem areas of the sites you visit, including details of why you found these aspects or functions problematic.

Take note of the types of content provided on the sites—do they have About Us pages, contact information, newsletters, articles, help or FAQ areas, legal information, and sitemaps? In addition to these points, identify the pieces of information that you find to be important or helpful, and those that are pointless or irrelevant. Chapter 3 contains more about the different types of content and web page elements you might want to keep in mind as you visit other web sites.

☑ **Compile a list of competitors' web sites that you'll visit regularly.**

You must check out the competition! In addition to researching their web sites, as we mentioned above, take time to find out what your competitors are doing, and plan to revisit their web sites regularly to stay up to date. If a competitor's site content is changed or updated frequently, consider taking screenshots of the pages—it's a great way to build up an invaluable virtual scrapbook of ideas.

☑ **Research the kinds of skills that will be needed to develop your web site.**

Listed below are some of the skills that are typically needed during the creation and maintenance of web sites. As you review this list, make a note of the skills that you have available now, as well as the skills that you'll need to source for your particular web project. You may need to allow for training costs, subcontracting costs, or both, within your project budget, so this is an important step!

HTML, XHTML, CSS
These markup skills are basic prerequisites for people who create web pages.

programming languages such as PHP, ASP, and Perl

database administration, using technologies such as SQL, MySQL, Oracle

graphic design
> Graphic designers need to be proficient with graphics programs such as Adobe Photoshop and Illustrator, and Macromedia Freehand.

photography

copywriting

editing

content management systems experience
> For those managing a large web site with a significant amount of content, some experience with implementing and maintaining a content management system is really important. Less critical is the knowledge of updating content, which is, or should be, the easy part! See Chapter 4 for checklists on content management.

project management

☑ **Research potential web site costs.**

Ask web site-savvy business associates and colleagues what they consider reasonable pricing for various elements of a web site project. Ask them for pointers to resources that they like or use themselves. You'll find especially helpful the feedback of a person whose web site has similar features and needs, and is a comparable size to your own.

Prices can be deceiving, so check out the details of any quote you receive. While some lower-cost services are quite good, others may end up costing you more in the long run. They may generate web site errors, generate periods of downtime, or deliver low quality work that doesn't support the professional image your business is aiming to project. On the other hand, don't assume that higher-cost services will always be the best. It's best not to make any assumptions at all. I recommend that you perform some research on the companies that you'll consider working with, and make sure that, as part of that research, you solicit recommendations from people and companies that you trust.

Keep notes about the typical prices for the services you've researched, and what services those prices include. We'll use these in the section on budgeting in Chapter 2.

☑ **Seek advice from others who have experience with web projects.**

Ask business associates and others you trust about their experiences, helpful tips, recommendations, and suggestions for working through a web site project.

☑ **Learn about current best practices and standards.**

By adhering to recommended best practices and standards, you can ensure that your web site functions more effectively, loads more quickly, and works in a multitude of browsers and alternative devices. You'll provide a better user experience, and you can save time and money in the process! Web site-related technology continually changes and improves, so make sure your site stays current. Avoid implementing technology that is too new to have been thoroughly time-tested. It's far better to use established, solid technologies that have proven track records. Not only should you be able to count these packages, but they're also likely to continually be updated and improved upon.

You've also come to the right place by reading this book—the ensuing chapters are devoted to best practices and standards. For a few specifics, though, see Chapter 5, Chapter 9, Chapter 10, and Chapter 11.

Developing a Web Site Style Guide

A web site style guide documents concise, helpful, and important instructions for the creation and maintenance of a web site and its content. It's important to keep the style guide well organized and to strike a balance between including too much detail, and skimping on specifics in the interests of keeping your style guide concise. The document must provide enough information to allow its users to maintain consistency across the site's communications elements, adhere to any legal requirements that affect the site, and ensure that the organization's branding efforts follow established conventions.

You might consider summarizing the style guide into a single-page reference that highlights the document's most important points and provides directions that allow users to find the specific details, templates, images, and other elements that will help them apply the style guide's advice on a daily basis.

This checklist identifies the key issues to keep in mind as you develop and maintain your web site style guide.

☑ **Provide and promote consistency among all of the web site's elements and content.**

☑ **Include writing style guidelines and clear examples that show users how to maintain consistent written communications throughout the web site.**

You might consider using a current, popular style guide as a basis for your own styles. Consider *The Chicago Manual of Style*, the *Publication Manual of the American Psychological Association*, or the *Economist Style Guide*.[4] In your own style guide's section on writing styles, highlight the usage of styles that are specific to your web site, and any differences between your styles and those advocated by the style guide to which your communications should adhere.

☑ **Include instructions about content publication and permissions.**

For example, will web content need approval by a specific person prior to being published by the web editor?

☑ **Include specifications for the usage of graphics and multimedia.**

☑ **Include guidelines for, and examples of, the use of logos and other branding elements.**

To preserve a specific corporate image, many companies do not allow their logos to be altered in any way. Changing the logo's colors, rotating or animating it, or using it as a watermark, often constitutes prohibited usage. Your style guide should clearly state conditions for the acceptable use of logos and other branding elements. Include web color codes, the minimum and maximum dimensions each element must exhibit, and any other conditions that will help ensure that your logo and branding elements project your organization's image correctly.

---

[4] The University of Chicago, *The Chicago Manual of Style, Fifteenth Edition* (Chicago: The University of Chicago Press, 2003); American Psychological Association, *Publication Manual of the American Psychological Association, Fifth Edition* (Washington, DC: American Psychological Association, 2002); The Economist, *Economist Style Guide, Eighth Edition* (London: Economist Books, 2003).

☑ **Include instructions for meeting, and text that addresses, the company's legal policies.**

Does your site need to display copyright information and notices, disclaimers, web site terms of use, or a privacy policy? Seek the advice of an attorney in your country for standard legal policies and text that's appropriate for use on your web site.

In your web site style guide, include instructions about where on the site any legal information should be used, and the specific text that must be displayed. Web page footers typically contain abbreviated legal information, such as links to the terms of use, a privacy policy, and/or a basic copyright notice, like this:

```
Copyright © 1996–2007 SKDesigns. All rights reserved.
```

More on Web Site Legalities

Tip

To learn more about web site legal policies, including copyright information, see my article, *The Legal Side*[5], and the U.S. Copyright Office's *Frequently Asked Questions about Copyright*[6].

☑ **Provide templates for the site's key web pages, along with instructions for, and examples of, their usage.**

Include guidelines for the structure of the site's HTML, CSS, and standard page layouts. Also include guidelines for the naming of web pages, files and directories, and protocols for internal and external page links.

In Chapter 2 we'll help you get started pulling together the information you'll include in your site style guide.

Learning from Others

Tip

For helpful insight as you create your web site style guide, it can be a good idea to review other web site style guides, noting which sections you find helpful, and which information is not helpful (make sure your own style guide doesn't include the latter information).

---

[5] http://websitetips.com/legal/
[6] http://www.copyright.gov/help/faq/

Check out the highly regarded *Web Style Guide: Basic Design Principles for Creating Web Sites*, Second Edition (Italy: Grafische SIZ, 2002) by Patrick Lynch and Sarah Horton for a helpful example of a good web site style guide. To find examples of web site style guides online, run a search on "web site style guide" or "Web site style guide" (using the surrounding quotes).

Managing Like Magic: Effective Organization

Whether you're planning to create a web site by yourself, or with a team of people, effectively organizing your project can help you stay on schedule and within budget so effortlessly that you'll begin to wonder whether you could start a sideline business as a magician!

The successful organization of a web site project depends on your breaking down the "big picture" into smaller parts, delegating tasks, and estimating the time that will be needed for each individual task. Here's a checklist to help you do exactly that.

Checklist 1.4

Break down your web site project into its major phases.

The major phases of a web site project usually include:

1. initial planning

2. content planning

3. design and development planning

4. implementation

5. after the launch

Within each major phase, create smaller, more manageable steps.

You can use this book's Table of Contents as a guide to identify the smaller steps involved in your web site project.

Prepare and follow a task list based on the above task breakdowns.

Once you've broken your project into smaller steps, you can create a task list that identifies what needs to be done, when, and by whom.

☑ Create a realistic schedule.

This may seem obvious, but the time required to complete the various stages of a web development project is often underestimated. So, as I mentioned above, when you're estimating the time a task might require, be sure to include a reasonable buffer—maybe even doubling or tripling the time you think you'll need.

Try to allow for the unexpected, such as unplanned appointments, software or computer glitches, and illness, and be sure to include time for unavoidable interruptions, including public holidays and so on. Set deadlines that reflect target dates for the completion of major and minor milestones. Many of us may have love-hate relationships with deadlines, but it's important to remember that deadlines are essential to helping us deliver work on time.

Project management tools can be especially valuable to those managing the development of medium to large web sites—especially those that integrate scheduling with Gantt charts and other visual time-tracking tools. We'll detail some more of these tools in just a moment.

For smaller web site projects, you could use your calendar or create a timeline chart—you might set a goal to complete your new web site within two months, for example. Then, set smaller goals that mark the completion of each item on your web site development task list.

Consider launching your new web site in phases to meet the project's identified short- and long-term goals. For example, earlier in this chapter I mentioned the example of launching the ecommerce facility of a web site by June 1, to sell teacher-related products. This might be a short-term goal for the site. The site's long-term goals might include adding articles to the site following that launch.

☑ Plan to update web site content regularly to keep it fresh and current.

Once your new web site is launched, regularly allocate time to keep the content fresh and up to date. Schedule time for ongoing web site updates and content maintenance, which might include the following:

❑ publish product updates

❑ undertake customer service tasks

❏ conduct site maintenance and error-checking

❏ update, edit, and manage text content

❏ make graphics-related additions

❏ undertake periodic web site evaluations

❏ implement front- and back-end programming updates and changes

❏ advertising and marketing tasks

☑ **Consider using helpful project management tools.**

A few examples that you might consider include Basecamp, by 37Signals;[7] dotProject,[8] an open-source solution; GoalPro, by Success Studios;[9] Microsoft Office Project;[10] and MindMapper, by SimTech.[11]

Working Together as a Team

Checklist 1.5

☑ **Communicate clearly.**

The project manager and team members need to know and understand the project's progress, including which tasks are being completed, and by whom. Keep the project manager and team members informed by setting up regular, consistent communications, such as phone conferences, in-person meetings, email updates, private online chat groups, and private online forums.[12] Follow up meetings and discussions in writing, to keep everyone informed, and minimize misunderstandings. These reports provide a handy reference, and ensure that you have a detailed paper trail of the project's evolution.

---

[7] http://www.basecamphq.com/
[8] http://www.dotproject.net/
[9] http://www.goalpro.com/
[10] http://office.microsoft.com/home/office.aspx?assetid=FX01085795
[11] http://www.mindmapper.com/
[12] Online chat tools that you might consider using include AOL Instant Messenger [http://aim.com/] and Miranda Instant Messenger [http://www.miranda-im.org/]; For IRC Channels, consider mIRC [http://www.mirc.com/] and ChatZilla [http://www.mozilla.org/projects/rt-messaging/chatzilla/].

☑ **Keep one master plan and one master schedule.** Make sure these documents are always current, accurate, and accessible to all team members.

☑ **Be supportive.**

The project manager and team members need to act professionally, and be helpful toward each other and the project manager.

☑ **Be positive and dependable.**

☑ **Be diplomatic and sensitive to others involved in the project.**

☑ **Stay flexible.**

Tip **Creating a Great Team**

The best teams tend to have a good time together, network well, and communicate clearly. To establish positive bonds within the team, create opportunities for team members to work *and* play together.

Summary

Effective planning helps web site projects stay on schedule and within budget, which ultimately gives the site a better chance of success. This chapter provided checklists to help you to plan effectively, make educated decisions, and begin to develop a web site style guide that we'll expand in upcoming chapters.

In Chapter 2, we'll build on this chapter with checklists that will help you to identify a strong focus for your project, begin to organize a development plan for your web site, and start to create your web site style guide.

2 What to Find Out: Initial Questions to Answer

You may have a clear vision of your dream house in your head. But it can be very challenging to try to communicate that vision to the professionals who will make your dream a reality.

"What would you like?" the architect asks from behind his large, expensive desk.

"Six bedrooms," you reply enthusiastically. "Oh, and it has to look *amazing*."

Your vision for your web site may be even more vague. Perhaps you know that you want a web site that reflects your company culture or positioning, but you're not sure what you need, or what to ask. How, then, can you plan your web site?

The checklists in this chapter will help you establish your target audience, identify the initial goals you have for the site, and determine the project budget.

Establishing your Target Audience

Determining who will visit your web site is the key to understanding why you need a web site, and identifying what it should include. Your site will enjoy the greatest possible success if you create it with those visitors in mind. It's hardly worth going through the turmoil of planning, documenting, and creating a web site if nobody's interested in using it.

Who will Visit and Why?

☑ **Determine the types of external visitors who will visit your site.**

Visitors to an organization's public web site might include current clients or customers, potential clients or customers, members of professional organizations, competitors, students, and educators. Visitors to the company's intranet site could include employees, management team members, marketing staff, and so on. The audience for the company's extranet site could involve product distributors, suppliers, affiliate companies, and collaborative businesses.

☑ **Determine the range of abilities and disabilities your visitors are likely to have.**

☑ **Determine the levels of Internet experience your visitors are likely to have.**

☑ **Determine the reasons why each different type of user will visit your site.**

If you can determine why your visitors will want to visit your site, you should find it reasonably easy to identify your site's primary purpose and goals. So, consider each user type in turn, and ask yourself what they'll want from your web site. What do they hope to achieve? For instance, among a range of possibilities, they may seek:

❑ corporate information about your company

❑ information about the products and services your business offers

❑ the ability to purchase products

❑ the ability to share information

❑ the ability to interact with a community

❑ entertainment

How will they Visit?

Few of us ever have the luxury of creating an intranet web site for a controlled environment in which all users have identical computers and software! Your site users will almost certainly visit using different computer configurations. Your web site should be accessible to all of them.

Unless you already have a site, and access to its server logs, you may not be able to answer these questions very easily. However, having identified who your site's users will be, and why they'll visit the site, you may be able to draw some conclusions about the systems and devices they're likely to use. Be sure to use current research to back up your expectations!

Checklist 2.2

 Identify the different browsers and alternative devices that visitors may use.

Users may employ any of a multitude of versions of Internet Explorer, Netscape, Opera, Safari, and may also access the site via PDAs, cell phones, or WebTV. Additionally, visitors could use speech recognition software or voice browsers.

 Identify the different computer platforms that visitors may use.

Visitors may use any of several versions of Microsoft Windows, Apple Macintosh, and Linux.

Determine the range of Internet connection speeds over which users will access your site.

Identifying your Initial Goals

After you've determined who your visitors are, and why they're visiting your web site, you can determine your site's primary goals and requirements.

Checklist 2.3

Identify your site's primary goals and requirements.

For example, if you believe that visitors will seek information about your products and services with the intention of purchasing online, your primary purpose may be to sell products through the web site.

Here are some of the other goals you may identify for your site:

The site will promote your business and develop your brand.
Promoting a business is the most important purpose for a business web site.[1] An important aspect of promoting a business is developing brand recognition among your target audience. You don't need to be Nike or IBM to have a brand image—everything about your web site will portray an image and give visitors an impression. That is your brand.

Tip   Domain Names and Branding

Your domain name is an important element in the promotion of your business and the development of your brand. Use your business name for your domain name whenever possible. Why? Because users will expect to find your business when they type your company name into their browser's address bar. Users will also remember your URL more easily if it's the same as your business or organization name. You should try to keep domain names as short as possible, so, if you have a long business name, consider using a logically abbreviated domain name in addition to your full business name.

The site will be used to sell new or existing products.

The site will help you reduce printing costs or call center overhead.
For example, if your business currently takes product orders by phone and mail, you may aim to cut back on both printing costs and call center overhead by setting up an online store.

The site will generate new business.

The site will provide entertainment.

The site will constitute your company intranet.
For more on intranets and intranet security, see the Intranet Journal[2] and Intranet Roadmap[3] sites.

---

[1] See also the article *Make Your Website Purposes Crystal Clear* [http://www.wilsonweb.com/wmta/purpose-clear.htm], by Dr. Ralph F. Wilson.
[2] http://intranetjournal.com/
[3] http://intranetroadmap.com/

The site will be your company extranet.
For more on extranets, see iStart,[4] New Zealand's ebusiness portal extranet, and Microsoft's *Extranet Access Management*[5] article, from their Identity and Access Management Series.

Identifying your Budget

Determining a web site budget is no easy task. A number of factors must be considered, including domain name registration, web site hosting, hardware, content management, site maintenance, and marketing—to name just a few! Use the following checklists as a guide to help you prepare your web site budget.

Domain Name Costs

Checklist 2.4

☑ **Itemize and budget for all the domain names that will be registered each year.**

Register Now!

As we saw earlier in this chapter, your domain name is an important part of building online brand recognition. If you haven't registered your domain yet, do so as soon as possible to make sure that you secure your first choice of domain. You can register your domain name and put it on hold, or "park" it, until you're ready to use it. Many registrars will park the domain names you register through them for no charge.

☑ **Consider the costs associated with purchasing more than one domain name.**

Why would you purchase more than one domain name? Brand protection! You may find it beneficial to own multiple domain names for brand protection purposes, including several top level domains (or TLDs) such as .com and .biz, as well as the TLD for your country (e.g., .us for companies in the United States, .co.uk for organizations in the United Kingdom, and .ca for Canadian businesses). If your organization is multinational, purchase domain names for the TLD of each country in which you operate. Amazon.com, Inc., for example, uses amazon.de for its German store, and

---

[4] http://www.istart.co.nz/extranet.htm
[5] http://www.microsoft.com/technet/security/topics/identity/idmanage/P3Extran.mspx

amazon.fr for its French store. Even though registration costs can start to add up, multiple TLD registrations are far less costly than paying attorneys to prosecute people who infringe your brand name or try to squat on your domain.

Redirect domain name variants to your main domain name. Domain name registrars usually provide redirect services—often for no charge. For example, I've registered variants of several of my domain names, and redirected them to their corresponding .com TLDs. To see this in action, type **http://skdesigns.net/** into your browser's address bar. Your browser automatically redirects to http://skdesigns.com/.

Consider purchasing domains that reflect common alternative spellings of your domain name—especially if your business or organization name is misspelled frequently. You can then redirect the misspelled domain to your correct domain name, and ensure that all those users who intend to visit your site actually reach it.

☑ **Don't infringe on trademarked names.**

It's best to consult with an attorney on legal issues like trademarks. To learn more about domain names and trademarks, though, check out these *Frequently Asked Questions (and Answers) about Domain Names and Trademarks*,[6] from the Chilling Effects Clearinghouse.

Web Hosting

To work out your hosting budget, you must first consider the requirements for your web site. The checklist below will help you do exactly that! Once you've completed it, you can use the information to research the costs of dependable web hosting services, and compare those costs against the investment required to purchase, house, run, and maintain your own servers. This process will help you determine the most cost-effective and overall best choice for your web site's hosting. Remember to allow for the projected growth of your site!

Tip

How Much for Hosting?

To research web hosting costs and offerings through offline sources, check out Internet magazines that feature performance tables for Internet Service Providers (ISPs) and hosting solutions.

---

[6] http://www.chillingeffects.org/domain/faq.cgi

You can also use search engines to uncover problems with potential web hosts. For example, if you've earmarked a few companies for consideration, try searching on Google for "COMPANYNAME hosting terrible/awful" (replacing the negative adjective as appropriate), or "COMPANYNAME hosting bad service." Imagine the kinds of words *you* might use in a letter of complaint to find out whether or not others have had negative experiences with your potential web hosts. Remember to check Google groups, too, not just results from web searches. It's amazing what you can uncover this way—you may well save yourself some heartache in the long run.

Checklist 2.5

☑ Determine the bandwidth allowance you require.

You can save bandwidth by optimizing your web site. We'll discuss this process in detail in Chapter 11.

Anticipating Bandwidth Needs

There are a number of online tools that have been designed to help you estimate your web site's bandwidth needs. To find these tools, run a search for "web site bandwidth calculator."

☑ Determine how much disk space your site will require.

The Disk Space Dilemma

Like bandwidth, you'll find a wide range of disk space options available through standard web hosting plans. Smaller sites may only need 20MB–30MB of space, but it's a good idea to buy more space than you need, so that your site has room for growth. Larger web sites may need 250MB–500MB of disk space; possibly more than that. For example, a personal diary to which you add a couple of small, 500px by 200px, photos might consume around 20MB of disk space in a year. On the other hand, a site that showcased classic TV advertisements as video files might require a minimum 500MB for storage. Double that volume might be required in the first year as more video files are added. For more about file sizes and the selection and management of content, including images and multimedia, see Chapter 3 and Chapter 4.

☑ **Determine the quality of hosting service you'll receive.**

Web hosting is a highly competitive industry, which is to your benefit. You don't need to settle for anything less than 99.9% guaranteed uptime. Look for references to redundant high-speed (T1 or T3) connections, frequent backups, backup generators that kick in if the host's electricity goes out, and off-site backup servers.

Check with the Better Business Bureau, or similar independent companies that monitor businesses, for positive feedback or complaints about the hosts you're considering. Look through the client lists of your potential web hosts, and contact a few of those client organizations to solicit their feedback about the service, uptime, and facilities they've received from the host in question. I've found that most people are glad to respond to these enquiries, at least with a short comment or two.

☑ **Determine the level of hosting support you'll need.**

Budget for 24-hour, seven-day telephone support.

☑ **Determine the training you'll need to support your web hosting arrangements.**

Budget for server hardware and software training and additional staff, if applicable. Include these costs if you're planning to purchase and maintain your own servers.

Identify your Server Needs

Checklist 2.6

☑ **Determine your needs for CGI use and access privileges.**

CGI (Common Gateway Interface) is nearly always a necessity for server-side programming. A CGI program, for example, might take data from an online form and place it into an email message, or turn the data into a database query.

☑ **Determine your needs for server-side scripting technologies such as PHP, ASP.NET, and others.**

For more on PHP, Perl, ASP, Cold Fusion, .NET, and other server-side technologies, see the official PHP site;[7] Perl.com, the Source for Perl;[8] and SitePoint's content on Server Side Coding, Server Side Essentials.[9]

☑ **Determine your needs for server-side includes (SSI).**

For more on SSI, see my Server-Side Includes (SSI) resource list.[10]

☑ **Determine your needs for a secure server (one that uses SSL).**

If you need to accept online payments or handle sensitive information, you'll need SSL to encrypt information that passes between the server and the visitor's web browser.

☑ **Determine you email requirements.**

Consider whether you'll need mailboxes, email forwarders, and email auto-responders. Web-based email access is a handy feature that allows staff to access their email via a web browser from any location—at home, at work, or on the road.

Branding and Marketing

Checklist 2.7

☑ **Consider using professional logo design services.**

Do you have a logo? Your logo is possibly the most visible and important part of your branding, so if you haven't had professional training in logo design, seriously consider hiring a professional. Get recommendations, review logo designers' portfolios and prices, and plan to work with your marketing expert to develop a logo that will best exemplify your organization's image.

---

[7] http://php.net/
[8] http://perl.com/
[9] http://www.sitepoint.com/subcat/server-side/
[10] http://websitetips.com/ssi/

If your business is brand new, you have a perfect opportunity to create a logo that's optimized for use online, and not restricted by existing branding requirements.

Tip 💡 Prepare your Logo Early

It's important to have your logo complete before the initial design work begins, as your web site's design—its colors, typography, style, and overall look and feel—will need to work closely with your logo.

☑ **Include costs for purchasing fonts, typography, and symbols, along with other branding-related expenses.**

Do you have existing letterhead, business cards, brochures, other print materials, press releases, or advertising? Your web site needs to maintain consistency with your other branding materials, including font and typographic treatments, the style used for bullets, arrows, and dividers, your writing style, use of white space, and more.

Perhaps you've decided to develop a new brand image that you'll launch with your new web site. As you do so, keep in mind all your business or organizational materials, and your marketing needs, and aim to creating consistent new materials that meet your communications requirements not just online, but through all media.

☑ **Factor in the cost of paid search directory and search engine submissions.**

You no longer need to submit your web site to multiple search engines. As long as your site has incoming links, search engine spiders will find it. That said, it's still important that you optimize your content for search engines. We'll address that particular topic in detail in Chapter 12, but also in Chapter 8, where we discuss the creation of search-engine friendly navigation systems.

It's still important to submit to search directories such as the dmoz Open Directory Project,[11] Looksmart[12] (for paid listings), and Yahoo![13] (free and paid listings).

---

[11] http://dmoz.org/add.html
[12] http://listings.looksmart.com/
[13] http://search.yahoo.com/info/submit.html

If you'd rather pay an expert to handle search directory and search engine submissions, or you'd like to handle these yourself after consulting with an expert, allow for these possibilities in your budget.

For more on search engines and directories, see Jennifer Laycock's Search Engine Guide,[14] Danny Sullivan's Search Engine Watch,[15] and Jill Whalen's High Rankings.[16]

☑ **Budget for online marketing expenses.**

Google AdWords[17] is highly recommended as a starting point for online advertising. Also, research independent web sites as sources of potential advertising opportunities, targeting industry-specific web sites for optimal results.

Hire an online marketing specialist to consult with you about marketing your web site generally, or to work with you to create a successful specific marketing, advertising, or viral campaign for the site. Be prepared to shop around, because you'll likely see some wild claims made by various consultants. Be sure to ask for recommendations from your colleagues and friends.

For more information on online advertising, see: avant|marketer,[18] Bruce Clay's Search Engine Promotion Tactics,[19] and Entrepreneur.com's Online Advertising Strategies for Small Business article index.[20]

☑ **Budget for offline advertising and promotions.**

Offline promotions can include many elements, such as distributing press releases; writing articles for industry magazines; newspapers, television, and radio advertising; yellow pages and other business directory advertisements; and direct mail. Other avenues that you might explore include print brochures, regular client newsletters, and the distribution of branded merchandise.

---

[14] http://www.searchengineguide.com/
[15] http://searchenginewatch.com/
[16] http://highrankings.com/
[17] http://adwords.google.com/
[18] http://www.avantmarketer.com/
[19] http://www.bruceclay.com/web_pt.htm
[20] http://www.entrepreneur.com/Your_Business/YB_Node/0,4507,469,00.html

Tip

Publish your URL

Include your web site URL and your email address on letterhead, business cards, brochures, and any other offline promotional materials.

☑ Include costs for training staff members in marketing, advertising, search engine strategies, and related branding and marketing tasks for your web site.

Bringing in the Experts

It may be to your web site's benefit to hire an expert or two for specific tasks: to help develop marketing copy, improve search engine optimization efforts, or to assist in some other expert capacity. This checklist identifies the different experts whose fees you might like to anticipate in your initial site budget.

Checklist 2.8

☑ **Include costs for a publicity agent or marketing specialist.**

You may decide to hire a publicity agent, marketing firm, or marketing expert to help you promote your new site.

☑ **Budget for the commissioning of content creators and editors.**

Your written content—which is integral to your branding—needs to be consistent with all your other promotional materials. Also, especially in the case of your site's homepage, or communications that sell products and services, expertise in writing compelling sales copy can make a huge difference to your bottom line.

If you'd like to learn more about writing marketing copy yourself, check out copywriting experts' web sites for plenty of articles, ideas, and books. In particular, see the sites of Nick Usborne[21] and Gerry McGovern.[22]

☑ **Include costs for an SEO (search engine optimization) copy expert.**

You might use an SEO copy expert to optimize a few key web pages on your site, including your homepage. If you'd like to tackle this task yourself, though, see Chapter 3 and Chapter 12.

---

[21] http://nickusborne.com/
[22] http://gerrymcgovern.com/

☑ Include the costs of employing and training staff who are involved with the web site's ongoing maintenance.

How Much is a Picture Worth?

☑ **Budget to pay licensing fees for the online use of royalty-free stock images and image collections.**

Royalty-free stock image collections to consider for use on your web site include Hemera Photo Objects[23] and Getty Images CDs.[24]

☑ **Include the costs of hiring professional photographers.**

☑ **Include costs for the creation and/or use of illustrations and other custom imagery.**

☑ **Include in your budget the costs of purchasing or hiring the hardware and software necessary to take photos, and scan and prepare images.**

☑ **Ensure your budget includes the necessary training costs for the creation of photography and graphics, and the processing of images for your web site.**

Tip 💡

Quality Counts!

As we'll see in Chapter 3, high quality images can help to give your site a more professional appearance, and boost its credibility. You don't need to spend a fortune, though. Unless you plan to use the photos or images in print communications, which require images of a higher resolution than is needed on the Web, you can save money by purchasing web-use, 72dpi imagery, rather than buying higher resolution, 300dpi, print-use images. A number of free or almost free professional-looking image resources are available on the Web, including iStockPhoto[25] and Free Stock Photos.[26]

---

[23] http://hemera.com/
[24] http://gettyimages.com/
[25] http://istockphoto.com/
[26] http://freestockphotos.com/

You can also cut costs by taking the photos yourself, or handing your good camera to the budding photographer among your staff.

Ecommerce

☑ **Include merchant account and related fees, or the fees charged by merchant account alternatives.**

Possible alternatives include PayPal,[27] and Kagi.[28]

☑ **Factor in the cost of secure server (SSL) facilities.**

☑ **Budget to purchase and run a shopping cart program.**

☑ **Include custom programming costs.**

☑ **Budget for product shipping, fulfillment, and related expenses.**

☑ **Include the cost of training staff to manage all aspects of your site's ecommerce capabilities, as needed.**

Computer Software and Hardware

☑ **Include the cost of purchasing hardware and software needed to write and edit content.**

To write text content for your site, you'll likely use a word processing program that's feature-rich and can assist with spell checking, grammar, and much more. Don't make the mistake of using something like Microsoft Word to convert the content into HTML pages, though! Use the specialist tools available for this purpose.

---

[27] http://paypal.com/
[28] http://kagi.com/

☑ **Factor into your budget the costs of web design and programming software.**

Again, it's possible to create your site using a plain text editor; however, dedicated markup editing software can speed up the work tremendously, in addition to helping designers and developers to catch errors and potential problems, which can reduce your overall development time. A few software tools you might consider include Bradsoft TopStyle,[29] Macromedia's HomeSite and Dreamweaver,[30] and Westciv's Layout Master and Style Master products.[31]

☑ **Budget to purchase software with which to create and manipulate graphics and photos.**

You'll need digital imaging software to create, edit, and optimize images and photos for your web site, as well as to create the initial web page designs and layouts. A few examples that you might consider are Adobe Photoshop, Photoshop Elements, and Illustrator,[32] Macromedia Fireworks,[33] and Corel Paint Shop Pro.[34]

☑ **Anticipate the costs of upgrading existing hardware and purchasing new hardware, such as high quality monitors, additional memory, and so on.**

☑ **If you don't already have one, budget to buy a digital camera (two megapixels or more), and purchase related training, software, and so on.**

☑ **If you don't already have one, include the cost of purchasing a scanner.**

---

[29] http://topstyle.com/
[30] http://macromedia.com/
[31] http://westciv.com/
[32] http://www.adobe.com/
[33] http://www.macromedia.com/
[34] http://www.corel.com/

Budget to buy a fax machine.

Your computer's fax capabilities may be sufficient. If not, though, allow for a fax machine, or possibly a combination fax/scanner/copier, in your project budget.

Include the costs of hardware and software required to work with media such as audio and video.

Include training costs in your budget as needed.

Summary

At the beginning of this chapter, you had no idea where to start your web site project. This chapter built on Chapter 1 by providing checklists to help you define your web site's target audience, and establish your site's primary goals. There was also a comprehensive checklist that outlined the various elements that can impact on your web site's budget, including web hosting, server requirements, and any external expert advice you may need. Consider and research each of these costs as you prepare your project budget—doing your homework now will save you a lot of heartache (and headaches!) down the track.

3

Preparing Web Site Content

You now have some idea of what you want from your web site. The next step is to get your content together and organize it for easy access. This is no simple task—especially if you're working on a large web site project—but it will make your life easier when the time comes to drop in, manage, and maintain the site's content.

The checklists in this chapter will help you prepare and organize your web site's content, as we look at everything from itemizing your content, to preparing copy and images for use on your web site.

Gathering and Itemizing Content

 Use physical file folders to organize print materials and notes.

 Save digital content to organized folders on your computer, or to a drive that's accessible to relevant project team members.

Save electronic versions of existing web site content to organized folders.

Tip

A Complete Content Inventory

As you itemize the content that's available, make helpful notes about its possible use on the web site. Create a chart or form, like the one in Table 3.1, into which you can write pertinent details for each existing content item. Include the following information, among any other details that are relevant to your specific project:

❑ the content item's title

❑ the item's filename and location

❑ the type and format of the content

❑ the item's file size, including dimensions for images

❑ the item's owners and authors

❑ the date on which the item was created, or last modified, or both

❑ the item's incoming and outgoing links, if applicable

❑ notes or comments that pertain to the item

The Link ID shown in the first column is a unique identification system that you'll create as you grow your inventory. If you're using a spreadsheet program such as Microsoft Excel, your link ID structure should be set up to allow you to add new content items in any location without messing up your numbering system.[1]

---

[1] For more on link IDs, see Janice Crotty Fraser's article, *Content Inventory & Information Architecture* [http://www.eruditiononline.com/04.04/content_inventory.htm], and Jeffrey Veen's *Doing a Content Inventory (Or, A Mind-Numbingly Detailed Odyssey through Your Web Site)* [http://www.adaptivepath.com/publications/essays/archives/000040.php].

Table 3.1. A sample web site inventory

ID	Name	Link URL	Subject	Type
1.0.1	About Us	/about/	Marketing	Paragraphs
1.2.1	Services	/services/	Marketing	Paragraphs
1.2.2	Design	/services/design/	Marketing	Paragraphs
1.2.3	Graphics	/services/graphics/	Marketing	Paragraphs
1.3.1	Contact	/contact/	Marketing	Form
1.4.1	FAQ	/faq/	Marketing	List items, descriptions
1.4.2	FAQ: Planning Your Design	/faq/plan/	Marketing	Paragraphs, list items, descriptions

☑ **Itemize common page elements and detail their content.**

Common web page elements are those that appear on every page—or nearly every page—of your site. Your logo, web site navigation, web site search, and copyright notice are all examples of common page elements.

☑ **Itemize each web page and detail the content it requires.**

Determine and itemize the content you'll need for each web page on your site. For example, your About Us page may contain an overview of your business and photos of key staff members. Your Contact Us page might contain the details of your business's office locations and opening hours, along with a contact form, phone and fax numbers, and an interactive map. Your Products page would likely contain product codes, descriptions, and images.

Providing Accessible Content

So, you've inventoried a bunch of existing content, and probably thrown in a bit of new content as well. How do you go about including all of this content on your web site in a way that makes it as accessible as possible to your users? Use the following checklist as a guide, though keep in mind that accessibility will be addressed in detail in Chapter 10.

☑ **Provide thorough, current information.**

☑ **Provide helpful links to other web sites and resources.**

☑ **Provide an accessible contact link.**

Create a link to your contact information from every page of your site. Provide several different ways for people to contact you—your email address, phone number, postal mail details, and fax number, for example—wherever the information is appropriate, including the About Us or Contact Us pages, and support pages. Where possible, consider noting a timeframe in which users can expect a response to their queries.

☑ **Provide helpful shopping information.**

If you're building a shopping site, provide helpful, accurate shipping and handling information, details of your returns policy, and other terms of business. Make sure this information is very easy to find. Perhaps include it in the product shopping subnavigation that appears on every product page—not just at the point of the sale's completion.

☑ **Provide an informative privacy policy.**

Your web site's privacy policy needs to explain clearly how your web site handles sensitive data, cookies, and related information. Make sure you adhere strictly to your policy.

☑ **Use plugins and alternative content formats judiciously.**

Use plugins and alternative formats sparingly as you strive to provide the most user-friendly, accessible web site you can. Use Macromedia Director and Flash, QuickTime, Adobe Acrobat, Real Media, Windows Media, and other file formats such as Microsoft Word and Microsoft PowerPoint with great discretion, and only where they're appropriate.

Preparing Web Copy

Your existing content may be stored in a variety of formats, such as Word, HTML, QuarkXPress, FrameMaker, Adobe Acrobat, or plain text documents, or in a database or content management system. You may also need to scan print materials to prepare them for use on your site.

Writing for the Web is different from writing for print, primarily because people don't read online—they scan the content.[2] As such, the content you publish on your web site needs to be more scannable than it would for a print publication, and you may need to revise or possibly rewrite your existing text to suit the medium.

Use the checklist below to help you write or edit your text, and prepare it as simply and as cleanly as possible for use online.

Checklist 3.3

- ☑ **Write concise sentences.**

- ☑ **Keep paragraphs short.**

- ☑ **Use subheadings to break up content.**

- ☑ **Use list formatting when possible.**

- ☑ **Provide a summary or overview of key points for longer articles before providing the details.**

- ☑ **Avoid using all capitals for titles.**

- ☑ **Provide clear, concise calls to action.**

- ☑ **Keep layout and formatting to a minimum.**

  Plain text (`.txt` format) is preferred for preparing your text content for inclusion into web documents. Written content is more flexible and easier to work with when it involves minimal formatting.

---

[2] For more on writing for the Web, see Jakob Nielsen's article, *How Users Read on the Web* [http://www.useit.com/alertbox/9710a.html], John Morkes's and Jakob Nielsen's *How to Write for the Web* [http://www.useit.com/papers/webwriting/writing.html], and Gerry McGovern's article *Writing for the Web* [http://www.gerrymcgovern.com/la/writing_for_web.pdf].

☑ **Avoid converting text content to HTML using word processing software.**

I haven't seen any satisfactory conversions of text to HTML through a word processor. Conversions from word processors typically end up requiring extra work, as the developer or designer must strip out the sea of extraneous markup created by the word processor behind the scenes. Also, these markup-bloated pages unnecessarily increase page load time, and, as a result, your bandwidth and web hosting fees.

 Tip

Tidy Up your HTML

If you inherit already-converted HTML content, you might decide use helpful HTML-stripping software, such as HTML Stripper or WebToData.[3] While utilities like HTML Tidy[4] will clean up HTML, it's generally faster and easier to strip out the HTML and start afresh. Remember to make and store backup copies of the original files before you strip the HTML from them.

☑ **Minimize the use of alternative formats for text content.**

To keep your web site user-friendly and widely accessible, reserve Adobe Acrobat (`.pdf`), Microsoft Word (`.doc`), Microsoft PowerPoint (`.ppt`), and other alternative formats for downloadable supplementary materials—don't use them for primary web content. If you're using an alternative format, utilize the file format's accessibility features to achieve optimal accessibility and deliver the most user-friendly content to your site visitors. Remember, you're providing the information for their use: make sure they can get to it!

Preparing Images

Checklist 3.4

☑ **Select high quality images to support your site's credibility.**

Studies show that high quality images increase site credibility,[5] and I think you'll agree that high quality images present a more professional appear-

---

[3] http://www.gltsoft.com/
[4] http://tidy.sourceforge.net/
[5] See B.J. Fogg's report,*Stanford-Makovsky Web Credibility Study 2002: Investigating what makes web sites credible today* [http://captology.stanford.edu/pdf/Stanford-MakovskyWebCredStudy2002-prelim.pdf].

ance. We've all been to web sites that display images with jagged edges, photos that aren't clear and sharp, graphics with inaccurate colors, and images that simply appear to have been degraded somehow—images like the one shown in Figure 3.1. We've also been to web sites whose images are clean and crisp, with smooth edges and gorgeous colors, like the one in Figure 3.2. Think about the impression you get from web sites with those very different image qualities.

Figure 3.1. A low-quality web graphic

Figure 3.2. A high-quality web graphic

Website Design

☑ Use photos that are in focus, are sharp, and exhibit good color contrast.

☑ Respect and obtain proper web-use licensing for the use of any images that you don't own.

☑ Select non-lossy formats for original images.

To maintain the high quality of imagery, non-lossy formats such as TIFF and PSD are usually a designer's first choice for original photographic images. For logos and other illustrations, vector-based formats, such as AI or EPS files, are preferred.

☑ Select illustrations, clipart, and other images that are sharp and have good color contrast.

☑ **Crop images, if required, to target their most important aspects.**

Cropping can also reduce image file size, improving page load time and reducing bandwidth.

☑ **Remove or diminish busy backgrounds, if required, to target the image's important aspects.**

☑ **Prepare thumbnail images for larger images.**

If, for example, your web site contains a photo gallery, you should prepare thumbnail images for use within the gallery. Displaying the larger images would increase the page's download time and your bandwidth usage. If, instead, you provide small thumbnails of these larger images, your visitors will be able to get an idea of what the photographs are (without having to wait ages for the page to display!) and, if they want to view a full-sized image, they can do so by clicking on its thumbnail.

☑ **Use appropriate, widely supported image file formats.**[6]

GIF is a lossless format that limits color usage to a maximum of 256 colors. The GIF format tends to work better with images that contain large blocks of a color, incorporate type, and/or need a transparent background. GIF format can work quite well with photos, clipart, and other images if these parameters are kept in mind.

An example of a transparent GIF image that contains solid color blocks and type is shown in Figure 3.3. As you can see, the transparent part of the image at the top is represented by a checkerboard pattern. When placed on a web page, as shown in the second image, the white background of the web page shows through.

---

[6] For more on choosing image formats, see Jason Cook's *Site Optimization Tutorial* [http://hotwired.lycos.com/webmonkey/98/26/index0a_page4.html?tw=design], and Wayne Fulton's article, *Image File Formats—which to use?* [http://www.scantips.com/basics09.html].

Figure 3.3. An image with a background that's 100% transparent

Services

Services

PNG, a lossless format, is widely supported by all modern browsers. Although modern browsers offer alpha transparency support, Internet Explorer 6 does not support PNG alpha transparency.[7] For this reason, I encourage you to use GIF for images that use transparency levels of 100%, and use PNG as much as possible otherwise.

 Tip

Try 4-UP

In recent versions of Photoshop/ImageReady, you can use the Photoshop/ImageReady four-pane, 4-UP viewer to compare optimized versions of file formats side by side in the same window, which makes it very easy to check the files' sizes and image quality. You can make adjustments to optimize your images, and compare the levels of quality and the file sizes as you work. The, choose whichever format is the best for that particular image—be it PNG, GIF, or JPG—and save the image. It's quick and easy!

---

[7] For more on the PNG format, see the W3C's document on the topic, at http://www.w3.org/Graphics/PNG/, and Gregg Roelofs's article, *Portable Network Graphics: An Open, Extensible Image Format with Lossless Compression* [http://www.libpng.org/pub/png/].

JPG format is a lossy format that usually is better suited than GIF for use with photos, though there are exceptions to this rule of thumb. To avoid blurring and image quality loss, carefully reduce the number of colors in the image as much as possible. If you're careful, you should be able to decrease the file's size for use online without incurring any noticeable quality loss. Notice the striking difference in the clarity of the images shown in Figure 3.4 and Figure 3.5. The image example in Figure 3.4 displays noticeable artifacts that blur the image; however, the example in Figure 3.5 remains clear, clean, and crisp with no artifacts.

Figure 3.4. Reducing image size with noticeable image quality loss

☑ **Resize images using a graphics program.**[8]

If you want to display your images at a specific size on your site, don't even think about simply changing the height and width attributes in your HTML markup! If you did so, you'd be increasing page load times unnecessarily, and potentially using huge amounts of bandwidth while losing web site visitors. Take a few moments to use a graphics program to size the image to the necessary dimensions.

---

[8] For more on the **IMG** element, see the W3C document, *Objects, Images, and Applets: 13.2 Including an image: the IMG element*
[http://www.w3.org/TR/1999/REC-html401-19991224/struct/objects.html#edef-IMG.].

Figure 3.5. Reducing image size properly, maintaining quality

 If you have a large number of images, batch process consistent treatments to save time.

Many graphics software products, such as Adobe Photoshop, give designers the ability to batch process images. For example, imagine if you had to resize 50 images to dimensions of 20x20 pixels. In Photoshop, you could record an *action* that resized any image to the required size, then use this action on all the other images that you need to resize.

Back Up Beforehand

Take extra care to back up your files before you run any automated process, as one rushed "time-saving" operation might have the opposite of the desired effect!

Summary

This chapter addressed the task of gathering content for use on your web site. We talked about the methods you could use to organize and itemize your content, including the specific content you'll use on each page of your site, and the content contained in common elements such as your company logo and tagline.

Finally, we discussed checklists that were designed to help you provide accessible content through your web site, write copy for the Web, and prepare images for use online.

4

Managing all the Content

Now that you've compiled your web site's content, it's time to figure out the best ways to deliver it to web users, and manage it easily. Remember this, my secret mantra for creating and maintaining professional web sites: "automation without compromising quality." Yes—it *is* possible to automate specific tasks associated with generating web content, preparing images, and so on, without degrading the quality of your content.

They key to figuring out how to manage your content is the process of exploring and understanding the options that are within your budget. Consider, in particular, the technology that's available and its costs, the skills needed to implement and run it, and the time you have available to manage your site content.

In this chapter, you'll find checklists to help you tailor an effective, workable approach to managing your site's content.

Assessing your Web Site Content

What types of content do you have? How much content do you have? Which content elements will be reused? Before you can decide how to manage your content, it's important to hone in on your specific content needs.

☑ **Take a content inventory.**

If you haven't already done so, take a content inventory. This can be really helpful in assessing how much content you have, what types of content you have, and what formats your content is stored in. For details on taking a content inventory, see Chapter 3.

☑ **Itemize your content.**

Do you have hundreds and thousands of text documents, each of which has its own individual image, or only a few articles and a handful of images? Include future projections of site growth in your itemization.

Look through your content inventory and itemize your existing and projected web site content into the following categories:

❏ type (e.g., articles, photographs, downloadable brochures, etc.)

❏ format (e.g., .txt, .jpg, .pdf, etc.)

❏ usage (e.g., Web only, marketing, print, etc.)

In addition to using your content on your web site, you might wish to use some of it in other communications, perhaps in a variety of file formats. It's important to note these possibilities so that you can revise and save the material appropriately. For example, if you intend to use your web copy in a print advertisement, you may need two different versions of the text. Similarly, if you're planning to use your web images in your print materials, you'll need to have both high- and low-resolution versions of those images, as image resolution requirements are higher for print than for the Web.

Check your Existing Content

note

If you have existing content, be sure to check that it meets the needs of your new web site, and can be exported without data loss.

You may find it helpful to itemize your content in a table or spreadsheet. If you have a lot of content, make life a bit easier by using new tables to itemize the content in the different sections of your web site.

Determining your Content Management Needs

You should now have at least some idea of how much content you have. The following checklist will help you determine what you'll need in order to manage all that content.

Checklist 4.2

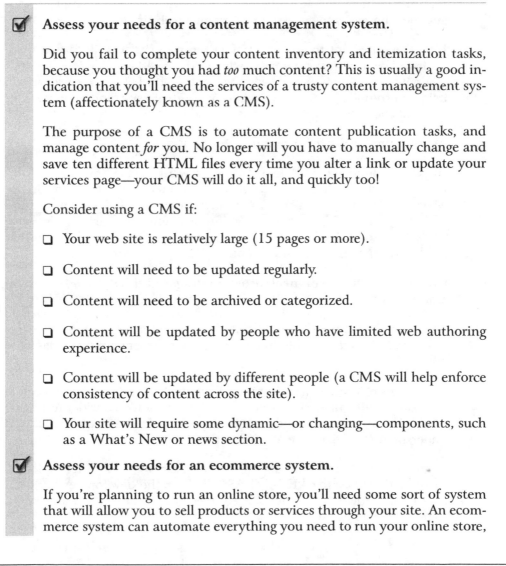

☑ **Assess your needs for a content management system.**

Did you fail to complete your content inventory and itemization tasks, because you thought you had *too* much content? This is usually a good indication that you'll need the services of a trusty content management system (affectionately known as a CMS).

The purpose of a CMS is to automate content publication tasks, and manage content *for* you. No longer will you have to manually change and save ten different HTML files every time you alter a link or update your services page—your CMS will do it all, and quickly too!

Consider using a CMS if:

❏ Your web site is relatively large (15 pages or more).

❏ Content will need to be updated regularly.

❏ Content will need to be archived or categorized.

❏ Content will be updated by people who have limited web authoring experience.

❏ Content will be updated by different people (a CMS will help enforce consistency of content across the site).

❏ Your site will require some dynamic—or changing—components, such as a What's New or news section.

☑ **Assess your needs for an ecommerce system.**

If you're planning to run an online store, you'll need some sort of system that will allow you to sell products or services through your site. An ecommerce system can automate everything you need to run your online store, providing you with the ability to add and update products in your product catalogue, accept and manage online payments, maintain customer and order information, and more.

If you've checked this option, see Appendix A for ecommerce-related checklists.

☑ **Assess your needs for HTML, XHTML, and/or CSS skills.**

As I mentioned previously, these markup skills are basic prerequisites for anyone who needs to create and maintain a web site.

If you've opted not to use a CMS for your web site, it's likely that these skills will be necessary for anyone who needs to add to or update the site's content. Even if you have decided to use a CMS, HTML knowledge will help you to understand the workings of your web site, and enhance your usage of the CMS.

☑ **Assess your needs for web authoring tools.**

If you have limited HTML knowledge, and want to save time, web authoring tools such as Adobe's Dreamweaver 8 (formerly from Macromedia) or Microsoft FrontPage can help you to manage your web site's content and layout efficiently. If you have a significant amount of content, but have chosen not to use a CMS, web authoring tools provide useful features that can help you manage the site's content.

☑ **Consider whether you need programming and database administration skills.**

Unless you're planning to build your own ecommerce or content management system, you probably won't need serious programming or database administration skills.

If you're using existing systems that will require heavy customization before they can be integrated with your web site, you should consider recruiting or developing at least a moderate programming skill-base, and gaining an understanding of database administration.

If you intend to build a specialized system, research the latest technologies. In particular, consider PHP and ASP.NET for the development of web-based applications, SQL and Oracle servers for storing data, and MySQL for database administration.

Building custom systems is beyond the scope of this book, but you may want to check out Kevin Yank's *Build Your Own Database Driven Website Using PHP & MySQL*, along with the other beginners' technology titles published by SitePoint.[1]

☑ **Assess your needs for image editing tools.**

If you're going to be working with images, you'll probably require some sort of image editing tool because, more often than not, you'll find that images in their raw form are rarely optimized for web use.

Image editing tools make it easy to optimize and manage the images you use on your web site.

As we saw in the section called "How Much is a Picture Worth?" in Chapter 2 in Chapter 2, there are many programs that allow you to create and edit images, most of which have built-in batch-processing capabilities. These tools can be invaluable to those who manage a site's content.

Web Authoring Tool Features

If you've decided that you don't require a CMS, and have opted to use a web authoring tool for your content management purposes, take a few moments to check that the software you're considering has the following features.

Checklist 4.3

☑ **The tool has a customizable, easy-to-use, user-friendly interface.**

Try online demos and study the product's screenshots, as well as downloading trial versions of the software whenever possible.

☑ **The tool offers template support.**

Templates enable the reuse of a single page layout and design across multiple pages. It allows you to maintain the consistency of your design, which helps support a professional appearance. Adding content straight into template pages is convenient and time-saving, and can generate cost savings, as less time is spent in the publishing process.

---

[1] http://www.sitepoint.com/books/

☑ **The tool provides permission controls and the ability to lock templates.**

Locking regions of templates is handy because it prevents users from making unwanted changes to page layouts when they're working on a file. Permission controls make it easy for content contributors to add content to a page without accessing the markup or locked-out regions of page templates.

☑ **The tool offers snippet or clip support.**

Check that the software allows you to create and store snippets of content and frequently used markup for use whenever they're needed. For example, Bradsoft TopStyle's Clip Library[2] and Macromedia Dreamweaver's Code Snippets and Library Items[3] provide easy drag-and-drop capabilities for snippets.

Tip **Clip Utilities**

In addition to HTML editing programs, other utilities enable you to manage templates and snippets regardless of the program you're using. ClipMate, by Thornsoft Development,[4] is one such program. ClipMate can store and organize templates and snippets, and allows them to be shared throughout a network, if required.

Content Management System Features

We were briefly introduced to the content management system earlier in the chapter, and thought that perhaps it could be our friend. Let's find out what makes this prospect so appealing.

A CMS includes programs that store, manage, display, and archive web site content. A good web CMS will help you organize and automate the management and publication of your data and content.

Ideally, a CMS makes adding and changing your web site content easy and convenient, even for those without HTML skills. It can streamline your workflow and allow you to publish content to your web site quickly. A CMS can also

---

[2] http://www.bradsoft.com/download/readme/readme30.asp#cliplib
[3] http://www.dwfaq.com/Snippets/
[4] http://www.thornsoft.com/

provide a centralized means of content editing, review, and approval, and often gives users the ability to create content components that can be used repeatedly.

A good web content management system should make the management of your web site content efficient and easy.

CMS in Review

For helpful feature directories and information on a range of CMS products, see: Bob Doyle's *CMS Faceted Product Directory*,[5] cmsInfo's *CMS Directories and Comparisons*,[6] the CMS Matrix,[7] and Adam C. Engst's article, *Help Us Choose among Content Management Systems*.[8]

Selecting a web site content management system that's best suited for your needs and budget can seem like a daunting task. There are literally thousands of possibilities! However, the following checklists will help guide you to choose a CMS that has features that correlate directly with your specific needs.

You might find it useful to create a Microsoft Excel chart to itemize the features you need in a web content management system. In your chart's columns, enter the names of content management systems you're considering, and list the features you want down the chart's left-hand side. Then, check off the features included in each CMS, and make note of the pricing and other helpful details. For an example, see the Excel chart prepared by the University of Texas during their CMS planning phase.[9]

Confirming CMS Support

IMPORTANT

Before you purchase a CMS, be sure to check that the web server that hosts your site will support your chosen CMS's requirements for databases and programming languages. Otherwise, it could all end in tears!

---

[5] http://www.cmsreview.com/
[6] http://www.cmsInfo.org/
[7] http://cmsmatrix.org/
[8] http://db.tidbits.com/getbits.acgi?tbart=07143
[9] Content Management System Steering Committee, *Selecting a Content Management System*, Content Management System, The University of Texas at Austin (March 2004) [http://www.utexas.edu/web/cms/about.html]; D. Cook, *Web Content Production and Delivery Requirements*, The University of Texas at Austin (March 2004) [http://www.utexas.edu/web/cms/content_management_specs.xls].

Features for you and your Staff

☑ **The tool has a customizable, easy-to-use, user-friendly interface.**

Try each product's online demos, and view screenshots of each CMS in action, as well as testing the trial versions of a variety of possible solutions. It will be more than worth the time and effort! Make sure you can customize the interface for your web site's specific needs, too.

☑ **The tool offers form-based text editing.**

Most content management systems support form-based text editing by default. This functionality will usually suffice for making simple text additions to the site with little or no formatting.

☑ **The tool supports WYSIWYG content editing.**

If you're adding content that requires text formatting and is to be accompanied by tables and images, it may be more convenient and time-effective to prepare and edit your web site content in a WYSIWYG editor, especially if your HTML knowledge is limited. WSIWYG editors work similarly to web authoring tools in that they create the markup for you; all you need to do is enter the content through an easy-to-use graphical user interface.

Your CMS may come with a WYSIWYG editor as a standard inclusion. If it doesn't, there are many third party editors available that can easily be incorporated into most CMS products.

Not all WYSIWYG Editors are Created Equal

Many WYSIWYG tools either create horrendous HTML, or add loads of extraneous, unnecessary markup to your files, so it's important to ensure that the WYSIWYG editor you choose creates clean, lean markup. It's always important to review and validate the markup behind the scenes. For more on creating standards-compliant markup, see Chapter 9.

☑ **The tool functions on multiple browsers and platforms.**

Some content management systems only work on the windows platform, and many are restricted to use within a single browser version. Make sure that the approach you choose offers the platform and browser options that you need.

☑ **The tool offers spellcheck functionality for content additions and editing.**

☑ **The tool offers staging server support.**

In the interests of quality assurance, testing, and workflow management, it's imperative that the tool you choose gives you the ability to publish content to a private staging or testing server that's separate from your live web site.

☑ **The tool provides for permission-based access.**

Especially when more than one person is involved in adding, changing, or deleting web site files, you may have a need for permissions-based access facilities. For example, your permissions setup might allow an administrator to access any part of the site, while an assistant in one of the company's departments might have access to make changes only to that department's web pages.

☑ **The tool supports automated version control and tracking.**

Version control will allow you to keep track of multiple versions of any given source file. A CMS that supports version control gives users the ability to view the differences between versions. This can help you to avoid overwriting files by mistake, give you the ability to roll back to earlier versions of files if problems arise, and identify the team members responsible for specific changes to files.

☑ **The tool allows for an unlimited number of content contributors.**

☑ **The tool permits annotations or comments for content review and changes.**

☑ **The tool provides email notifications of progress through steps in the workflow.**

☑ **The tool offers centralized content and document management features.**

☑ **The tool offers stability, reliability, and excellent performance overall.**

☑ **The tool is affordable.**

Confirm the CMS License

Be sure to check the licensing agreements for the tool you choose. Will you pay for each processor that uses the system? Costs can quadruple very easily when a system is used within an organization, so read the small print.

☑ **The tool offers excellent after-sales support.**

Once you choose a CMS, double-check that the customer support for the product is top-notch, and available 24 hours a day, seven days a week.

A Big Investment

A content management system can be a big investment both financially and in terms of the hours you'll spend implementing it, so it pays to do your homework thoroughly. This section has offered a number of possible features that could serve your project's needs, but everyone's requirements are different. Compare and contrast as many different CMS solutions as possible, and be sure to check the costs of each very carefully. Cut corners with a CMS and you may not reap the benefits in the long term. By the same token, don't spend money on features that you really don't need. For more on choosing a CMS, see Gerry McGovern's article titled, *Don't Make these Mistakes when Buying Content Management Software*,[10] and Michael Seifert's article, *Choosing a Content Management System, An objective market overview*.[11]

---

[10] http://www.gerrymcgovern.com/nt/2004/nt_2004_03_29_CMS.htm
[11] http://www.sitecore.net/upload/choosing_a_content_management_system_002.pdf

Content Publication Features

☑ **The tool supports content lifecycle management.**

If, on some areas of your web site, the information will be valid only for a limited amount of time—for instance, a What's New section—check that your CMS has content lifecycle management capabilities. These features will make it easy to keep track of time-critical content effectively and appropriately.

It's also important to keep track of aging content that, at some point, needs to be updated, archived, or removed from the site. That's not too difficult to manage on smaller web sites, but it can become an impossible task on larger sites. Lifecycle management can help automate this process.

☑ **The CMS allows for the scheduling of publications.**

You may need to have some of your documents published at a specific date and time. For example, as author of a regular column for the web site, you may decide to write several columns in advance before your vacation. You need them to publish automatically on the specified dates while you're away. Similarly, if you plan to launch a new product on a specific date, you may want your web site to be updated with the new product's promotional content at the stroke of midnight on that date. Scheduling capabilities are designed to make these otherwise laborious tasks easy.

☑ **The tool dynamically or automatically generates indexes or lists.**

☑ **The tool automates the cross-referencing and interlinking of content and other data on the site.**

☑ **The tool offers customizable directory structures and directory names.**

☑ **The tool supports customizable filenames and the creation of search-engine friendly, human-friendly URLs.**

See Chapter 7 for more on directory structure, directory names, and filenames.

☑ **The tool has customizable categorization options.**

These options give you the ability to assign published text or articles to the categories and/or subcategories of your choosing.

☑ **The tool has flexible, customizable archiving options.**

In particular, seek the ability to auto-generate archives by category, by department (especially helpful for intranets), by document title, by day, by week, by month, by year, and so on.

☑ **The tool allows for the easy management and use of images, multimedia, and other web site content formats.**

Some content management systems automate some basic image manipulation tasks such as thumbnail creation and image borders.

☑ **The tool facilitates the easy management of email subscriptions.**

☑ **The tool provides detailed activity logs and traffic reports.**

Ideally, the tool you choose should offer visitor reports, search term reports, and control panel logs. Activity reports can depict the numbers of new and repeat visitors, and their activity by time period (each hour, day, week, month, and year).

Also helpful are reports that illustrate a visitor's route through your web site, which can quickly highlight significant dropout points. As well as revealing which pages users visit most, and how they get to those pages, this information can help you to see where you're losing visitors' interest, allowing you to make the appropriate changes to keep users interested.

Control panel logs are a useful way to keep track of who has been working on your web site, what work they've done, and when they logged in to do it.

Behind-the-Scenes Features

☑ **The CMS is flexible, scalable, and nonproprietary.**

A web site CMS must allow for you, as the client, to make easy changes and improvements; it must permit growth, and be built from extensible code. And, as we saw above, the ability to repurpose or reuse your content is critical. Someday, your site may incorporate a different content management system, change server platforms, or undergo other changes. Your content should remain available regardless of the CMS you've chosen. A vendor-neutral, non-proprietary, standards-based content management system is a wise approach to managing your content.

☑ **The tool provides automated, scheduled backups.**

☑ **The tool offers support for multiple platforms.**

Be sure to check that your CMS supports all the major platforms, including Windows, Mac, and Linux.

☑ **The CMS offers support for popular scripting packages.**

Opt for a CMS that supports current popular scripting languages, such as JavaScript, PHP, ASP.net, and ASP.

☑ **The tool provides custom template support and integration.**

A web CMS must integrate with your web site's templates. You should not be required to use the pre-configured templates that come with the CMS.

☑ **The tool separates content from presentation.**

By keeping your site's content separate from its presentation, you achieve the flexibility required to make swift, far-reaching changes to the site's content. Since the content is separate from the look and feel of the site, even design changes to your web site are easy to implement.

☑ **The tool produces standards-compliant XHTML, HTML, XML and CSS code.**

In addition to creating standards-based output, some content management systems and markup editing tools have modules or plugins that allow you to validate your pages individually, or in batches. Check to be sure that the tool you've chosen will do this for you.

☑ **The tool provides support for W3C Web Accessibility Guidelines, and applicable government requirements.**

Some content management systems and markup editing tools will test the site's compliance with the W3C WAI (Web Accessibility Guidelines), U.S. Section 508, and other government requirements. In addition, you can access standalone tools that test and make recommendations about your site's accessibility, and a few of these tools will even make corrections. See Chapter 10 for more on this topic, including helpful accessibility checklists.

☑ **The tool validates internal and external hyperlinks.**

☑ **The CMS integrates with existing applications and processes.**

☑ **The tool generates dynamic pages.**

These are typically pages that are generated on the fly using the information stored in the CMS database.

☑ **The tool generates static pages.**

You may wish to incorporate a page that contains information that's not linked to the CMS data, or create a page that has a different look and feel from the rest of the site. Your CMS should give you the ability to create static or "standalone" pages like these.

☑ **The CMS lets you generate and manage metadata.**

Summary

This chapter's checklists were designed to help you figure out how to manage your content, and deliver it to the Web in the most time-efficient, convenient, and easily managed way. They should help you do this with the minimum amount of stress, allowing you to maintain a consistent, professional web site.

In this chapter, I shared my secret to creating and maintaining professional web sites: using automation whenever possible, but without compromising quality. I also provided checklists that will help you to automate many content management tasks.

We've made a lot of progress in these first four chapters, that's for sure! Now that you've planned, chosen, prepared, and figured out how to manage your content, you're ready to launch into the next chapter, whose checklists will help you create user-friendly web sites.

5 Web Site Usability: Focusing on the User

How often have you walked into a store with the intention of making a purchase, only to leave frustrated and empty-handed when you couldn't find the item you wanted?

I expected no better in a recent shopping adventure to a gigantic electronics warehouse. Yet I was pleasantly surprised when I found what I needed quickly *and* easily, despite the store's size. In addition to a large store map and an information booth positioned right at the store's front door, large colorful signs were painted on the warehouse walls to show the location of each major section. Products were well organized and clearly labeled, and a large Checkout sign directed me to the cashiers once I'd picked up the items I needed. I left feeling extremely satisfied, knowing that this is where I'll be making all my future electronics purchases.

Like the electronics store, a user-friendly web site that encourages visitors to return is one that allows those visitors to find information and complete tasks swiftly and simply. Truly user-friendly web sites provide visitors with multiple ways to find the information and functionality they need. Helpful navigation and search tools, fast-loading pages, and content that's easy to access, scan, and understand, are central to making the user experience effortless and enjoyable. But, as you know, in creating a user-friendly site, we need to integrate many different elements in ways that meet the needs of the target users we identified in Chapter 2. This chapter's checklists will help you to focus on your target users, and ensure that you don't forget any important elements as you work to create a usable site.

Creating a User-friendly Index Page

First impressions last—a maxim that certainly holds true for visitors to a web site.

Let's reconsider my great shopping experience for a moment. As I walked into that store and was greeted by its colorful, informative signs, I felt comfortable and in control of my shopping expedition. Your visitors need to feel a similar sense of security when they first arrive at your web site.

When the index page of your site has loaded, your visitors should be able to answer all of the following questions:

❏ Where am I?

❏ What is this site about?

❏ What content can I find here?

❏ What can I do here?

❏ How do I find information?

The following checklists will help you make your homepage as user-friendly as possible, so that visitors can find the answers to these questions at a glance, without being frustrated or intimidated.

Checklist 5.1

☑ **Provide obvious identification for your web site.**

Prominently display your logo and a meaningful tagline on the site's homepage. In some site designs, the organization's logo and tagline are displayed slightly larger on the homepage than on the inner pages.

☑ **Provide an overview of what your web site has to offer.**

Provide an overview of your web site's content and features, and the way in which the site is organized. For example, you might spotlight sale items, or the newest or most popular content, with a link to each item. Consider providing hyperlink teasers—snippets of content from within your web site, such as the example from SitePoint's homepage[1] shown in Figure 5.1—to grab users' attention and draw them into the site. Give visitors a reason to move off your homepage into the site, while providing a helpful overview that puts them in control of the user experience.

Figure 5.1. Hyperlink teaser and content snippet

New Articles, Fresh Thinking RSS

Why You Don't Need a Usability Lab
by Elizabeth Neal - Oct 8th, 2004

You know it's time to get serious about your Website's usability. Now you just have to convince your boss to spring for an elaborate usability lab with all the latest gadgetry... or do you? Elizabeth shows how easy usability testing can be as she debunks the myth of the hi-tech usability lab.

☑ **Provide fresh content.**

Update your homepage content frequently—even by refreshing a hyperlink to new content. Consider adding to your homepage a What's New section—a CMS should allow you to do this easily. You could also rotate a range of content items through the homepage to provide visitors with different information snippets each time they visit.

☑ **Provide shortcuts to your site's most frequently visited pages.**

Shortcuts makes using your site's key functionality more convenient for visitors. They also give you the opportunity to highlight your site's most popular content on your homepage.

---

[1] http://sitepoint.com/

Provide easy access to your site's login tools, and direct links to registration forms and account information.

Direct links to login tools, registration forms, and account information are particularly important if your web site sells products, or requires users to register and login before they can access content or functionality.

 Prominently display the site's search box.

 Provide a direct link to your sitemap.

This will allow your visitors to see, with one click, an overview of all the information that's available on your site.

Ensuring your Web Site Focuses on Users

Your web site needs to be created for your users. Just like the electronics warehouse I visited, your web site must be so convenient and easy to use that visitors don't even have to think about it. Your visitors should be able to find the information they need easily, and do what they need to do without waiting, becoming frustrated, getting lost, or stumbling across web site errors that prevent them from accomplishing their goals. Here's a checklist of key points to keep in mind as you plan, build, and review your site's usability.

Checklist 5.2

 Give users the chance to provide themselves with self-service.

Create easy-to-follow navigation, provide several different methods by which users can find information, and label pages clearly. Examples are shown in Figure 5.1, which depicts a teaser with a link that leads directly to a specific content item, and Figure 5.2, which shows a global navigation system that provides access to the key sections of the web site. Your visitors should use your help and sitemap pages only as a last resort.

 Provide predictable and consistent global navigation.

Figure 5.2 shows an example of the global navigation for the site of a fictitious company, MyByz. Note that this global navigation system contains links to all the vital company information—including the Products, About, and Contact pages—as well as links to essential site features such as Help

and Search. For more on developing consistent and effective site navigation, see Chapter 8.

Figure 5.2. Global navigation

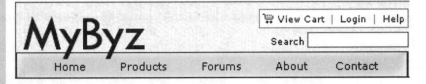

☑ **Display "You are Here"-type cues for users.**

Display an accurate, helpful page title on every single page of your site. Include cues within the global and sectional navigation, as well as bread-crumb navigation trails, to indicate users' current locations within the site. In Figure 5.3, the users have clicked on the Products global navigation item on the MyByz web site; now, as they move around within the Products section, the Products navigation item remains highlighted to orientate the user. As you can see, the subnavigation for that content section also helps to indicate to users the options available within that section.

Figure 5.3. Providing "you are here"-type cues for users

☑ **Support multiple methods by which users can reach or find content.**

Make the most of global and sectional navigation, and on anything other than the smallest web sites, include a sitemap, links to help and further assistance, and a search facility.

☑ **Provide easy access to help and contact information.**

Include links to your site's help and contact information on every page of your web site. Include these links in your site's global navigation, the page footer that sits at the bottom of every page, or both. Amazon.com, Nordstrom.com, and other large ecommerce sites provide links to help information from the top of every page, near the View Cart links; Contact Us links are displayed at the bottom of every page. Figure 5.2 and Figure 5.3 show that MyByz has adopted a similar method on its site.

☑ **Provide friendly, helpful information about potential errors.**

We'll discuss this in detail a little later in this chapter.

☑ **Ensure that your pages load quickly for all users.**

Optimize your web pages to ensure that they load as quickly as possible. Also, cater to all the possible Internet connection speeds that your target audience may use, including those on dial-up and broadband.

☑ **Accommodate a wide range of user abilities, disabilities, browsers, and alternative devices.**

Again, we'll deal with this issue in detail later in this chapter.

☑ **Use color effectively.**

Use color effectively to enhance visual cues—and the overall visitor experience!—while accommodating a wide range of viewing devices and user needs. Use color to distinguish hyperlinks, provide navigational cues, and direct user focus to certain areas of your web site. Chapter 6 provides detailed checklists to help you achieve these aims and more.

☑ **Provide scannable pages.**

Trust me: your visitors do *not* want to scroll though pages and pages of information before they find what they need. If you provide this kind of content, your users won't ever come back! Create information pages that are easy to scan and make all the key information readily available to your users.

☑ **Speak your visitors' language.**

It's up to your site to speak in the visitor's language, not the other way around. Write your content from your visitors' perspective, using words that they'll understand immediately, and keep the tone consistent throughout your site—through your content, your navigation, everything.

☑ **Use instantly recognizable and relevant hyperlinks.**

Make sure that your hyperlink style is different from your regular text style, and that your hyperlink text accurately tells users where the hyperlink will lead. The common way to distinguish hyperlinks from text is to underline the link, and display it in a different color. Color can also be used to differentiate between visited and unvisited hyperlinks.

Be careful to ensure that your link text gives users a clear indication of where the link leads. The link text depicted in Figure 5.4 doesn't provide any clues about the content that users can access by clicking on it.

Figure 5.4. Poor hyperlink text

Try <u>this</u>.

The hyperlink text in Figure 5.5 does a much better job of telling users exactly where the hyperlink will lead—to "our new polka-dot jackets."

Figure 5.5. Better hyperlink text

Learn more about **<u>our new polka-dot jackets</u>**.

Another reason to avoid vague hyperlink text is that, to bookmark a page, some users right-click on a link, or drag it directly to their desktop. Vague hyperlink text can make bookmarks created like this difficult or impossible to identify.

A better options is to make use of the `title` attribute to provide a tooltip that displays when users hover the cursor over the link.[2] Text within the `title` attribute can provide valuable supplementary information, as is illustrated in Figure 5.6.

Figure 5.6. Using `title` to display a tooltip

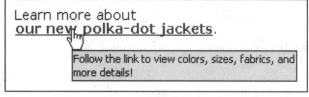

☑ **Ensure that your pages are bookmark-friendly.**

Create permanent URLs for each of your web pages, avoid the use of frames, and don't create hyperlinks that require JavaScript—such links are often useless for the purposes of bookmarking.

☑ **Make sure your site's functionality and features behave predictably.**

Sometimes surprises can be good, but they can just as easily backfire—especially online! Don't take these chances where your web site is concerned. Make sure your visitors always know what they're getting, and where they can get it from.

☑ **User-test throughout the design and development processes.**

To eliminate and avoid usability problems before you launch your web site, conduct user testing throughout the site's entire design and development processes—even during the project's earliest stages.[3] See also Chapter 14 for checklists and tips on testing your web site.

---

[2] For more on using the `title` attribute, see the W3C documents, *Links: Link Text* in the HTML Techniques for Web Content Accessibility Guidelines 1.0 [http://www.w3.org/TR/WCAG10-HTML-TECHS/#link-text], and *The Global Structure of an HTML Document: The Title Attribute* in the HTML 4.01 Specification [http://www.w3.org/TR/html401/struct/global.html#h-7.4.3].
[3] Kelly Goto and Emily Cotler, *Testing for Usability* in *Web ReDesign: Workflow that Works* (Indianapolis: New Riders, 2002), 205–225.

Providing Fast-loading Web Pages

Although your site's actual page load time is an important element of its usability, your users' perceptions of whether or not your site loads quickly are also important. For example, if visitors have to wait to click hyperlinks, read page content, run a site search, or interact with a web page, they'll perceive that the page loads too slowly, which increases the likelihood that they'll leave the site. So it's important that you ensure that users can accomplish their goals as soon as possible—this will boost user satisfaction and the chances of visitors staying on your site.[4] Use the following checklist to help reduce your web site's actual page load times *and* its perceived page load times.

Checklist 5.3

☑ **Accommodate a wide range of user connection speeds.**

Although reports continue to reflect the rapid growth of broadband throughout the world, there remains a large percentage of dial up (narrowband) users.[5]

☑ **Optimize your web page markup.**

To help keep markup and scripting to a minimum within each page, separate the page's content from its presentation, and externalize the page's CSS and scripting. This approach offers an added bonus in that it makes your web site easier to manage, too! Avoid using tables to lay out your web pages; instead, use CSS to recreate table-based layouts while ensuring quicker page load times.

☑ **Use minimal graphics per page, to save page load times and bandwidth.**

---

[4] Andrew B. King, *Flow in Web Design* in *Speed up Your Site: Website Optimization* (Indianapolis: New Riders, 2003), 29–37; Christine Perfetti and Lori Landesman, *The Truth About Download Time*, User Interface Engineering (January 31, 2001) [http://www.uie.com/articles/download_time/].
[5] Robyn Greenspan, *Global Broadband Tops 123M*, ClickZ Stats: Trends and Statistics (September 17, 2004) [http://www.clickz.com/stats/markets/broadband/article.php/3409671]; Andrew B. King, *Beach, Blanket, Broadband! – US Broadband Penetration Grows to 51.4% Among Active Internet Users – September 2004 Bandwidth Report*, The Bandwidth Report (September 19, 2004) [http://websiteoptimization.com/bw/0409/].

☑ **Optimize images and alternative file formats, including multimedia files.**

Where possible, compress images, audio, and video files to keep the download times to a minimum.

☑ **Promote "flow" by providing a fast response to user interactions, and minimizing distractions.**

Flow occurs when a user immensely enjoys and focuses on an activity, even to the point of losing a sense of self and time. To create greater opportunities for flow to occur around your web site, it's important that you offer plenty of swiftly-responsive interactivity, clear navigation and feedback, an uncluttered layout, and site credibility.[6]

☑ **Load useful content first.**

Try to display useful content during the first few seconds in which your web page loads.

The sooner users can interact with a page, the longer they will wait for the page to load. However, studies show that those users will leave if they have to wait for more than about eight seconds to do something.[7]

Accommodating User Abilities, Disabilities, Browsers, and Alternative Devices

Checklist 5.4

☑ **Provide a flexible web site design that works in a wide range of screen resolutions and window sizes, and with alternative devices.**

Your page design must be fluid and flexible if it is to display well and function effectively on small screens as well as at larger resolutions. We'll discuss the techniques you can use to ensure that your site is flexible and standards-compliant in Chapter 9, and we'll deal specifically with accessibility in Chapter 10. For now, though, keep in mind that your site should be developed to work across browsers, platforms, and devices. So, for instance, use external style sheets to target and support alternative media,

---

[6] Andrew B. King, *Speed up Your Site: Website Optimization* (Indianapolis: New Riders, 2003), 36–37.
[7] Andrew B. King, *Speed up Your Site: Website Optimization* (Indianapolis: New Riders, 2003), 25.

such as handheld devices and printers. And avoid fixed-width designs, which can be problematic for users with lower screen resolutions.

✓ Use scalable font sizes.

An important element of user-centric design is to create your site in such a way that it caters to the preferences and needs of individual visitors. For instance, allow users that may be visually impaired to alter the size of fonts displayed on your pages via their browsers. To support this functionality, you must use scalable font sizes in your markup (such as em measurements), rather than fixed font sizing (such as pixel measurements).

✓ Avoid using frames if possible.

Frames can prevent users from bookmarking pages, but in terms of the broader questions of site accessibility, they can be a nightmare. Framed pages have the potential to trap other web sites within your pages; they can prevent search engines from properly indexing your pages (unless you include links on each frame page to link back into the web site proper); and they can cause significant problems for users of screen-reader technology. Though the correct implementation of frames can help alleviate these issues,[8] framed pages can remain a challenge in terms of accessibility and for users of alternative devices. For users of voice browsers and keystroke technology, each frame becomes a separate page, and most PDAs and cell phones can't access framed pages at all. In the long run, it's better to avoid using frames altogether.

✓ Provide printable versions of your web site.

Take advantage of the CSS `print` media type to specify rules for print layouts, and eliminate the need to create an alternative print version of your web site's content. Creating a customized print version of the site gives you the opportunity, for example, to hide web site-only areas of your pages—such as the site's navigation—and to specify a more printer-friendly version of your organization's logo. However, make sure you provide scalable font sizes for your print style sheet and, where possible, use black text on a white background.

---

[8] See Jim Byrne's article, *Accessibility and Frames – Some Notes* [http://www.mcu.org.uk/articles/noframes.html], David Austin's *Website Design Philosophy* [http://www.speechutilities.com/about_this_website.htm], and the tutorial *Creating Accessible Frames* [http://www.webaim.org/techniques/frames/], by Utah State University.

Ensuring Predictability

When you're creating a user-friendly web site, it's important to remember that your visitors don't like to think, they don't like to wait, and they're not really into surprises. We've all made the Predictability = Boring association in the past, but when it comes to your web site, Predictability = Efficiency.

Creating a user-centered web site involves working out the finer details on behalf of your users, so that site visitors don't have to hunt for any functionality or information themselves. This checklist will help you ensure that your site behaves as predictably—and efficiently!—as possible.

Checklist 5.5

☑ **Provide clear, predictable, consistent web site and page architecture.**

We'll address the questions of architecture in detail in Chapter 7.

☑ **Include important web site and page identifiers, navigation elements, and location cues on every page.**

This includes your web site identification, such as your company name and logo, the name of the web page, links to major sections of the site, as well as local and sectional navigation, You are Here cues, and a web site search. See Figure 5.2 and Figure 5.3 for examples.

☑ **Keep existing browser functionality enabled.**

Your site's users rely on the basic functionality of their browsers. To reduce the risk of upsetting your visitors, ensure that the existing browser functionality still works:

❑ Don't disable the browser's back button.

❑ Don't disable the right-click mouse button functionality.

❑ Don't force hyperlinks to open in a new window (unless users have been warned to expect this behavior).

❑ As we discussed earlier, size fonts using scalable rather than fixed measurements, otherwise your visitors will not be able to increase or decrease the size of page text using their browser preferences.

Using Conventional Practices

Users expect to see global site navigation, search tools, underlined hyperlinks, and specific labels for shopping functionality, your homepage, and so on. Moreover, they expect to find these cues at certain locations on your web pages. This checklist will help you to ensure that your site meets user expectations by adhering to these conventions.

Checklist 5.6

☑ **Underline hyperlink text, and display links in a different color from surrounding text.**

On a web page, underlined text is used to identify clickable hyperlinks. Especially within body content, underline hyperlinks, and make them a different color from the surrounding text, so they'll be obvious to your site visitors.

Some web site designs remove underlining within obvious global navigation systems. Yet, these systems often display an underline, or some other visual cue, when users mouse over the navigation links. Don't break this convention unless you have very compelling reasons, and have considered alternative solutions.

☑ **Avoid underlining text that is not a hyperlink.**

Since underlined text is used to identify clickable hyperlinks online, don't underline text that's not a hyperlink. To emphasize snippets of your site's text content, use italics for emphasis, and bold for greater emphasis.

☑ **Differentiate between visited and unvisited hyperlinks.**

Usability experts continue to find that differentiating between visited and unvisited hyperlinks is critical to users' enjoyment of a web site. Color is the most common way to differentiate between visited and unvisited hyperlinks, but be sure to choose colors that are clear to vision-impaired visitors, and those using alternative displays. It's also important not to rely solely on color for important functionality or cues. Chapter 6 covers the selection and application of appropriate web site colors in detail.

Note that it's also common for web site designers *not* to use color or appearance to differentiate between visited and unvisited links, especially for aesthetic reasons within navigation bars. While it may be acceptable to break the rule in this case, reinforce the user's orientation with You Are

Here indicators. And always ensure that visited links in the main content area of the page *are* differentiated from unvisited links.

☑ **Apply easily recognized, commonly used labels.**

Use easily recognized, common terms for labeling your navigation and other web objects, such as your Home, Search, About, Contact, and News pages.

☑ **Place web objects where users expect to find them.**

Place web objects in conventional locations—this is where users expect to find them![9] Don't make them hunt.

☑ **Place your logo at the top-left of every web page, and link that logo to your homepage on every page except Home.**

☑ **Place a Home link near the top-left of each web page, or in your global navigation.**

☑ **For web sites that offer account management and/or shopping cart facilities, place View Cart and/or Manage Account functions near the top-right of each relevant page.**

☑ **Place a local web site search form at the top of each web page.**

Learn the Rules Before you Break them!

note

It's important to know and understand the common practices and defacto standards of web usability before you weigh the possible benefits and risks of breaking out of that mold. For example, for years now, we've seen web site navigation located on the left of a web page. However, mouse users must move the mouse across the page to access the navigation on the left, then move the mouse to the far right to use the browser's scroll bar. If the web

---

[9] Heidi K. Adkisson, *Identifying De-Facto Standards for E-Commerce Web Sites*, (master's thesis, University of Washington, 2002); Michael L. Bernard, *How Should Information be Positioned in a Typical Website?* Criteria for Optimal Web Design (Designing for Usability), Software Usability Research Lab (March 30, 2003) [http://psychology.wichita.edu/optimalweb/position.htm]; Jakob Nielsen, *Designing Web Usability* (Indianapolis: New Riders, 2000).

site navigation were located at the right-hand side of a web page, there would be no need for this left-to-right-to-left-again movement.

Should you break the mold, or follow convention? Before you break any rules, you need first to understand why those rules exist, and the possible consequences of breaking them—chief among them the likelihood that you'll confuse users. Check out the studies noted above, and understand as much as you can about web site usability before you try to bend the rules.

Providing User-friendly Corrections for User Errors

It's important that users who make errors on your site are able to fix them quickly and easily. An error message must be friendly and concise; it must explain the error clearly, and show the user how to fix the problem.

Checklist 5.7

Provide obvious, clear error messages that explain how the user can resolve the error.

If a user provides an incorrect username or password, for example, be sure your web site's error message states this simply, and helps the user make the required correction:

"Your username didn't work. Sorry! Please check your spelling and try again. Click here to get help, or to check that your subscription hasn't expired."

Error messages that address issues with local site search results are notoriously poor. If a user performs a search that returns no results, or returns too many, provide options that actually help the user to get what he or she wants. For instance, include links to an advanced search function, and to more detailed search instructions. Consider displaying a link to the site map, too, especially in the event that no search results are returned.

Use consistent error message content, formats, and locations.

Being consistent with your use of colors, fonts, text, and your approach to handling user errors will save users time and energy—once they've seen one error message, they'll know what to expect from all the error messages at your site. They'll also gain confidence in your web site and have a stronger impression of your brand.[10]

---

[10] Matthew Linderman and Jason Fried, *Defensive Design for the Web* (Indianapolis: New Riders, 2004), 26.

Use color and text to highlight user errors and explain how to fix the problem.

For example, if you're displaying an error at the top of a form page, clearly explain the error and the possible ways in which users can fix it. Use color and highlighting—for instance, red, bold text in a centered box—to make the error message obvious. In addition, use the same color and highlighting at the problem area of the form, so users know exactly which section/s they need to correct. Figure 5.7 shows this kind of error message in action.

Figure 5.7. A helpful error message

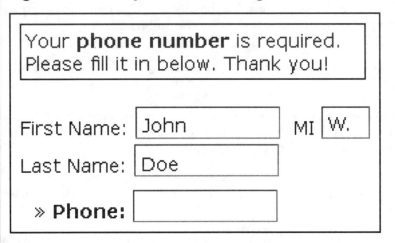

Eliminate the need for back-and-forth clicking.

If users neglect to fill out a field in an online form, or fail to fill out a field properly, allow them to fix their mistakes without back-and-forth clicking between the error message and the form itself. Provide the error message and the ability to fix the error on the same page, as per the solution depicted in Figure 5.7.

Don't make users have to retype correct information.

It's not uncommon for users to neglect to fill out fields in a form—sometimes, the user's browser crashes, or there's an interruption as the person tries to fill out the form. Save user data as it's typed, and let users know that you're doing so.[11] The exception to this rule is, of course, password fields.

☑ **Provide concise instructions.**

Although you need to be clear when you provide instructions, avoid wordiness: keep your instructions concise. Good instructions will reduce the number of errors made by your site visitors, and decrease the likelihood of users becoming intimidated by the error messages. Note how wordy the instructions in the error message in Figure 5.8 are when compared to those in Figure 5.9—this message eliminates unnecessary words while providing helpful instructions.

Figure 5.8. Instructions and form are too wordy

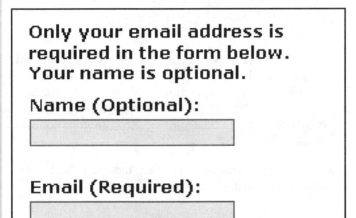

Only your email address is required in the form below. Your name is optional.

Name (Optional):

Email (Required):

---

[11] Linderman and Fried, 86; Alex Osipov, *Save Form Data with Cookies*, Acky.net: JavaScript Tutorials (July 23, 2001) [http://www.acky.net/tutorials/javascripts/cookies/].

Figure 5.9. Concise instructions and form

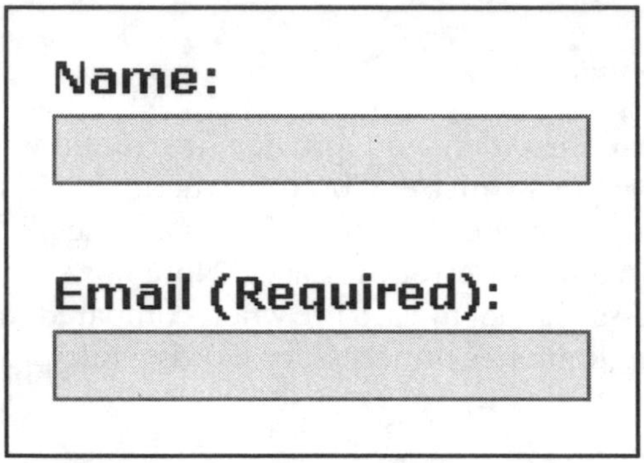

Name:

Email (Required):

Summary

This chapter provided checklists to help you create a user-friendly web site—one that helps users to find and do what they need easily and quickly, and provides information that's easy to scan and understand. We reviewed checklists that identified how to create fast-loading pages, and promoted the application of predictable, consistent behaviors that make sites easy to understand, and simple to use.

Now that we've covered the nuts and bolts of pure usability, let's move on to discover how color can be used most effectively on web sites.

6

Color

I think most of us would agree that the world would be a pretty boring place without color—as would your web site! Color is a primary building block of visual design that enhances your site's aesthetic qualities, and allows it to have a lasting impression on visitors. Color can also boost the usability of your site, drawing visitors' attention to certain areas of a web page, improving readability, enhancing raw functionality, and highlighting the visual organization of content, pages, and the site as a whole.

The effective use of color can make a valuable difference in your site's success. This chapter provides checklists that will help you to provide a positive first impression for visitors, enhance your site's functionality, and use the most appropriate colors for accurate display on a wide range of computer monitors and other devices.

Preparing a Color-friendly Work Environment

To avoid unwelcome, ugly surprises as you apply colors to your site design, it's important to keep the colors you use as accurate as possible—especially if you're preparing images for use on your web site. To create accurate colors for your web site, you'll need to adjust your hardware and software. This checklist will help you to view and work with colors accurately.

☑ **Position your monitors in areas with subdued light, out of strong or direct light.**

☑ **Use color-neutral, daylight-balanced lighting in your work area.**

OTT-LITE Technology[1] is one well-known provider of suitable lighting.

☑ **Set your displays to 24-bit or 32-bit color (True Color).**

Windows users can access the appropriate options by clicking Start > Control Panel > Display. Then, in the Display Properties window, click the Settings tab. Macintosh users need to click System Settings > Display.

☑ **Set your display contrast to its maximum unless the image display is too bright or harsh on this setting.**

Set your display gamma to 2.2 (Windows users) or 1.8 (Macintosh users).[2]

☑ **Calibrate your displays to the sRGB ICC profile.**

Especially important, in this regard, are computer displays that you use to work with and produce images for your web site. You've probably already noticed that a web site's colors can look quite different on various computer displays—maybe you've even had clients tell you the colors you've used on their web sites are "all wrong," even though you've employed their corporate colors. There are millions of computer displays in the world, and they can employ a wide range of settings, including color space—the range of color that the display is capable of reproducing. No two devices are exactly alike. The goal of the ICC (International Color Consortium)[3] is to standardize vendor-neutral, cross-platform, device-independent color profiles.

To manage the colors in web site images, use the sRGB color profile. Although, increasingly, the sRGB color profile is being used as the default

---

[1] http://ottlite.com/
[2] For more on display gamma, see Norman Koren's article, *Making Fine Prints in your Digital Darkroom: Monitor Calibration and Gamma*
[http://www.normankoren.com/makingfineprints1A.html#Monitorsetup].
[3] http://www.color.org/

display, millions of existing displays still use other profiles. Nonetheless, using the sRGB color profile will help you ensure that the colors in your images display as close to the intended colors as possible.

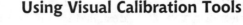

Using Visual Calibration Tools

Tip

Visual calibration is offered within Adobe products, such as Adobe Gamma for Windows, and Monitor Calibrator for Macintosh. To access this functionality in Windows, click Edit on the menu bar, then click Color Settings. Macintosh users must click Photoshop on the menu bar, then click Color Settings. Then, in the Working Spaces box, select sRGB IE61966-2.1. For higher levels of accuracy, try calibration software such as X-rite,[4] Color Savvy,[5] Alwan Color Expertise,[6] or Gretag-Macbeth.[7]

Choosing a Color Scheme

Color matters to users, whether they know it or not. In fact, a usability study found that "the best predictor for the overall judgment by typical users of a web site was its beauty."[8] Harmonious colors engage web site visitors and provide an inner sense of order, resulting in a peaceful visual experience that's less likely to intimidate or frustrate them. The use of triadic color schemes—three colors the same distance apart on the color wheel—achieves this inner sense of order the best.[9]

The key to choosing a harmonious color scheme for your web site lies in your branding: choose a color scheme that works well with your existing logo and company colors. The following checklist will help you to choose the right colors for your web site.

---

[4] http://www.xrite.com/
[5] http://www.colorsavvy.com/
[6] http://www.alwancolor.com/
[7] http://www.gretagmacbethstore.com/
[8] Laurie Brady and Christine Phillips, *Aesthetics and Usability: A Look at Color and Balance*, Usability News (May 1, 2003) [http://psychology.wichita.edu/surl/usabilitynews/51/aesthetics.htm].
[9] Leatrice Eiseman, *Pantone Guide to Communicating with Color* (Cincinnati: Grafix Press, 2000), 11; Vader, Beverly, *Choosing a Color Palette*, Encyclopedia of Educational Technology (no date) [http://coe.sdsu.edu/eet/Articles/colorwheel/start.htm].

☑ **Base your web site's color scheme on your branding and logo colors.**

Color is an important aspect in building recognition of your brand. Stay consistent by basing your web site's design on your branding, including the colors used in your logo.

Getting to Know the Color Triads

Triadic colors can be bright and strong, such as the primary triad of red, yellow, and blue, and the secondary triad colors of orange, purple, and green. For more subtle hues, lighten, darken, or add gray to triadic colors to create an endless variety of interesting, eye-pleasing color combinations.

To help you choose attractive colors, use a color wheel, such as the Primary color wheel (mixed from red, yellow, and blue), the Secondary color wheel (mixed from orange, green, and violet), the Tertiary color wheel (one primary and one secondary color mixed together), or the Visual color wheel (mixed from red, green, and blue). The Visual color wheel's RGB primaries are used for computer monitors, cameras, scanners, and other digital technologies, and the secondary (subtractive) triad is CMY (cyan, magenta, yellow), a printing standard.

Add color wheels, such as those from The Color Wheel Company,[10] to your bookmarks—they're very handy reference tools. Make use of other color palette and color scheme tools as you choose web site color schemes; try VisiBone's Color References,[11] Dominique Trapp's Color Harmony Guide,[12] and Color Wheel Pro.[13] For helpful software and more online color tools, visit WebsiteTips.com's Color section.[14]

To read more about using color on your web site, try the excellent book by Mimi Cooper and Arlene Matthews, *Color Smart: How to Use Color to Enhance Your Business and Personal Life* (New York: Pocket Books, 2000), and Leatrice Eiseman's *Pantone Guide to Communicating with Color* (Cincinnati: Grafix Press, 2000).

---

[10] http://colorwheelco.com/
[11] http://visibone.com/color/
[12] http://www.ideabook.com/color.htm
[13] http://color-wheel-pro.com/
[14] http://websitetips.com/color/

☑ **Use a neutral, subtle color scheme for your web site to help direct the focus to your products or services.**

Neutral doesn't have to mean dull and boring, of course! But, if you're going to get users to focus on your products or services, your web site colors must remain fairly neutral. For example, if you visit an art gallery, you'll notice that the walls and interior colors are neutral colors. This allows visitors to focus on the art—the surrounding colors don't distract visitors from the works themselves.

Branding and logo colors may intentionally be strong, as this is a great way to grab attention. If you're working with a strong palette like this, you might choose to use paler shades of the branding and logo colors to create a more neutral color scheme for the site, reserving the strong colors for use in small accents here and there. One example of this approach in action is the color scheme at Amazon.com. The Amazon logo uses black text and a light-orange color on a white background. The color scheme doesn't use the orange prominently, but shades of it are applied throughout the web site as accents: a darker shade of this orange is used for heading text and arrows, and to create a light-orange background bar at the bottom of each page. Amazon.com's global navigation tabs are a neutral, subtle color.

☑ **Use color to convey meaning.**

Some brands define themselves, at least in part, by color—look at Coca-Cola (red and white) or McDonald's (red and yellow), for example. When you plan your web site's color scheme, don't leave your choices to chance. Understand what colors mean, and use them effectively, keeping in mind the cultural differences mentioned next.

☑ **Consider the different meanings associated with colors in particular cultures.**

Each region of the world has its own predominant colors, distinctive palettes, and color associations. For example, in the United States, red is often associated with power, love, passion, and rage. By comparison, in China, red is the color of weddings, and red, pink, and burgundy are associated with good luck, good health, and prosperity.[15] As you choose your web site colors, be sure to use colors that are appropriate for the cultures and countries in which your target markets or audiences live.

---

[15] Mimi Cooper with Arlene Matthews, *Color Smart: How to Use Color to Enhance Your Business and Personal Life* (New York: Pocket Books, 2000), 117.

Tip

Discovering the True Meanings of Color

Three helpful books that detail the cross-cultural meanings of colors are Leatrice Eiseman's *Pantone Guide to Communicating with Color* (Cincinnati: Grafix Press, 2000), her new book, *The Color Answer Book: 100+ Frequently Asked Color Questions for Home, Health and Happiness* (Herndon, Virginia: Capital Books, Inc., 2003), and Mimi Cooper and Arlene Matthews' *Color Smart: How to Use Color to Enhance Your Business and Personal Life* (New York: Pocket Books, 2000).

☑ **Use no more than six colors in your web site color scheme, if possible.**

Studies show that using more than six colors can slow down the time users take to search through information. While other studies suggest that as many as nine colors may be acceptable, provided those colors are separated within the color space,[16] I think it's a good idea to remember that old cliché—"better safe than sorry"—and to create color schemes that use a maximum of six colors.

☑ **Avoid placing blocks of saturated, complementary colors next to one another.**

When you place next to each other saturated complementary colors, such as red and blue-green, yellow and dark blue, or purple and yellow-green, you'll see a flickering effect. This effect is actually generated as your eyes' focus shifts quickly back and forth, as it's unable to settle on either complementary color. Not surprisingly, this effect causes eye strain![17]

☑ **Test for color differences, inconsistencies, and problems using a variety of displays, resolutions, and platforms.**

While your web site colors will look different on nearly every display, it's important to check for unsightly problems. By testing on a variety of displays and resolutions, you can see if your web site colors shift in undesirable ways, and then adjust your images, your CSS, or both, to eradicate any problems. For example, you may have a logo image that blends seamlessly

---

[16] H. Smallman and R. Boynton, *Segregation of Basic Colors in an Information Display*, Journal of the Optical Society of America A, 10, 1985–1994 (1990); U. Derefeldt and H. Marmolin, *Search Time: Color Coding and Color Code Size*, (Paper presented at the First Annual Conference on Human Decision Making and Manual Control, 1981.)

[17] See Victor R. Stanwick's article, *Avoiding Problems with Adjacent Colors* [http://www.fast-consulting.com/color/coloravoidingproblems.htm].

against your site header's background color on one monitor; however, you may find the two elements appear in different shades on another display.

New flat-panel LCD (liquid crystal display) monitors tend to be brighter and crisper than CRT (cathode ray tube) displays and older LCD displays; images generally appear lighter on Macintosh computers than on Windows PCs, due to the different gamma settings used. Lower-cost laptops are inclined to sacrifice accuracy in color reproduction.[18] Color displays on PDAs and cell phones are even less predictable, and if your web site is targeting alternative device users, keep in mind that plenty of older PDAs with black-and-white displays are still in use.

Using Color to Enhance Functionality

As well as creating a serene browsing experience for your visitors, color can be used to enhance the functionality of your web site. The following checklist provides pointers on how best to use color to improve the functional aspects of your site.

Checklist 6.3

☑ Use color to direct user focus.

Use color to focus user attention on certain sections on a page. For instance, you might use red to highlight a sale item, or apply a yellow NEW! icon to attract attention to new articles, products, or services. Yellow is the brightest and most reflective of all the primary colors, while red causes the most active physiological responses. While yellow and red command attention, it's best use them judiciously—too much of these bright colors can be exhausting and distracting.[19] Brighter colors stand out from darker colors, warm colors stand out more from a cool background,[20] and saturated colors (intense, pure colors to which no gray has been added) stand out more than their less-saturated counterparts.

The NEW! icon in Figure 6.1 shows how we can draw attention to new items in stock through the use of color and bold text—even in this grayscale example. The shaded background and bold text attracts our focus.

---

[18] For more on this, see Joe Gillespie's article, *Paper vs. Pixels—Part 2* [http://www.wpdfd.com/editorial/wpd0904news.htm#feature2].
[19] Cooper and Matthews, 25, 39, 50; Eiseman, 19.
[20] Color wheels visually illustrate color temperature, i.e., warm vs cool colors. Warm colors include red-violet, red, red-orange, orange, yellow-orange, and yellow. Cooler colors are yellow-green, green, blue-green, blue, and blue-violet.

Figure 6.1. Using color to direct user focus

- **NEW!** Version 8 of our graphics software now available!
- **NEW!** Version 2.1 Update of our print software now available!
- Same old stuff here, though
- More of our same old stuff here, too

This NEW! icon is achievable with a mixture of text and CSS, which eliminates the need to create a graphic, and helps to minimize page load times and bandwidth usage.

☑ **Use colors consistently to avoid user confusion.**

Use colors consistently throughout your site. For example, if you choose dark red for your main headings and dark blue for article titles, don't decide to use dark blue for main headings in a particular section, and some other color for the titles of articles displayed there. Consistency reduces confusion. Perhaps your color scheme uses a different color for each section—blue for electronics products, and green for software, for example. That's fine. If, in the blue section, you use navy blue for the main headings, and in the green section, you use green for the main headings, don't diverge from this standard. Stay consistent within the color scheme you've created.

See Figure 6.3 through Figure 6.5 below for examples of color schemes in action. And don't forget that your site will be easier to manage and maintain if you use CSS to designate the colors displayed on your pages.

☑ **Use color to distinguish hyperlinks from regular text.**

Designate a color for styling hyperlinks that makes them stand out from surrounding text. Make sure you underline hyperlinks as well, especially within your text content, so that you're not solely relying on users to distinguish the color in order to identify the links. I sometimes style hyperlinks bold, to make them even more obvious.

☑ **Avoid using purple to style unvisited hyperlinks.**

☑ **Avoid using blue to style visited hyperlinks.**

Browser defaults use blue for unvisited links and purple for visited links, so if you switch these colors, it's very likely that you'll confuse your site visitors.

☑ **Where possible, use CSS, instead of graphics, to create web site colors.**

You can use CSS for a multitude of web site color purposes. Using CSS instead of graphics reduces page load times and bandwidth use, and results in a web site that's infinitely easier to maintain than one created without CSS. For example, if you use CSS to create borders around photographs, instead of adding those borders to the actual photographs themselves, you'll be able to change border colors and styles for photographs site-wide, simply by changing the CSS rules for the photograph borders. As we saw above, Figure 6.1 depicts a NEW! icon created using CSS instead of a graphic, saving bandwidth and page load time. Figure 6.2 uses CSS to add color and style—and a drop cap—to the headings on a page.

Figure 6.2. Using CSS to apply colors and style to headings

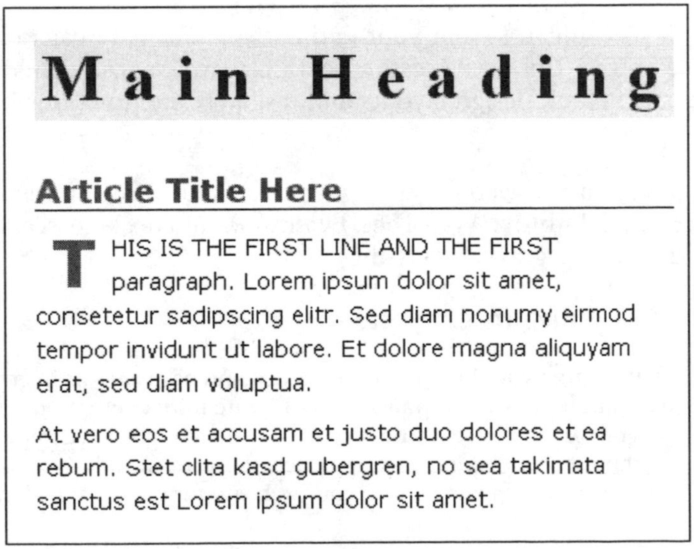

Main Heading

Article Title Here

THIS IS THE FIRST LINE AND THE FIRST paragraph. Lorem ipsum dolor sit amet, consetetur sadipscing elitr. Sed diam nonumy eirmod tempor invidunt ut labore. Et dolore magna aliquyam erat, sed diam voluptua.

At vero eos et accusam et justo duo dolores et ea rebum. Stet clita kasd gubergren, no sea takimata sanctus est Lorem ipsum dolor sit amet.

You can also use CSS to create design accents, to color particular web site functions, and to designate media-appropriate colors for specific media.[21] For additional checklists and tips on CSS and web site design, see Chapter 9 and Chapter 13.

Perform a "wireframe" test to ensure that you're catering for various user preferences and disabilities.

Users can customize their browser settings to turn off colors, alter font sizes, and select fonts; they can also choose to use their own style sheets. Rather than being alarmed by this fact, embrace this user-friendly flexibility by ensuring that your web site design makes sense in black-and-white—especially its navigation and other important functions. Test your design without color to make sure it's still user-friendly and works well.

Many graphics programs offer a grayscale feature, which makes checking your design layouts in grayscale easy to do. If you need to, simply take a screenshot of the web page in question, then open the screenshot image in your graphics program. Alternatively, in Photoshop CS, select Image > Mode > Grayscale from the menu bar to access this functionality. If you're using your design files, create a duplicate copy first!

On Mac OS X, you can switch your entire display to grayscale: click on System Preferences > Universal Access > Set Display to Grayscale. This feature makes it easy to check design layouts and test web site functions in grayscale.

Windows users can test web pages in grayscale using a free online testing tool called the Colorblind Web Page Filter.[22] Also, check to see if your particular display has grayscale settings.

Tip

Designing in Grayscale

Try creating your initial web site design and page layouts in grayscale. Graphic designers learn in school to create initial designs and layouts in grayscale because it's important that the designs have impact even without color. Taking this approach for your site design and page layouts will help ensure that your web site functions, and that visual

---

[21] For more on the topic, see Elika Etemad's and Jorunn D. Newth's article, *Pocket-Sized Design: Taking Your web site to the Small Screen* [http://www.alistapart.com/articles/pocket/], and the W3C's *Media Types* in Cascading Style Sheets [http://www.w3.org/TR/CSS21/media.html], part of Level 2 Revision 1 in the CSS 2.1 Specification.

[22] http://colorfilter.wickline.org/

cues won't depend solely on color in order to make sense.[23] Designs that work well in grayscale are solid—though color will enhance them, they won't depend on color in order to succeed.

If you've created wireframes to plan your site's information architecture, it's a good idea to use those wireframes to create your web site design and page layouts. For more on information architecture, wireframes, and design, see Chapter 7 and Chapter 13.

☑ **Use color to emphasize the organization of information and provide visual cues.**

When you use color to organize information, you have the opportunity to give your web site visitors subtle cues that make your web site easier to navigate and your pages quickly comprehensible. For example, the major sections of some web sites are organized by color. Amazon.com uses green for its Books section, blue for Electronics, and dark red and light-orange for the Today's Deals area. Amazon.com changes some of these section colors on its local sites to suit the cultural color preferences of those sites' specific users.

Figure 6.3. Using color to create visual cues

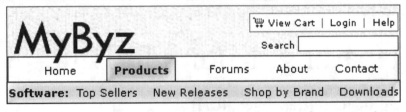

Graphics Software

Lorem ipsum dolor sit amet, consetetur sadipscing elitr, sed diam nonumy eirmod tempor invidunt ut labore et dolore magna aliquyam erat, sed diam voluptua.

Figure 6.3 shows how colors have been used as visual navigation cues on the MyByz site. You can use color as a visual cue for headings—try using

---

[23] For more on creating grayscale designs, see Heather Quinn's article, *Where / What Vision Systems and Visual Design* [http://www.evolt.org/article/rating/22/60261/] and the DevX article, *Design with Color* [http://www.devx.com/projectcool/Article/19987].

different colors for headings and subheadings, as well as differentiating them using the font sizes and page layout, as shown in Figure 6.4.

Figure 6.4. Headings: creating visual cues using color and size

Heading, Midnight Blue
Article Title, Medium Teal

Text is black. Background is white to provide contrast for better legibility. Lorem ipsum dolor sit amet, consetetur sadipscing elitr, sed diam nonumy eirmod tempor invidunt ut labore et dolore magna aliquyam erat, sed diam voluptua.

In Figure 6.5, the main heading uses a different font from that used in the article title heading, providing an additional visual cue.

Figure 6.5. Headings: creating visual cues with color, size, and font

Heading, Midnight Blue
Article Title, Medium Teal, and Different Font

Text is black. Background is white to provide contrast for better legibility. Lorem ipsum dolor sit amet, consetetur sadipscing elitr, sed diam nonumy eirmod tempor invidunt ut labore et dolore magna aliquyam erat, sed diam voluptua.

These text effects are easily achieved using CSS.

Don't rely solely on color to communicate important visual cues.

Your use of color in the organization of information should enhance the user experience; the user experience should not depend upon it. When your web site doesn't solely rely on color to communicate important visual cues, your web site will be more device-independent, and therefore more usable. This approach also ensures that visually impaired site visitors can use your web site easily.

As an example, consider Amazon.com's navigation. It doesn't depend solely on color in order to be usable or understandable; nor does the navigation system for the fictional MyByz.com site shown in Figure 6.3. The navigation makes sense in grayscale, which means that it will be accessible by those with color blindness and other visual disabilities.

Using Color to Enhance Readability

Checklist 6.4

For best legibility, use colors that provide a strong contrast between the page background and the text.

Use solid, light-colored backgrounds behind dark-colored text for page content areas.

Black text against a solid white background provides the best contrast and is typically the easiest text to read.

Avoid displaying patterns, textures, and colorful backgrounds behind text.

Summary

This chapter identified the important considerations affecting the best use of color on your web site. It explained how to set up a color-friendly work environment, provided guidelines to help you choose a color scheme for your web site, and showed how best to use that color scheme to enhance the functionality of your web site. I also included references to color wheels and other helpful tools that will prove very valuable as you work with color on your web site.

Well, that's the fun stuff taken care of! Let's move on to what are generally seen to be the more "serious" details (though I think they sound more serious than they really are!), starting with information architecture.

7

Information Architecture

Imagine that some site owners take all the content from their online store, including hundreds of articles and all the computer products the site sells, and throw it all off a ten-story balcony. The content, articles, and products land on the pavement below, scattered over a 500 meter radius, in pieces. It's your job to find all the pieces, somehow put everything back together correctly, organize it all logically, and design a new store for the site owners—all within eight weeks!

How do you feel? That's exactly how I felt when I was faced with a recent web site redesign project. And if you've ever had anything to do with information architecture, you will probably already have felt like this once or twice yourself.

This chapter focuses on creating a well-organized order for your web site's content—creating order from what may initially seem like a chaotic mass of materials thrown off a ten-story balcony. Organizing your content is beneficial both to your site's visitors, and those who maintain it. The checklists in this chapter will help you to organize and structure the information for your web site, and keep it that way.

Laying the Foundations

Checklist 7.1

☑ **Determine how users will interact with your web site.**

Will they be want to purchase products? Will they be seeking information? Will they try to register for a newsletter? Work out how your visitors will use your web site, then document their interactions and all of the steps involved in each task that they'll undertake.

 Tip

Creating Personas Can Help

Creating personas can help tremendously as you determine and document how users will interact with your site. Personas are users that you create on the basis of your research of the real users of your web site.[1] For example, imagine several types of users who would visit your web site. Give them fun names—make a game of it—and pretend that you're each of these different people moving around and using the site.

Imagine you have a photography-related web site, for example. One user might be a professional photographer who's looking for specific equipment to purchase. She's new to the Internet and has bought a computer only recently. Become that user, thinking like her as you move around your web site. How would she find that special equipment easily? Document each step along the way, from finding your web site, to completing a purchase.

To learn more about personas, see Christina Wodtke's terrific book, *Information Architecture: Blueprints for the Web*, cited above.

☑ **Document the steps involved for each user activity.**

You'll use this information to map out the information your web site needs to offer.

☑ **Allow for a range of Internet experiences and a variety of skill levels among users.**

Your users could include a person who's just started taking lessons on how to use a computer, to someone who's been a programming guru for the

---

[1] Christina Wodtke, [From A to C by Way of B] in *Information Architecture: Blueprints for the Web* (Indianapolis: New Riders, 2002), 152–188.

last twenty years. One might have just completed setting up wireless Internet access; another might not be able to point out the browser's address bar. Consider all skill levels as you profile your users.

☑ **Allow for a variety of user abilities and disabilities.**

Your web site structure needs to cater to a wide range of visitor abilities and disabilities, including the provision of access to those using alternative devices and adaptive technology. For example, you should include within your markup ways for these users to skip past navigation, or skip past long content to navigation. We'll discuss accessibility more in Chapter 10.

Improving Findability

It's important to organize your web site's information architecture so that users can find content easily. Information architects refer to this characteristic as the site's **findability**.[2] The findability of your content plays an important role in the success of your site.

Checklist 7.2

☑ **Organize content from visitors' perspectives.**

You might be inclined to arrange your web site's information architecture to reflect the structure of your company, for example. However, what might (or might not!) work within your company often won't make sense to your web site visitors.[3] For this reason, it's critical to consider carefully the different perspectives of audience members as you organize the information on your web site.

☑ **Visually group pieces of information into manageable units.**

The Rule of Seven

You may have come across the rule of grouping no more than seven items into a single group—pay no heed, it is a mere myth![4] So don't feel that you must have no more than seven items in your global navigation! Group content, functionality, and tasks on a logical basis.

---

[2] Wodtke, 126–128.
[3] See Peter Merholz's article, *The Pendulum Returns: Unifying the Online Presence of Decentralized Organizations, Part 1 of 2* [http://www.adaptivepath.com/publications/essays/archives/000028.php].
[4] IAwiki, *Breadth vs. Depth in Site Architecture* [http://www.iawiki.net/BroadVsDeepHierarchy], IAwiki (July 2, 2004); James Kalbach, *The Myth of 'Seven, Plus or Minus 2'* [http://www.ddj.com/documents/s=4058/nam1012431804/], Dr. Dobb's Journal (January 14, 2002).

☑ **Visually group similar kinds of information together.**

☑ **Visually separate different information.**

To separate information groups visually, use whitespace, color, borders, and other visual styles.

☑ **Create multiple ways to find information on your web site.**

In addition to your navigation tools, include a local web site search and a sitemap. You might also provide a listing of the most popular pages, most popular products, deals of the day, and so on.

☑ **Plan to monitor your site's search and activity logs.**

Closely monitor your server activity logs to see what users are looking for, and to ascertain whether they're using search due to navigation problems or because of some weakness that's inherent in your web site's architecture. If your statistics software is up to the task, you may be able to ascertain at which point visitors give up trying to click through to their destinations, and resort to using the search instead. You can use this information to determine which areas of your web site need findability enhancements.

Organizing for Success

I love organizing. So much so, in fact, that I've organized my entire multimedia collection. It just so happens that my love for organization has made my life *so* much more convenient—I rarely have trouble finding anything. I've sorted the collection by type first—DVDs, CDs, cassette tapes, and vinyl records—and then in alphabetical order. I've also organized my CDs into several main categories, such as classical music, rock 'n' roll, healing music, and audio books. I've used a combination of two types of organization schemes for my CD collection—a technique that's also important for your web site.

Organization Schemes

Organization schemes and organization structures make up your web site's organizational system. The way you organize your site's content will have a strong influence on your web site's navigation, directory structures, and indexing. It makes sense that the way in which your content is organized will influence the labels you use in your navigation, directories, page headings, and more.

Even though you might be jumping the gun, and thinking about how you'll compile your web site, it's critical to focus first on grouping your content logically. If, first, you focus on grouping your content with your users in mind, ultimately, you'll create a better, more logical, and more usable site. So put your compilation thoughts on the back-burner for the moment as you use these checklists to organize your content.

Checklist 7.3

☑ **Use an exact organization scheme for users who know what they want.**

Exact organization schemes—alphabetical, chronological, or geographical schemes, for example—are easy to use and maintain. You'll typically find archives of press releases, newsletters, and magazine articles organized by release date in chronological order. Archives for magazine articles may use chronological order to list the magazine issues first, and may then employ either alphabetical organization for the articles' titles, or numerical ordering to list the articles by the page numbers on which they appear.

☑ **Use an ambiguous organization scheme for users who may not know what they want.**

Despite their name, ambiguous organization schemes, such as organization by topic, task, or audience, can be used to group related items in meaningful ways. You'll find an abundance of web sites that use these organization schemes. Amazon.com, for example, organizes products by category to help users—across the top of each page of the site appear navigation tabs that read Books, Apparel & Accessories, Electronics, Toys & Games and so on.

☑ **Use both schemes when possible.**[5]

Providing multiple ways for visitors to access information allows your site to satisfy all the different reasons why people will visit it. Some visitors will know exactly what they're looking for, while others may have only a very vague idea, or wish to browse. Your site should cater for both extremes, and everything in between!

---

[5] Louis Rosenfeld and Peter Morville, *Information Architecture for the World Wide Web, Second Edition* (Sebastopol: O'Reilly & Associates, Inc., 2002), 74.

The value of using both systems is obvious in my own Brainstorms and Raves[6] web site archives. Visitors can access all of the articles or weblog posts in a variety of ways—by category, by title, by cited links, or by date (year, month, week, and day). A local site search is also available. The site's users employ all these different methods to access the content on the site, so this is certainly not a case of overkill. On the contrary—this approach provides a variety of ways for users to find content quickly and easily at the web site, and it's very easy to maintain through a content management system.

Organizing Content Structure

The structure of your web site's information, based on a hierarchy, databases, hyperlinked text, or a combination of these means, defines how your visitors will navigate through your web site. Here's a checklist that highlights a number of points that you should consider as your organize your web site's information.

Checklist 7.4

☑ **Organize content into groups.**

Organize your content into groups, for instance, alphabetically, chronologically, or geographically; by a person or group; by task (register, pay a bill, etc.); or by visitor type (individuals, business, clients, press). Various methods are available to help you organize your content, including card sorting, free-listing, affinity diagrams, mind mapping and idea maps, and persona design or scenario development.[7]

Card sorting involves writing down the name of each content item on a separate card, asking others (separately) to sort them into groups, and collating the results to help determine how you should organize your web site information.

Freelisting can be a pre-cursor to card sorting. Before someone sorts existing information, it can be helpful to explore and determine what content categories might be appropriate for your site, as well as how they're related.[8]

---

[6] http://brainstormsandraves.com/archives/
[7] For more detail on these techniques, see the IAwiki's *Techniques for IA* [http://www.iawiki.net/TechniquesForIA] article, and James Robertson's article, *Information Design Using Card Sorting* [http://www.steptwo.com.au/papers/cardsorting].
[8] See the article by Rashmi Sinha, titled *Beyond Cardsorting: Free-listing Methods to Explore User Categorizations* [http://www.boxesandarrows.com/view/beyond_cardsorting_free_listing_methods_to_explore_user_categorizations], for more on this.

Affinity diagrams are similar to card sorting, but can help to show how items or groups relate to each other.[9]

Mind and idea maps can be helpful in promoting "freeform" brainstorming without the constraints of a hierarchical structure, the results of which can then be used to create outlines or otherwise organize information.[10]

When recently I began to redesign a client's information architecture, I started by identifying the different kinds of content he had. His self-made web site with over 200 web pages lacked navigation, organization, labeling, and consistency. I had no index or sitemap, and no local search. After completing a detailed content inventory, I sorted content in large categories—products, services, and articles, and "miscellaneous" for everything else. I then evaluated subcategories and sorted accordingly. Content about products, for example, was broken into product subcategories, including books, videos, software, and microphone sections.

☑ **Determine logical hierarchies.**

Web site hierarchies may be broad and shallow, narrow and deep, or somewhere between. Broad, shallow hierarchies provide more options for web site users initially, while narrow, deep hierarchies provide just a few options that require the user to click through more pages and levels in the hierarchy. Figure 7.1 and Figure 7.2 show examples of these two approaches.

Figure 7.1. Broad and shallow web site hierarchy

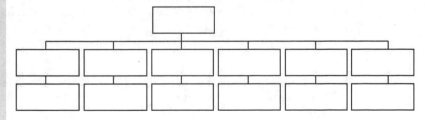

---

[9] See the IAwiki's article on Affinity Diagrams [http://www.iawiki.net/AffinityDiagrams] for more on this.

[10] See Heidi Adkisson's article, *Mind Mapping & Composition* [http://www.iathink.com/2003/10/mind_mapping_co.html], and Robin Good's article, *Mind Mapping and Visual Concepts Diagramming* [http://www.masternewmedia.org/2002/10/31/mind_mapping_and_visual_concepts_diagramming.htm] for more on mind and idea mapping.

Figure 7.2. Narrow and deep web site hierarchy

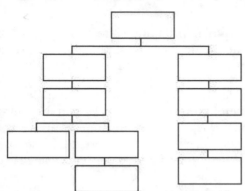

Strike a balance between these approaches:[11] provide sufficient options to be helpful to users without providing so many options that you overwhelm them.

The Three-click Myth

The "three-click" rule is just a myth … but it's not a bad myth!

You've probably come across the "three-click" rule, which states that you must provide access to whatever the user needs within three clicks of their current location, otherwise users will become frustrated and leave. However, recent usability studies reveal that the three-click rule is indeed just a myth: the number of clicks is not the key factor in users' frustration or success. When visitors complain about having to make too many clicks, they're most likely complaining about the symptom rather than the cause of the problem—a lack of good find-ability.

Myths aside, the three-click rule isn't a bad idea! It's a simple and effective way to ensure that your site visitors find information quickly and easily.

☑ Identify related information.

An article categorized in a particular group might also be suited to inclusion in another group. For example, you may have an article on low-calorie fish

---

[11] Rosenfeld and Morville, 69.

and chips in your Favorite Recipes category; it may also work well in the Healthy Eating category.

☑ **Use faceted classifications and hierarchies to help users view information in a variety of ways.**

Amazon.com's global tabbed navigation provides categorized organization by product type, including categories such as Books, Electronics, Toys & Games, and Kitchen & Housewares. In addition, you can view products in the categories of New Releases, Top Sellers, and Today's Deals. You can also use the search tool, browse any of the stores in the left-side column, or choose from other categories on the page, such as The Page You Made, Recommended For You, and New and Future Releases. Amazon.com provides a range of ways by which users can find anything. Indeed, if you have the underlying metadata and structure in place, your site can provide a variety of navigation options and ways to use information, all of them based on users' needs. This approach, called **faceted classification**, can provide tremendous flexibility to your system, giving users greater opportunities to find the information, use the functionality, or complete the tasks they want.[12] Don't feel forced to apply only one category to any given product or article—hedge your bets!

☑ **Ensure that your web site's labeling system uses clear, short, consistent labels that your visitors will understand.**

Labels are possibly the most obvious way to show visitors how your content is organized. Headings, navigation, and contextual links are among the labels that communicate your site's organization to users at a glance. Avoid jargon. Labels must convey sequence, as in the case of headings and subheadings. Often, labels also need to provide directions for your site visitors, for instance, where to start, where to go next, and what action to take.[13]

☑ **Diagram your content's information architecture.**

Diagram your content's information architecture and directory structure using storyboarding, sitemapping, or a combination of these techniques.

---

[12] William Denton, *How to Make a Faceted Classification and Put It On the Web*, Miskatonic University Press (November, 2003) [http://www.miskatonic.org/library/facet-web-howto.html]; Rosenfeld and Morville, 207.
[13] Rosenfeld and Morville, 76-105.

Test and tweak this architecture as required throughout the design and development process.[14]

Sitemapping Tools

Tip

To create sitemaps for new web sites, you might like to try tools such as SmartDraw,[15] or Microsoft Visio.[16] To create sitemaps of existing web sites, try Powermapper,[17] or Site Map Pro.[18]

Cybergeography.org has published a number of examples of sitemaps online, at *An Atlas of Cyberspaces: Maps of Web Sites*.[19]

Preparing Web Page Information Architecture

If you think of a web site's information architecture as being similar to the architecture of that dream home we were building a few chapters back, the information architecture of the individual web pages corresponds to the structure and organization of details in the individual rooms of that home.

Checklist 7.5

☑ **Organize web page content logically, predictably, and consistently.**

☑ **Emphasize important content.**

Headings, for example, are usually displayed in larger, bolder text with more white space around them than typical sentences of body text. Sub-headings are often displayed in slightly smaller bold text than headings, usually in a different color, a different font, or both. You can emphasize other content items using colors or bold text, or by placing important content in a box or other "structure" at a suitable location on the page.

---

[14] For more on this, see Troy Janisch's article, *How Good Does Your Web Site Look on Paper?* [http://evolt.org/article/rdf/22/60331/], and Carolyn Snyder's book, *Paper Prototyping: The Fast and Easy Way to Design and Refine User Interfaces* (San Francisco: Morgan Kauffman Publishers, 2003).
[15] http://www.smartdraw.com/
[16] http://microsoft.com/office/visio/
[17] http://www.powermapper.com/
[18] http://www.sitemappro.com/
[19] http://www.cybergeography.org/atlas/web_sites.html

☑ **Create mockups, such as sketches, wireframes, and paper prototypes to reflect each of your web page architecture needs.**

Your homepage will most likely have different information architecture needs from other pages. Main pages for sections might require a table of contents or similar listing approach. Ecommerce pages will have their own special information architecture requirements. It's important to sketch out the information architecture requirements for each of these different needs, or pages. Then, perform usability testing to ensure that the pages meet user needs, and that the information architecture for each page type works well.

 Tip

Paper Prototyping

When figuring out a web page's architecture, sketching ideas with pencil and paper is a tried-and-true approach. Paper prototypes are effective, as they aid visualization and are an invaluable testing tool. What's most important is to work out a solid web page architecture carefully and thoughtfully for each type of web page you need.[20]

☑ **Group corporate information items together.**

This includes navigation links that lead to content about your company, press releases, employment opportunities, and investor information. This makes it easy for those who are interested in this information to find it.[21]

☑ **If you place ads on your homepage, place them on the outer parts of the page,[22] and make sure they're clearly differentiated from web site content.**

---

[20] For more on paper prototyping, see Troy Janisch's article, *How Good Does Your Web Site Look on Paper?* [http://evolt.org/article/rdf/22/60331/] and Carolyn Snyder's book, *Paper Prototyping: The Fast and Easy Way to Design and Refine User Interfaces*, (San Francisco: Morgan Kauffman Publishers, 2003).
[21] Jakob Nielsen and Marie Tahir, *Homepage Usability: 50 Websites Deconstructed* (Indianapolis: New Riders Publishing, 2002), 12.
[22] Andrew B. King, *New Riders Interviews Jakob Nielsen and Marie Tahir*, WebReference Update Newsletter (October 8, 2001) [http://www.webreference.com/new/011011.html].

Information Architecture for Ecommerce Pages

Amazon.com is a model of a great ecommerce site—they do an excellent job. The checklist below is inspired by Amazon.com's influence, along with studies from top information architects and usability experts.

Checklist 7.6

☑ **Make the shopping cart easy to find from anywhere on your web site.**

Provide multiple entry points to the shopping cart so that users can see what's in their cart, add items, and complete their orders whenever they choose to, and without hassle. Figure 7.3 shows the shopping cart icon and label, reading View Cart, in the web site's global navigation. You can also see the top-of-the-page global navigation and the Cart, Checkout bottom-of-the-page global navigation.

Figure 7.3. Shopping cart links

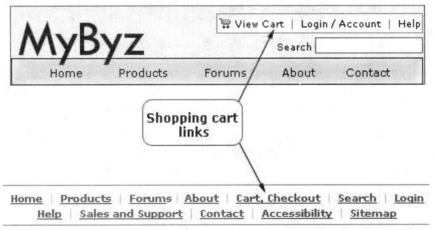

☑ **For each product on a web page, display a clear, at-a-glance view of the item's name, price, current availability, an item description, shipping options, and Add to Cart or Add to Wish List links.**

Figure 7.4 shows how this information may be shown on the product page in an ecommerce page's architecture.

Figure 7.4. An item's at-a-glance view

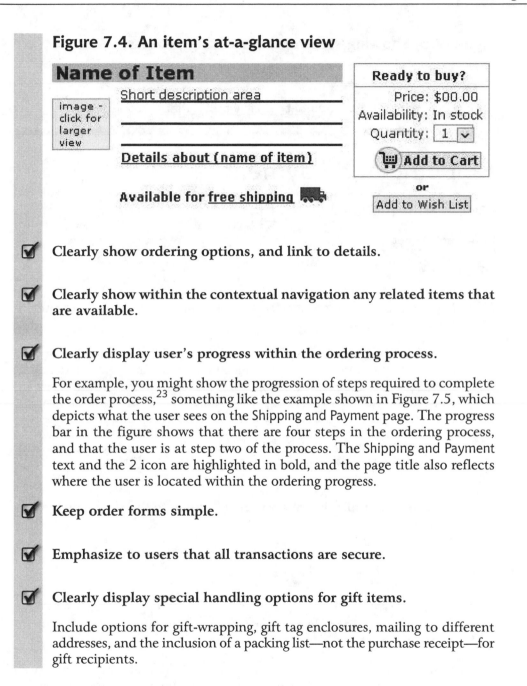

☑ **Clearly show ordering options, and link to details.**

☑ **Clearly show within the contextual navigation any related items that are available.**

☑ **Clearly display user's progress within the ordering process.**

For example, you might show the progression of steps required to complete the order process,[23] something like the example shown in Figure 7.5, which depicts what the user sees on the Shipping and Payment page. The progress bar in the figure shows that there are four steps in the ordering process, and that the user is at step two of the process. The Shipping and Payment text and the 2 icon are highlighted in bold, and the page title also reflects where the user is located within the ordering progress.

☑ **Keep order forms simple.**

☑ **Emphasize to users that all transactions are secure.**

☑ **Clearly display special handling options for gift items.**

Include options for gift-wrapping, gift tag enclosures, mailing to different addresses, and the inclusion of a packing list—not the purchase receipt—for gift recipients.

---

[23] Wodtke, 207.

Figure 7.5. Showing steps in the ordering process

Shipping and Payment

☑ **If your ecommerce store sells internationally, design menus and information accordingly.**

Include pricing for a variety of currencies, or provide information on currency exchange rate policies. If you are unable to handle international orders, be sure to make this clear up-front. It can be a very frustrating experience for a customer to begin to place an order only to find that they cannot complete it because the delivery address is not acceptable.

☑ **Clearly show options that allow customers to modify the quantity of each item being purchased.**

☑ **Provide clear links that allow users to return to the shopping process from their carts.**

Organizing Directories

Checklist 7.7

☑ **Base your user-friendly directory structure on your content's information architecture.**

Your content's information architecture is the natural basis for your web site's directory structures—store content about your company in the `about` directory, and store newsletters in the `newsletters` directory, for example.

You might consider creating directories by topic, by date, and by security needs (i.e., password-protected areas, restricted files, etc.).

☑ **Use conventional practice to create guessable, user-friendly, consistent directory names.**

A conventional practice has developed among software company web sites to make finding products easy. You'll find that quite a few web sites offer software products in directories that use the company's name with the .com TLD, followed by `/products/` and the product name.[24] Table 7.1 lists just a few sites that follow this conventional practice:

Table 7.1. Directory names and conventional practice

Product	Domain	Directory structure	
		Products	Product name
Adobe Photoshop	http://adobe.com/	products/	photoshop/
Macromedia Flash	http://macromedia.com/	products/	flash/
Barebones BBEdit	http://barebones.com/	products/	bbedit/
Jasc Paint Shop Pro	http://jasc.com/	products/	paintshoppro/

Before you decide on your directory names, investigate web sites that are easy to navigate. For example, on many web sites, you can type in the company name and the .com TLD, then **/about/** or **/contact/** into your browser's address bar to access the corresponding content. Figure 7.6 shows many of the commonly used root-level directory names.[25]

---

[24] See, in particular, Jesse James Garrett's article, *User-Centered URL Design* [http://www.adaptivepath.com/publications/essays/archives/000058.php] for more on this topic.
[25] See Greg Knauss's article, *A Standard for Site Organization* [http://www.theobvious.com/archive/1998/11/02.html].

Figure 7.6. Conventional-practice directory names

about
contact
forums
images
help
legal
newsletter
press
products
services
sitemap

Catering to URL "Hackers"

Remember that some people enjoy "URL hacking"—trying to guess the addresses of pages on your site, instead of using your web site's navigation tools to access those pages. A user might simply edit the current web address from

http://somesite.com/recipes/indian/curry/spicy/

to

http://somesite.com/recipes/indian/

and hit **Enter**. Your web site should be able to cater to these users. In Figure 7.7, the user would expect to access an index page for all the Indian recipes on the site.

Plan ahead for the growth of your directory structure.

If you were to create a web site for your gourmet cooking store, you'd probably like to include a section for recipes. After all, visitors can read a recipe, and, if they like it, buy the ingredients at your store! So you create a `recipes` directory to store your recipe pages. Instead of putting all of your recipe pages in the `recipes` directory, though, you'd be wise to add categories for existing recipes and store the pages in each category accordingly, something like the directory structure example shown in Figure 7.7.

Figure 7.7. A directory structure that allows for growth

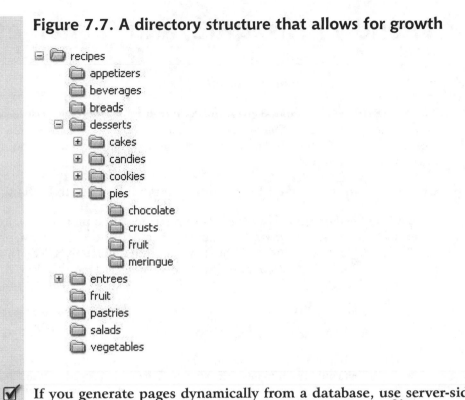

If you generate pages dynamically from a database, use server-side scripting to create easy-to-remember permanent URLs.[26]

Allow for secure areas in your directory structure.

Rather than storing sensitive or secure information throughout your directories, set up secure directories specifically to store sensitive information. This approach makes the content and site much easier to manage![27]

---

[26] See Ralf S. Engelschall's article, *A User's Guide to URL Rewriting with the Apache Webserver* [http://www.engelschall.com/pw/apache/rewriteguide/].
[27] See Paul Chin's article, titled *Intranet Content Organization* [http://www.intranetjournal.com/articles/200309/ij_09_18_03a.html].

Using Friendly URIs, URLs, and Filenames

Checklist 7.8

☑ **Use human-readable, consistent filenames.**

Make sure that each filename gives an accurate hint of the page's content, and that it creates a URL that anyone can easily read, write, and remember. Consistency facilitates the all-important predictability, and promotes easier web site maintenance.

☑ **Create human-friendly URLs, including database-generated URLs.**

Dynamically generated URLs often contain strings of command punctuation, such as & (ampersand), % (percentage), + (plus), and $ (dollar) signs, which are not human-friendly. To create more human-friendly URLs that are easy to remember and communicate, you could use server-side URL rewriting techniques, or have your web site CMS generate static pages that use friendly URLs.[28]

 Using Robots Exclusion Files

If your web site CMS or other application provides sorting features that could result in more than one URL being generated for the same content, include directions to exclude the duplicates within your `ro-bots.txt` file[29] to help search engine crawlers. (A `robots.txt` text file gives permissions and instructions to search engine robots about directories and filenames; for instance, it's commonly used to tell the bots which areas to avoid indexing.)

☑ **Keep filenames and directory names as short as possible.**

☑ **Use lowercase letters and numbers as first choices for directory names and filenames.**

---

[28] For more on this topic, see Avi Rappoport's article, *Generating Simple URLs for Search Engines* [http://www.searchtools.com/robots/goodurls.html].
[29] See Martijn Koster's article, *Robots Exclusion* [http://www.robotstxt.org/wc/exclusion.html] for more on this.

☑ **Avoid the use of mixed-case or all-capitals for filenames and directories.**

Use all lowercase letters. This helps maintain consistency and avoids potential problems with servers that use case-sensitive URLs, such as UNIX—especially important if you change web hosts.

☑ **Limit the use of underscores, hyphens, and periods in filenames and directory names.**

☑ **Avoid using special characters in filenames or directory names.**

Examples of special characters to avoid are ?, %, #, /, \, :, ;, $, ^.

☑ **Avoid character spaces in filenames.**

Use underscores if you need to replace spaces; however, minimize their use.

☑ **Create filenames and locations with a view to permanence and the long term.**

Unlike files that you move around on your computer, a URL is associated with each web page on your server. Therefore, if you move a web page, you need to redirect users to the new URL to avoid frustrating them, and to make sure search engines find your new page. Links from other web sites are an important aspect of the Web, and play a critical role in search engine rankings. Create all of your filenames with permanence, and the long term, in mind.[30]

☑ **Redirect the URLS of pages that have been moved or removed.**

Your first choice should be to use server-side redirect techniques, such as Apache mod_rewrite, IIS ReWrite, or ISAPI ReWrite.[31] If server-side redirecting isn't an option, though, consider using client-side redirects.

---

[30] For more on this, see my article, *Friday Feast #55: Friendly, Lasting URLs* [http://brainstormsandraves.com/archives/2003/08/08/friday_feast_55_friendly_lasting_urls/], and Jakob Nielsen's report, URL as UI [http://www.useit.com/alertbox/990321.html].
[31] For more, see the Apache HTTP Server Documentation Project's, *Module mod_rewrite URL Rewriting Engine* in Apache HTTP Server Version 1.3 (2004) [http://httpd.apache.org/docs/mod/mod_rewrite.html], and Matt Foley's tutorial, *Top 10 IIS Tips* [http://www.sitepoint.com/article/top-10-iis-tips].

Hiding Filename Extensions as Much as Possible

You can help retain the longevity and permanence of your URIs (Universal or Uniform Resource Identifiers) by eliminating file extensions such as .php, .cfm, and others. Doing so can also make your filenames easier to remember.[32]

Checklist 7.9

☑ **Create your web site's file directory structure to use directory defaults for web page filenames.**

For example, don't create an About page on your server in the root directory, as appears in the example shown in Figure 7.8.

Figure 7.8. Avoiding URIs with filename extensions

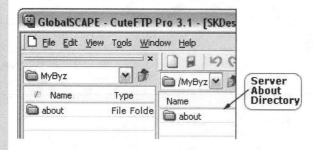

Instead, create an about directory folder, as shown below in Figure 7.9.

Figure 7.9. Correctly creating and structuring directory folders

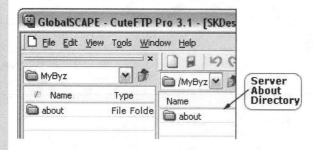

---

[32] For more on this topic, see Tim Berners-Lee's article, *Cool URIs Don't Change* [http://www.w3.org/Provider/Style/URI.html], and Victor Engmark's *Make Readable URIs* [http://www.w3.org/QA/Tips/readable-uri].

For your web page URI, use the server's directory default filename, such as `index.html`, `index.shtml`, or `default.htm`—check with your ISP to ascertain the defaults on your server. If you do so, the default web page will load automatically when a URL points to a directory name, rather than a filename. This approach can be easy to remember and maintain, and hides implementation information.[33]

The URL that's used to access the web page in Figure 7.8 above, from the fictional MyByz web site, is http://mybyz.com/about.shtml. Figure 7.10 provides a more user-friendly approach—the URL is http://mybyz.com/about/.

Figure 7.10. The about directory folder with default web page

You can use this directory name within your site markup. See the next point for details on hiding the server directory default `index.shtml` in your site's markup, too.

In your site's markup, hide filename extensions as much as possible.

This approach provides a more human-friendly URI, gives you the flexibility to change the underlying technology—e.g., to convert your web site from ASP to PHP—without breaking URIs, and can even help to generate smaller file sizes, as you won't need to specify entire filenames. For example, in your site markup, have your hyperlinks refer to directories:

```
<a href="/about/">About</a>
```

---

[33] Again, Victor Engmark's article titled *Make Readable URIs* [http://www.w3.org/QA/Tips/readable-uri], has more on this.

```
<a href="/about/johndoe/">About John Doe</a>
```

Avoid creating hyperlinks that contain filenames and their extensions:

```
<a href="/about/index.shtml">About</a>
```

```
<a href="/about/johndoe/index.shtml">About John Doe</a>
```

Summary

In this chapter, we reviewed checklists that will help you plan and organize your web site's information architecture. We discussed the importance of basing your site structure on user needs, and organizing the site to optimize its findability. We also saw checklists designed to help you organize your web site for success, and organize the information architecture for all your web pages, including ecommerce pages.

The last section provided checklists that will help create your web site directory structures, filenames, and user-friendly URIs and URLs. In Chapter 8, we'll translate the information architecture we developed in this chapter to your web site's navigation.

8

Navigation

Much like a street map is designed to help you find your way, or explore your surroundings, the goal of a web site's navigation system is to help users explore and to find their way through the web site.

Wendy Peck, in *Web Menus with Beauty and Brains*, states, "Excellent navigation is the result of gathering great amounts of relevant information and considering every aspect of site goals and visitor expectations ... a menu is the public presentation of how well you have done your homework and is a wonderful measure of your planning focus."[1]

The checklists in this chapter will help you to create a truly user-friendly web site navigation system—one that helps your site visitors explore and find their way around your site both easily and efficiently.

Golden Rules for Effective Web Site Navigation

Your web site's navigation must be easy to use, convenient, and appropriately labeled if it is to be helpful to your visitors. The information architecture of your

---

[1] Wendy Peck, *Web Menus with Beauty and Brains* (New York: Hungry Minds, 2002), 5.

web site shapes the characteristics of your navigation systems, so if you haven't yet established an information architecture for your site, Chapter 7 has the checklists and tips you'll need. The following checklist identifies the key considerations that underpin the success of an online navigation system.

Checklist 8.1

☑ **Create the navigation system with users in mind.**

☑ **Place the navigation system where users expect to find it.**

Users arrive at your web site with established expectations about where they'll be able to find the navigation systems. Figure 8.1 shows the most common locations for web sites' global, local or section, and contextual navigation systems.[2]

The common locations identified in Figure 8.1 aren't prescriptive: you aren't absolutely required to follow these conventions. However, it's important to know where users typically expect to find navigation, and to understand and be aware of the common practices. Consider breaking these conventions only if you have a compelling reason, and if you decide to do so, bear in mind the potential consequences—break from the standard, and you risk confusing users.

☑ **Ensure that the navigation system accommodates the various ways in which visitors want to access content and functionality on your site.**

It's important that you know how users will use your web site. Only then can you can create a navigation system that meets their needs. As we saw in Chapter 7, developing user profiles and studying the tasks each user type will want to complete—as well as how they'll complete those tasks—is crucial to understanding the ways in which your site will be used. This process impacts on the site's organization as well as its navigation.

For example, I recently needed to develop a navigation system that met a variety of visitor needs and purposes. This system, which was to be used

---

[2] Heidi K. Adkisson, *Identifying De-Facto Standards for E-Commerce Web Sites* (master's thesis, University of Washington, 2002); Michael L. Bernard, *How Should Information be Positioned in a Typical Website? Criteria for Optimal Web Design* (Designing for Usability), Software Usability Research Lab (March 30, 2003) [http://psychology.wichita.edu/optimalweb/position.htm]; Keith Instone, *An Open Discussion on Web Navigation* (paper presented at the Puget Sound SIGCHI, September 16, 2002), 5 [http://user-experience.org/uefiles/presentations/KEI-WebNav-20020916.pdf]; Jakob Nielsen, *Designing Web Usability* (Indianapolis: New Riders, 2000), 207.

Figure 8.1. Predictable locations for navigation systems

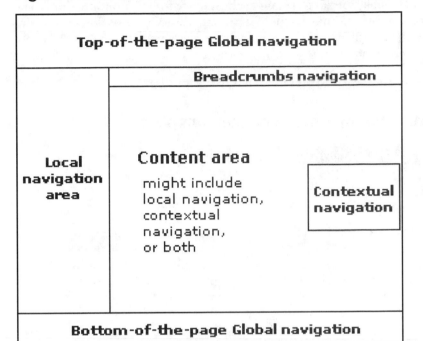

on a site that sold specialized software products, had to cater to the following groups:

❑ new users of the software who knew little or nothing about it

❑ advanced users looking for tips to optimize their usage of the software

❑ visitors who were interested in purchasing products related to the software

❑ potential consulting clients

Figure 8.2 shows the solution we created. To suit new users, we placed the Hints, Recommendations category at the top of the left-side navigation column that begins with a subcategory called New to Speech Recognition. This was followed by the label User Profiles, which contained information to help people select the software that was appropriate to various lines of work or disabilities, as well as speaking directly to those who wanted to make volume purchases of the software. The next label in the system reads Dragon NaturallySpeaking Hints—a subcategory for existing software users. This is followed by links to specific products, and information about consulting services. The Products category appears immediately below the Hints, Recommendations category because users saw this as the next most important area of the web site. As Figure 8.2 shows, this navigation system was located on the left-hand side of the site.[3]

Figure 8.2. A user-based navigation system

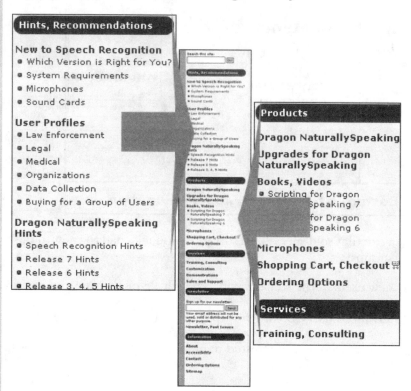

In addition to this left-hand navigation system, a global navigation bar appears across the page, providing access to top-level categories and help, as Figure 8.3 illustrates.

---

[3] This image shows the homepage of Softnet Systems, Inc. [http://pcspeak.com/] at October 15, 2004.

Figure 8.3. A navigation bar with top-level categories and help links

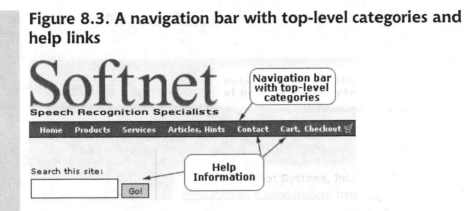

☑ **Provide multiple ways for users to access information.**

Some visitors will know exactly what they're looking for, while others will be less sure, or may want to browse. Your web site's global navigation should provide links to the site's main sections, but you might need local or section navigation, too. A site search feature may also be useful, and for sections that contain large volumes of information, you might include a section index. Contextual navigation could be used to provide links to articles or other information that relates specifically to the content on the page.

If it is to be most helpful to your visitors, your web site will probably need to incorporate a combination of navigation types. The Amazon.com web site, for example, provides users with a variety of ways to find information:

top-of-page global navigation
> Amazon.com's global navigation provides links to several main sections. Amazon.com is constantly adding more stores and categories to the site, so, to prevent the global navigation from becoming overwhelming,[4] several main sections are displayed alongside a See More Stores link—this takes users to an index page that lists all the stores available. The global navigation also contains links to the user's shopping cart, wish list, and account, as well as help, as you can see in Figure 8.4.

---

[4] A funny parody that shows how navigation can be overwhelming is provided at *Amazon 2001: A Navigation Odyssey* [http://www.dack.com/web/amazon.html].

Figure 8.4. Amazon.com top-of-page global navigation

local/section navigation

When you click a tab in the site's global navigation, the global navigation displays local/section navigation for categories within that main category. So, if the users clicks the Electronics tab, the categories Browse Brands & Products, Top Sellers, Camera & Photo, Computers, Software, and Audio & Video are displayed, as Figure 8.5 illustrates.

Figure 8.5. Amazon.com top-of-page local navigation

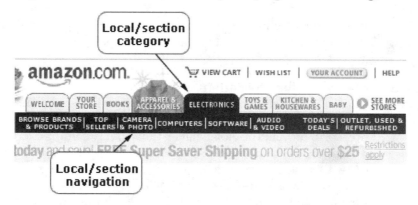

The left-hand column still provides site and web search options, as well as a more detailed local/section navigation system that adds subcategories to each of the main sections in the Electronics category.

more local/section navigation: main section content area
    The Electronics section's main content area provides personalized electronics recommendations, links to sale items, Cool Technology Gadgets, Featured Categories, a Showcase, and more.

more local/section navigation: right column
    The column on the right has links to top-selling electronics items and more personalized Favorite Stores recommendations.

As you can see, "navigation" can include a range of on-page elements—it's not just about navigation bars that run across or down the side of the page. By studying the different needs of your site's users, and the tasks they want to undertake at your site, you'll come to understand which parts of the site are the most important, and the different ways in which users will expect or need to access particular content or functionality.

The Project Gutenberg web site[5] also provides multiple ways for visitors to find books within a Book Catalog that contains more than 13,000 ebooks. Despite the growing number of books, the site's owners provide several ways to search the catalogue, which makes it easy to find books or just to browse the collection. The site's navigation and search methods include:

❑ browse by author, title, language, or recently posted

❑ database and full text search

❑ a Top 100 Books listing

❑ simple and advanced searches

❑ the Project Gutenberg Catalog in RDF/XML format

❑ directory listings

❑ a downloadable text file containing a chronological index

❑ ftp and http mirror sites

In Figure 8.6, the Gutenberg Project's Book Catalog section navigation includes navigation for authors, titles, and language, in alphabetical order.

---

[5] http://gutenberg.net/

Figure 8.6. Local navigation with multiple choices

Freshness: updated nightly.

Authors: A B C D E F G H I J K L M N O P Q R S T U V W X Y Z other

Titles: A B C D E F G H I J K L M N O P Q R S T U V W X Y Z other

Languages: Aleut Bulgarian Catalan Chinese Czech Danish Dutch English Esperanto Finnish French German Greek Hebrew Italian Japanese Khasi Korean Latin Lithuanian Middle English Nahuatl North American Indian Norwegian Polish Portuguese Romanian Russian Sanskrit Serbian Slovak Spanish Swedish Tagalog Welsh Yiddish

Recent: last 24 hours last 7 days last 30 days

Once content is stored in a database, displaying lists in a variety of ways is usually a simple matter. The Project Gutenberg web site doesn't currently provide listings ordered by year of publication, native country of the writer, or genre, which I think would be helpful navigation additions. Since this information is already included in their database, they could easily add these lists to their navigation choices, or at least include the options within their Advanced Search page.

Use the sitemap you created as you developed the site's information architecture to inform the development of your site's navigation.

The sitemap you created as you developed the site's information architecture should be translated, at least to some degree, into the site's navigation. If you haven't already created a sitemap, see Chapter 7.

☑ **Ensure that your navigation system provides context and flexibility to reinforce your information architecture hierarchy.**[6]

Visitors need to be able to move laterally and vertically within your navigation system to access the different parts of your web site. At the same time, you don't want this flexibility to be overwhelming. It works well—especially on larger sites—to provide a combination of global, local, contextual, internal, and supplementary navigation. The Amazon.com site, which we discussed above, exemplifies this point. Figure 8.7 depicts the global navigation, local/section navigation (Software), and supplemental navigation (Search) on the fictional MyByz web site. In addition, the structural breadcrumb trail (another local/section navigation element), provides context, showing where, specifically, the visitor is located within the structure of the web site.

Figure 8.7. A navigation system providing context

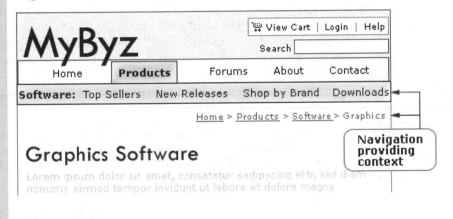

☑ **Create and implement a consistent navigation system throughout your web site.**

Once you've determined the global, local/section, internal, and supplementary navigation details for your web site, implement those systems consistently on every single page.

---

[6] Louis Rosenfeld and Peter Morville, *Information Architecture for the World Wide Web, Second Edition* (Sebastopol: O'Reilly & Associates, Inc., 2002), 112.

☑ **Use templates, server-side includes (SSI), or similar technologies to simplify the maintenance, and support the consistency, of your navigation system.**

Sensible use of "include" directives—that is, having every page use a single file that controls a given navigation area—can make the difference between maintaining a single navigation file, or, potentially, hundreds of them.

☑ **Explain your navigation system in your web site style guide.**

To help ensure the site-wide implementation and consistency of your navigation system—especially if the site is to be maintained by developers other than yourself—include specific details of its implementation in your web site style guide.

☑ **Use navigation labels that are concise, conventional, and easily understood.**

Poor navigation labels will undermine even the best site structure. Avoid using jargon—use words that your visitors will understand easily. And be sure to use concise, conventional labels, such as Home, Contact (or Contact Us), About (or About Us), wherever you can.

Tip

Form Follows Function

As the American sculptor Horatio Greenough once famously declared, "form follows function."[7] Your navigation needs—including the labels you choose—should shape your design, not the other way around. Determine the information architecture and navigation first, before you create the site's visual design.

☑ **If you use icons within your navigation, use them as enhancements, not as the only visual cues.**

For example, in Figure 8.8 the shopping cart icon that appears beside the View Cart navigation label provides a visual cue for that link. However, it would be bad for the site's usability if we were to remove the View Cart label and use only the icon. Users of text-only browsers, or visitors who browsed

---

[7] Peter-Paul Koch took this to heart in his *Form Follows Function* [http://www.digital-web.com/articles/form_follows_function/] article for Digital Web Magazine in 2003.

with images turned off, would not see the graphic icon, and may not realize that the link existed.

Figure 8.8. Using icons as visual enhancements

Icons that Work

If you use icons to enhance the visual cues on your site, be certain that they are well understood. Complete detailed user testing before you decide to use icons, and use conventional icon symbols whenever possible.

☑ **If you use graphics in navigation areas, be sure to cater to visitors who use low-bandwidth connections and/or alternative devices.**

While graphic navigation bars can look great, it's important to remember that not all users have high-resolution monitors and speedy web connections. It's a good idea to create any graphically-based navigation system with bandwidth conservation in mind. Optimize graphics to improve your page load times, and include the `alt` or `title` attribute to support visitors who browse with images turned off, or using alternative devices.

One easy way to conserve bandwidth while keeping your site looking fantastic is to use CSS. You can use CSS to create many visual effects, including borders, background colors, tabs, mouse hovers, and more. Not only does this approach minimize the use of graphics, which, in turn, helps reduce bandwidth and page load times, but it also has the added bonus of supporting the site's accessibility.[8]

☑ **Avoid using Flash to create your web site's navigation.**

If your site visitors don't have Flash (or the correct version of Flash) installed, or can't use Flash for some reason, they won't be able to use your

---

[8] For helpful examples and details on using CSS, see Dan Cederholm, *Web Standards Solutions: The Markup and Style Handbook* (Berkeley: friends of ED, an Apress Company, 2004), 10–13.

site. While you can take steps to ensure that your Flash files are accessible, unfortunately, this can be a particularly challenging task.[9] If you choose to use Flash for navigation, be sure to include an additional HTML-based text navigation to ensure that your site is accessible to all users.

If you use JavaScript to create or enhance navigation elements, make sure your navigation works without it.

Your web site visitors may have JavaScript disabled, and your navigation must be usable by those who rely on assistive technologies. As such, we must be careful in our use of JavaScript in navigation. If you want to create a rollover effect, consider using CSS instead. If you want an expanding and collapsing navigation system, be sure that it can be used without scripting. Take a look at the local navigation system at Brainstorms and Raves,[10] which uses CSS and DOM-based expandable and collapsible navigation menus that are cross-browser and cross-platform compatible, and accessibility-friendly. They're proof that the usability of such systems can be guaranteed.[11] Figure 8.9 shows the menus in their collapsed and expanded states.

Site visitors who have turned off JavaScript, or use alternative devices such as screen readers, can click the Toggle Show/Hide link to access the alternative navigation.

Keep in mind the browser features that are used to access your web site.

Whether you're creating an intranet, extranet, or public web site, the vast majority of your visitors will use a web browser such as Internet Explorer, Firefox, Safari, Mozilla, or Opera. Some of your visitors will use PDAs, cell phones, and screen readers. All these browsers provide built-in navigation features, such as Back and Forward buttons or functions, History, and Bookmarks or Favorites. By default, unvisited links display in blue, while visited links are purple. In addition, when users pass their cursor over a hyperlink in a typical web browser, the destination URL appears in the status bar—usually at the bottom of the browser view window. Keep these

[9] Jared Smith has written a good article on the subject, *Creating Accessible Macromedia Flash Content* [http://www.webaim.org/techniques/flash/].
[10] http://brainstormsandraves.com/
[11] For more on creating accessible menus like this, see Jeffrey Zeldman, *Designing with Web Standards* (Indianapolis: New Riders, 2003), 372–77. For other scripting options, see SitePoint's book, *DHTML Utopia: Modern Web Design Using JavaScript & DOM*, by Stuart Langridge.

Figure 8.9. An expanding and collapsing navigation menu

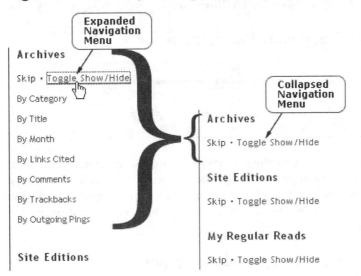

points in mind as you develop your navigation system, to ensure that the end result is usable across different browsers, platforms, and devices.

☑ Don't disable browser navigation features.

Make sure your web site navigation doesn't disable browser functions, such as the Back and Forward functions. Methods such as JavaScript redirects, frames, or opening links in new windows can all override or disable the browser's native functionality. Thoroughly test your web site to ensure that your navigation doesn't impact negatively on browser navigation features.

Creating User-centered Global Navigation

Your web site's global navigation should appear on every page, and provide consistent access to functionality that visitors may need at any time while they're using your site.

Global navigation typically takes two formats—it appears across the top of the page, or along its left-hand side; often, it's also displayed in simple text-link form across the bottom of the page. Whether at the top or left of the page, the global navigation usually provides links to important content, top-level categories, and help information and tools, as Figure 8.10 illustrates.

Figure 8.10. Top-of-page global navigation

The bottom-of-page navigation typically repeats the top-of-page navigation system alongside extra links to other important, but less frequently accessed areas of the site: legal and contact information, or the sitemap, for example. Figure 8.11 shows an example of bottom-of-page navigation; it corresponds to the top-of-page navigation we saw in Figure 8.10.

Figure 8.11. Bottom-of-page global navigation

Home | Products | Forum | About | Cart, Checkout | Search | Login
Help | Sales and Support | Contact | Accessibility | Sitemap

Privacy | Terms of Use | Copyright © 2004 MyByz, Inc. All rights reserved.

Checklist 8.2

☑ **Include a link to your homepage in your global navigation.**

Most top-of-page global navigation systems include the company logo. Make your company logo a clickable link to your homepage, but also be sure to create a separate link to Home in your global navigation. Not all users will realize that the logo is a clickable link, so including a Home link in the global navigation is the most user-friendly approach—don't think that it's redundant! The examples in Figure 8.10 and Figure 8.11 depict the Home navigation item as part of the global navigation.

Top-left, Center-bottom

Users expect to find links to the homepage in the top-left corner, and in the center of the bottom of every web page.[12]

---

[12] Heidi P. Adkisson, *Global "Home" Link*, Web Design Practices (2003) [http://webdesignpractices.com/navigation/globalhome.html]; Michael Bernard, *Examining User Expectations for the Location of Common E-Commerce Web Objects*, Usability News (April 1, 2002) [http://psychology.wichita.edu/surl/usabilitynews/41/web_object-ecom.htm].

☑ **Include links to all of your web site's top-level sections in your global navigation.**

☑ **Include links to your web site's help information in your global navigation.**

Help information might include links to a shopping cart, a sitemap, web site help, contact information, or details about your company, as Figure 8.12 illustrates.

Figure 8.12. Displaying help information within the global navigation

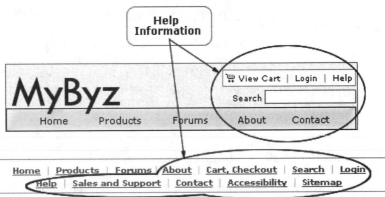

☑ **Provide contextual clues that identify the user's current location.**

Keep in mind that your visitors can arrive on any page of your site—not just the homepage—as they might follow direct links from other sites, search engines, or directories. Providing context to show users where they're located within the overall site structure will help these visitors, as well as those who began at your homepage.

Structural breadcrumb trail navigation is a good way to provide context, as it shows exactly where the user is located within the web site. Displaying local/section navigation adjacent to the global navigation bar, and using visual color cues, can also successfully show context. In Figure 8.13, local/section navigation with visual color cues, and a structural breadcrumb trail navigation system, provide context for visitors.

Figure 8.13. Providing context with local/section and structural breadcrumb trail navigation systems

What are "Structural" Breadcrumb Trails?

"Structural" breadcrumb trails are different from "true" breadcrumb trails that track the user's literal path through a web site, like the breadcrumb trails at Peter-Paul Koch's QuirksMode web site.[13] Structural breadcrumb trails reflect the contextual structure of the site, to show the user where they are located within the web site hierarchy at any point in time.

Use minimal global navigation on form pages.

Eliminate navigation elements that aren't required to fill out online forms, but do provide a link out of the form process—especially in the case of multi-step processes such as registration or purchase. Providing only essential navigation elements can help customers to stay focused while ensuring that they still have a way to leave the form page if they choose to.[14] For example, in Figure 8.14, the top-of-page global navigation has been removed; minimal bottom-of-page global navigation is displayed, and a Back to shopping link is provided on the customer Sign In page—the first step in the purchase process.

---

[13] http://www.quirksmode.org/about/faq.html#feature
[14] Matthew Linderman with Jason Fried, *Defensive Design for the Web: How to Improve Error Messages, Help, Forms, and Other Crisis Points* (Indianapolis: New Riders, 2004), 156–59; Christina Wodtke, *Information Architecture: Blueprints for the Web* (Indianapolis: New Riders, 2003), 206.

Figure 8.14. Using minimal navigation on form page

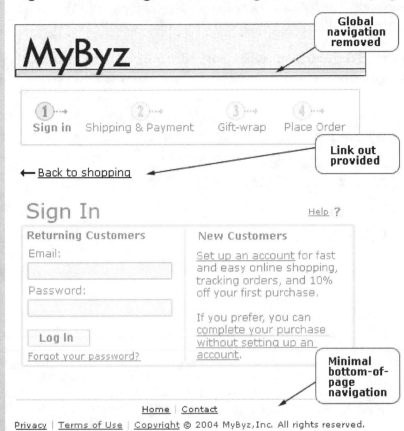

Creating Local or Section Navigation

Local navigation allows users to move easily between categories or sections within a web site. For larger sites, local navigation often lets users move between both categories and subcategories of content.

Checklist 8.3

☑ **Complement your web site's global navigation with local navigation.**

Local navigation expands upon the main content categories, allowing users to explore grouped content within those categories. In Figure 8.15, the main category, Products, is complemented by a local navigation menu that contains the subcategories, Top Sellers, New Releases, Shop by Brand, and Downloads. These local navigation sections complement the Products category—they fit logically with, and relate to, the label Products.

Figure 8.15. Local navigation complementing global navigation

Similarly, if you click on the main categories at PriceGrabber.com,[15] you'll notice that it uses a similar approach, but incorporates visual color cues to make navigation clearer and easier to use.

The left-side navigation column can also be used for local/section navigation. In Figure 8.16, the top-level global navigation categories (Home, Products) are complemented by local navigation subcategories (Software) that are broken down even further into subcategories, as the Graphics subsection shows.

☑ **Use local and internal navigation to link to more detailed information.**

When a section of the site includes a lot of detailed information, it's helpful to provide users with a brief overview, such as a bulleted list, of the content the section contains. Provide with each bulleted item a link that allows users to drill down to more in-depth information if they wish.

Let's imagine you're creating an online folio for a web design company. The parent product page might provide links to categories such as Web, Print, and Multimedia. On this page, under each main category heading, you could include an overview of the work the company had completed. For example, under Web, you could display thumbnail screenshots of the

---

[15] http://www.pricegrabber.com/

Figure 8.16. Complementary global and local navigation

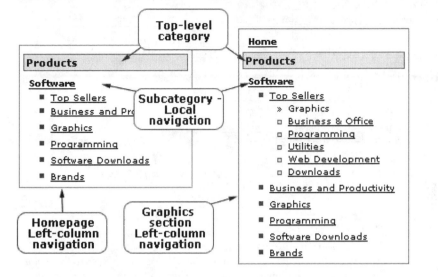

sites created, along with the sites' URLs, a brief description of each project, and a link to more information. You could then provide a detailed case study, larger screenshots, and customer testimonials to meet the needs of users who wished to drill down further. This structure is illustrated in Figure 8.17. Note that if several pages are required for the product, local or internal navigation links could join these "sibling" pages, allowing users to move easily between them. All of these pages should, of course, link back to the parent product page, as well as to the section's main page.

SitePoint uses this approach to organize its Books section.[16] If you visit one of the book pages, such as *The CSS Anthology: 101 Essential Tips, Tricks & Hacks*,[17] a bulleted list highlights the book's features under the book's title heading. This list is followed by an overview of the book. The left-hand local navigation includes links to more detailed information, including the navigation items Table of Contents, Sample Chapters, Reader Reviews, Browse the Index, and more, as shown in Figure 8.18.

Don't Create Unnecessary Pages

It's not always necessary to create extra pages to provide more detail. Page file size is a major factor in the cost of site hosting and bandwidth

---

[16] http://sitepoint.com/books/
[17] http://www.sitepoint.com/books/cssant1/

Figure 8.17. Local and internal navigation links

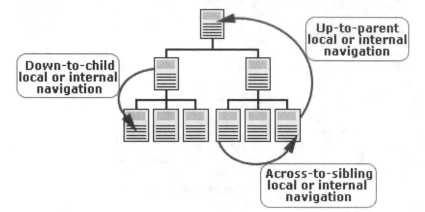

usage—as well as how easily users are able to access your site's content—so don't create extra pages unless they're really needed. If the file size of your page stays remains small even after you include specific products highlights and details, there may be no need to create extra pages for this information—especially if you provide thumbnail images that link to full size versions. Include internal navigation to provide an at-a-glance view of the page content and to allow convenient navigation within the page itself.

☑ **For web sites that have subsites, or sections with subcategories, consider including subcategory navigation within the global navigation.**

A user-friendly approach to navigation that's especially suited to larger web sites is to include direct links from the web site's homepage to *subcategory* pages (otherwise known as "grandchild-level" pages, because they are three levels deep in the site, and are usually accessed through a top-level navigation item, then a section navigation item). This approach can deliver a helpful overview of the content that's available on the web site, and provide users with quick, easy access to that content. The navigation system in Figure 8.19 shows the top-level main section links (Design and Layout, Client Side Coding), and grandchild-level subcategory links that are displayed on SitePoint's homepage.[18]

---

[18] http://sitepoint.com/

Figure 8.18. SitePoint Books local and internal navigation links

Microsoft takes a different approach, including left-hand navigation links to its main subsites only from its homepage.[19] The homepage provides left-hand navigation links to main subsites, such as the Product Families category, which links to the Windows, Office, and Windows Server System subsections, among others. Clicking Office takes you to the Microsoft Office subsite.[20] Although each subsite (except MSN, which has a different look and feel) has its own local left-hand navigation, within each of Microsoft's subsites the top-of-page global navigation includes links to the Microsoft homepage and the sitemap, as well as a search box that allows users to search the entire Microsoft.com site. This approach provides local naviga-

---

[19] http://microsoft.com
[20] http://office.microsoft.com/

Figure 8.19. Main section links and subcategory links (grandchild-level) from homepage

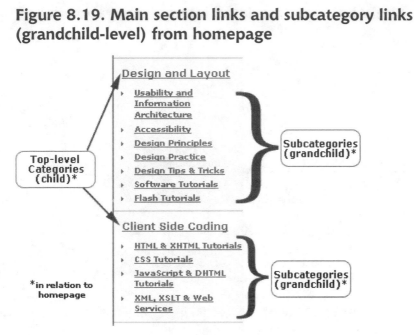

tion that helps users move within a subsite, while providing global navigation features that allow users to browse the whole of the site, no matter where they're actually located within the overall structure.

☑ **Use structural breadcrumb navigation to add context for users.**

Breadcrumb navigation contains hyperlinks that reflect a web site's category hierarchy in sequential order, providing context and cues about where the visitor is located within the web site. Figure 8.20, Figure 8.21, and Figure 8.22 show sequential screenshots of structural breadcrumb navigation from three of SitePoint's pages. The first, Figure 8.20, is at the top-level category section, Before You Code. Note that Home is a clickable link, but the structural breadcrumb for the current page, Before You Code, is not clickable.

Within the Before You Code section, users can click on several subcategories, including Site Planning. Figure 8.21 shows the structural breadcrumb navigation for the Site Planning subcategory. Again, the current page is not a clickable link.

Figure 8.20. Structural breadcrumb navigation: top-level category section

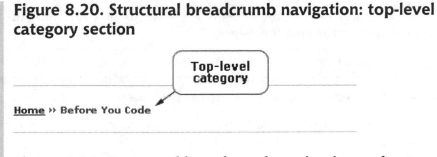

Figure 8.21. Structural breadcrumb navigation: subcategory

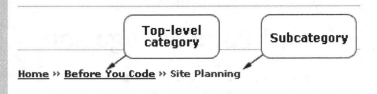

From the Site Planning subcategory, users can click an article link to view that article content. Figure 8.22 shows the structural breadcrumb navigation for one of these articles. SitePoint has chosen to break the article across six web pages, and the structural breadcrumb navigation provides links to all of them.

Figure 8.22. Structural breadcrumb navigation: article, content

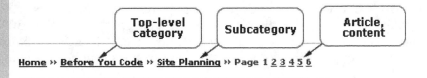

Although usability experts are still researching this form of navigation, they're finding that structural breadcrumb navigation helps reduce user search time, clicks, and errors.[21]

---

[21] Michael L Bernard, *Criteria for Optimal Web Design (Designing for Usability): What is the Best Way to Arrange Menus*, Optimal Web Design, Software Usability Research Lab (March 31, 2003) [http://psychology.wichita.edu/optimalweb/menu.htm]; Bonnie Lida Rogers and Barbara Chaparro, *Breadcrumb Navigation: Further Investigation of Usage*, Usability News (May 2, 2003) [http://psychology.wichita.edu/surl/usabilitynews/52/breadcrumb.htm].

Create local navigation systems for sections of your web site that contain more than a few pages.

If you give a local structure to each section of your site, users will feel more comfortable and more welcome, and it will be easier for them to navigate and find information.[22]

 Create a user-friendly table of contents for each section of your web site.

If you have a few pages within a section, it's helpful to provide a table of contents to help users move quickly to the content they want.

Providing Internal Page Navigation

Internal page navigation can be helpful on pages of your web site that contain a lot of information and require some degree of organization. Here's a checklist to help you include user-friendly internal page navigation on your site.

Checklist 8.4

 For longer pages, create a tables of contents whose items link to each heading or subheading on the page.

A table of contents provides helpful information and makes navigating the page easier and faster. Some would argue that content that spans more than a couple of screens should be split across multiple pages to improve page load times, and if you have a site that's supported by advertising, more pages will mean more ad impressions. The disadvantage to this approach is that with each click to a subsequent page, you lose users: 75% of users will fail to click through to a second page, and fewer than 50% of those who do will click through to a third page.[23] There's no point in having the opportunity for all those ad impressions if nobody is going to see the ads!

Offering Long Content as a Download

If you have content that spans more than a few screens, such as a white paper, presentation, or research paper, consider providing that content as a downloadable document for offline reading. For more on alternative document formats, see Chapter 4.

---

[22] Nielsen, 222–24.
[23] Wodtke, 19.

☑ **If content is broken across several pages, include links to all those pages from each page of content.**

☑ **If content is broken across several pages, give users the option to view it all on one page.**

Make your View on a Single Page option available on all the pages of the document, not just the first page.

☑ **Provide Top of Page links for pages that span more than two screens.**

Top of Page links aid usability and accessibility, as they take the user directly to the top of the page, where the global navigation is likely to be placed, eradicating the need for laborious scrolling. A simple text link is usually sufficient, although graphical Up arrows are also helpful in addition to the text link. See Figure 8.23 for an example.

☑ **For longer pages, include Top of Page links at regular intervals.**

You could include a Top of Page link at the end of a content block, for example, like the one in Figure 8.23—an alphabetical listing from the Brainstorms and Raves web site.[24]

Figure 8.23. Recurring Top of Page links

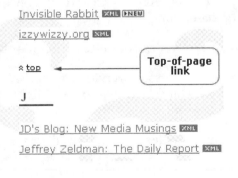

---

[24] http://brainstormsandraves.com/links/

Adding Supplemental Navigation

Large, complex web sites often need a sitemap, a site index, and a site search. This section contains checklists to help you develop these tools for your site.

Creating Sitemaps

A sitemap typically is a concise, one-page outline of the architecture of the entire site, which links to main content categories and subcategories. Sitemaps should reinforce your information hierarchy and promote user exploration, as they provide an excellent opportunity for your site visitors to get an at-a-glance view of what your web site offers.[25] The design of a sitemap greatly influences its usability. Here's a checklist to help you ensure that yours is both user-friendly and effective.

Checklist 8.5

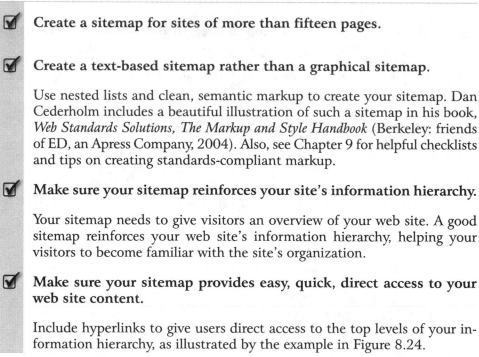

☑ **Create a sitemap for sites of more than fifteen pages.**

☑ **Create a text-based sitemap rather than a graphical sitemap.**

Use nested lists and clean, semantic markup to create your sitemap. Dan Cederholm includes a beautiful illustration of such a sitemap in his book, *Web Standards Solutions, The Markup and Style Handbook* (Berkeley: friends of ED, an Apress Company, 2004). Also, see Chapter 9 for helpful checklists and tips on creating standards-compliant markup.

☑ **Make sure your sitemap reinforces your site's information hierarchy.**

Your sitemap needs to give visitors an overview of your web site. A good sitemap reinforces your web site's information hierarchy, helping your visitors to become familiar with the site's organization.

☑ **Make sure your sitemap provides easy, quick, direct access to your web site content.**

Include hyperlinks to give users direct access to the top levels of your information hierarchy, as illustrated by the example in Figure 8.24.

---

[25] Jesse James Garrett, *The Elements of User Experience: User-centered Design for the Web* (New York: AIGA / Indianapolis: New Riders, 2003), 131.

Figure 8.24. A small web site sitemap

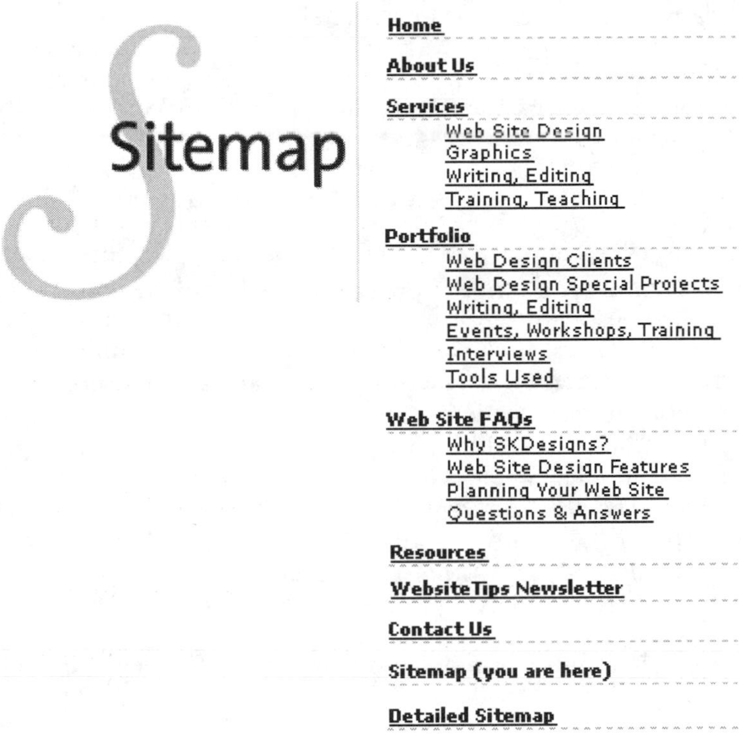

Sitemap

Home

About Us

Services
  Web Site Design
  Graphics
  Writing, Editing
  Training, Teaching

Portfolio
  Web Design Clients
  Web Design Special Projects
  Writing, Editing
  Events, Workshops, Training
  Interviews
  Tools Used

Web Site FAQs
  Why SKDesigns?
  Web Site Design Features
  Planning Your Web Site
  Questions & Answers

Resources

Website Tips Newsletter

Contact Us

Sitemap (you are here)

Detailed Sitemap

☑ **Make sure your sitemap supplements existing navigation, rather than being a last resort for users, or an excuse for poor global navigation.**

If visitors find that your navigation labels are ambiguous or the site's navigation is poor, they might use the sitemap to try to find what they're seeking[26] … assuming they don't leave the web site in frustration first! Make sure your sitemap acts only as a supplement, not a band-aid.

Creating Site Indexes

Large, complex web sites may need both a sitemap and a site index. A site index doesn't rely on the site's information hierarchy. Instead, like a book index, it uses

---

[26] Eric L. Reiss, *Practical Information Architecture: a Hands-on Approach to Structuring Successful Websites* (New York: Addison-Wesley, 2000), 132.

an exact organization scheme approach, such as alphabetical or chronological organization.[27] Site indexes are most helpful for users who already know what they're seeking and want to access it immediately.

Checklist 8.6

 Create your site index based on the terms that users actually look for.

Analyze search logs and user research information to ascertain which terms are important.

For each term in your index, provide a listing of the documents indexed with that term.

You can create indexes for smaller web sites manually. Owners of web sites that use a content management system—especially larger web sites—might employ the CMS's capabilities with metadata, and a list of equivalent terms (or "controlled vocabularies"). Creating metadata and controlled vocabularies is beyond the scope of this book, but check out the chapter on this topic in Louis Rosenfeld and Peter Morville's article, *Thesauri, Controlled Vocabularies, and Metadata* in their book, *Information Architecture for the World Wide Web*, Second Edition (Sebastopol: O'Reilly, 2002).

Remember to update your site index regularly to keep it current and accurate.

A current, accurate index is most useful and helpful to your web site visitors. If you have a content management system, consider automating these important updates.

Creating Search

Determine Whether or not you Need a Search Feature

Checklist 8.7

Include a search feature if your web site has too much information to browse easily, or if users expect it.

Unless your web site comprises only a few pages, users will usually expect a search feature to be available.

---

[27] See Chapter 7 for more on organizing your web site.

☑ **Include a search feature if you have highly dynamic content.**

Don't Need Search?

Tip

If you've determined that you don't need a search feature, at least recognize that you might need one at some point. It would be wise to bear in mind the impact of adding a search box to your web site at a later date; therefore, consider reserving an area for the search box: leave it blank, or consider using a decorative holding image of some kind.

Developing a Search Feature

Checklist 8.8

☑ **Include a search box within the global or local navigation on every page of your site.**

When you design your navigation system and create your page architecture, keep in mind recent usability studies that show that users expect to find a search box at the top of the page—in particular, at the center of the top of the page, or at the top-left of the page.[28] Figure 8.25 shows a search box positioned near the top-left of the Softnet Systems homepage,[29] above the left-hand local navigation.

You'll find the search box for the MyByz web site in the top-of-page global navigation; we've also included a link to a search page in the bottom-of-page global navigation, as Figure 8.26 shows.

☑ **For search options with restricted scope, clearly state the scope of the search in both the search box and the results pages.**

Scoping, or restricting a search to a particular area of a web site, or specific content, can be a helpful feature, especially for larger web sites. Scoped search can also help keep search results to a manageable number. For example, allowing users to search only within a particular category of products can help refine the results of a product search. Using Amazon.com's search feature, for example, you can search all products or select one of the many

---

[28] Heidi P. Adkisson, *Search*, Web Design Practices (2003) [http://webdesignpractices.com/functions/search.html]; Michael Bernard, *Examining User Expectations for the Location of Common E-Commerce Web Objects*, Usability News (April 1, 2002) [http://psychology.wichita.edu/surl/usabilitynews/41/web_object-ecom.htm].
[29] http://pcspeak.com/

Figure 8.25. Search box feature near top left of page

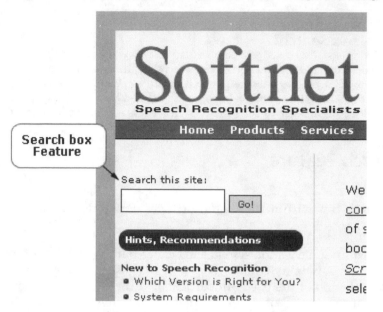

Figure 8.26. Search feature in top- and bottom-of-the-page global navigation

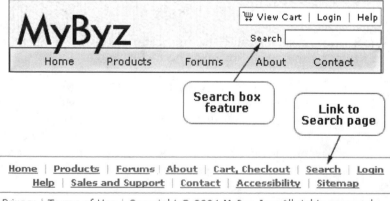

categories to receive more refined results. To prevent confusion, it's important to clarify the scope of the search up-front.

☑ **Ensure that search results are sorted to present the best matches first.**[30]

☑ **Organize search results in groups according to the web site structure.**

For example, the SitePoint web site has five main sections at the time of writing: Articles, Books, Blogs, Marketplace, and Forums. It groups its search results according to this structure, so you'll find articles together, blog posts together, and so forth.

☑ **Keep page abstracts short on search results pages.**

☑ **For advanced search, provide brief, helpful instructions.**

☑ **Allow users to search within their current results to help narrow their search.**

☑ **Provide helpful options when a search yields no results.**

In the case of a failed search, offer a method to revise the search, search tips to help improve the results, links to an advanced search facility, more detailed search instructions, a link to the site map, and, if you have one, a link to your web site's index.

☑ **Make sure your search results program eliminates duplications within the search results list.**

This includes URLs that, though they're different, actually point to the same page, for instance:

http://mybyz.com/products
http://mybyz.com/products/
http://mybyz.com/products/index.html

---

[30] Jakob Nielsen, *Designing Web Usability: The Practice of Simplicity* (Indianapolis: New Riders, 2000), 230.

☑ **Enhance search destination pages, for instance, by highlighting the user's search terms.**

Highlighting the user's search terms on the pages they access through the search results allows users to scan those pages to find exactly what they're looking for. It also lets them quickly assess the relevance of that information to their needs.

A Good Search is Worth the Effort!

Users find it extremely frustrating when a web site's search tool provides inaccurate or unhelpful results. Make sure you test your search facility well, and customize it closely to your users' needs. For more on search tools, including installation and configuration tips, see Avi Rappoport's Search Tools web site.[31]

Summary

A web site navigation system needs to provide visitors with an easy and convenient way to explore and move through your web site. This chapter's checklists covered the key points that you should address as you build a user-friendly web site navigation system, including tips on creating good global, local/section, internal page, and supplemental navigation, including sitemaps, indexes, and search.

Next, we take a different tack! Chapter 9 explores the important questions of creating your site using code that embraces current best-practices and meets the recommendations of the World Wide Web Consortium.

---

[31] http://searchtools.com/

Best Coding Practice: W3C Standards and Recommendations

Think back to that dream house you were building, and imagine that it's completed and you've moved in. What would happen if you came home one day to find that your front door had been pushed down, your floors were all flooded, and your neighbor was lying at the bottom of the stairs, unconscious?

Don't worry: this *won't* happen because, although you may not have been aware of it at the time, your house was built to standards that are designed to prevent such disasters from occurring. Your doors are a standard thickness for security purposes, your plumbing is made to handle a standard level of water pressure, and your stairs are a standard height and depth to ensure they're as safe as possible. These are just a few of the aspects of your house that need to be standardized. To ensure that your home is safe and comfortable for you and your visitors, a lot more building standards will have been followed by the builders of your dream house. You may be surprised to learn that most aspects of your home adhere to specific standards—especially when you realize that Bob next door has had to follow *exactly the same* standards, even though his home is completely different from yours.

On the Web, the W3C (World Wide Web Consortium) provides recommendations that must be followed by all of us: web site designers and developers, browser makers, and the creators of software that helps us construct web sites. Despite its superior sounding title, the World Wide Web Consortium is not some higher authority that tries to force these recommendations onto an unreceptive audience.

Its advice is usually eagerly heeded by those designers, developers, browser makers, and software developers!

Even though the standards exist, there are endless ways to build a web site, just as there are endless ways to build a house. The motivation behind the development of standards is to create a basis from which we can build web sites—or homes—that anybody can use. In the case of the Web, the standards help us to ensure that anybody, anywhere, on any connection, using any system, can access our web sites and have them work as expected.

The W3C's long-term goals for the Web are to promote universal access, semantics, and an environment that's built on trust.[1] The checklists in this chapter are devoted to helping you create well-structured markup and CSS and, thereby, to achieve the best possible results for your web site.

Magic Markup

Creating meaningful structural markup allows CSS to more effectively ensure the site-wide consistency of your layouts and designs. Unlike "tag soup"—any nonstandard, poorly structured markup that, though it may be understood by the developers as they create the web site, becomes almost unintelligible when they return to it later—anyone who works on your web site will be able to understand heading elements, list item elements, paragraph elements, and other markup that's used for its intended purpose. Search engines and alternative devices also rely on correctly structured markup to do their jobs, so a standards-compliant approach to web development has numerous benefits beyond simply making it easy for you to maintain your site. Use the checklists below to help ensure that your web site uses well-executed structural markup.

Checklist 9.1

☑ **Use consistent markup.**

☑ **Use the correct DOCTYPE.**

Browsers look for the DOCTYPE, or document type declaration, at the top of every web page; it tells the browser how to render that page and, as such,

---

[1] W3C, *W3C Mission* in About the World Wide Web Consortium (W3C), (October 14, 2004) [http://www.w3.org/Consortium/#mission].

is essential if web pages are to display and function properly in newer, standards-based browsers.[2]

Tip 💡

Accessing DOCTYPE Templates

The Web Standards Project (WaSP) web site's Learn section[3] provides free structural templates to help designers and developers create conforming HTML and XHTML documents that include the proper DOCTYPE. You're welcome to download and use them, and they're a great way to start your web site development work.

☑ **Validate your code.**

Use the W3C Validator to validate your markup. Two services are offered: a CSS Validation Service,[4] and a Markup Validation Service.[5] If you validate your code frequently during its development, you'll find errors and problems quickly, and you'll be able to fix them more easily than if you left the validation until later. Don't wait until you complete an entire page or—worse yet—an entire site!

☑ **Include the correct character encoding with the Content-Type <meta> tag on every web page.**

For example, here's the opening code for a document that is written to the XHTML 1.0 Strict DOCTYPE, and uses the ISO-8859-1 (aka Latin 1) character encoding. Note the use of a <meta http-equiv="Content-Type"> tag to specify the character encoding.

```
<!DOCTYPE html PUBLIC "-//W3C//DTD XHTML 1.0 Strict//EN"
    "http://www.w3.org/TR/xhtml1/DTD/xhtml1-strict.dtd">
<html xmlns="http://www.w3.org/1999/xhtml"
    xml:lang="en" lang="en">
<head>
<title>Nifty New XHTML document</title>
<meta http-equiv="Content-Type"
    content="text/html; charset=iso-8859-1" />
```

---

[2] For more on creating standards-compliant sites, see Jeffrey Zeldman's article, *Fix Your Site With the Right DOCTYPE!* [http://www.alistapart.com/articles/doctype/], and *My Web Site is Standard! And Yours?* [http://www.w3.org/QA/2002/04/Web-Quality] by Karl Dubost.
[3] http://www.webstandards.org/learn/templates/
[4] http://jigsaw.w3.org/css-validator/
[5] http://validator.w3.org/

Note that the W3C standard for XHTML recommends that documents also begin with an XML declaration that specifies the character encoding like this:

```
<?xml version="1.0" encoding="ISO-8859-1"?>
```

Unfortunately, this declaration causes Internet Explorer 6 to ignore the DOCTYPE that follows it. This bug has been corrected in Internet Explorer 7, but until Internet Explorer 6 passes from common use the XML declaration is best omitted. Be aware that this may cause some XML-aware software to interpret your documents using the default UTF-8 encoding.[6]

☑ **Encode reserved HTML characters as HTML character entities.**

Encoding reserved characters as HTML character entities allows them to be interpreted correctly by browsers and other agents. If they're not encoded, browsers may misinterpret the characters, for instance, taking < to mean the start of an HTML tag, or & to indicate the start of a character entity reference. Table 9.1 identifies a few of the more common reserved characters, and identifies their correct codes.[7]

Table 9.1. Encode reserved HTML entities

Character Name	Entity Name	Entity Number	Character
Quotation mark	&quot;	&#34;	"
Ampersand	&amp;	&#38;	&
Less-than symbol	&lt;	&#60;	<
Greater-than symbol	&gt;	&#62;	>

☑ **Include the title element on each page.**

The words that you include within the title element (located within the head element of your web pages) become a user-friendly page title that's helpful to search engines, site users, and your web site's local search facility alike.

---

[6] Since ISO-8859-1 is a strict subset of UTF-8, this is not usually an issue for English language documents or for languages that make use of the same character set.
[7] For more on this, see *HTML Document Representation: Character Entity References*, in HTML 4.01 Specification: W3C Recommendation 24 December 1999 (December 24, 1999) [http://www.w3.org/TR/REC-html40/charset.html].

```
<!DOCTYPE html PUBLIC "-//W3C//DTD XHTML 1.0 Strict//EN"
    "http://www.w3.org/TR/xhtml1/DTD/xhtml1-strict.dtd">
<html xmlns="http://www.w3.org/1999/xhtml"
    xml:lang="en" lang="en">
<head>
<title>What's new in Microsoft Office 2004</title>
</head>
```

The markup above creates a title that can be displayed by the browser that renders that web page. The text within the `title` element is displayed only in the browser's title bar—it's not visible anywhere on the web page itself—as Figure 9.1 illustrates.

Figure 9.1. Applying the TITLE element in the browser window

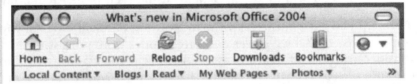

The `title` element is not the same as the `title` attribute. The attribute can be applied almost to any element as a means of providing additional information, like so:

```
<a href="http://movabletype.org/" title="Popular publishing
    system, primarily for weblogs, but configurable for web
    site publishing, too">Movable Type</a>
```

☑ **Include `meta` elements to aid your web site's search engine rankings.**

For more on `meta` element content, see Chapter 3.

☑ **Avoid using proprietary markup or scripts.**

Such scripts may be nonstandard, so it's best to avoid them.

☑ **Avoid using deprecated markup.**

Since future versions of W3C Recommendations will eliminate the elements and attributes that have been marked as "deprecated," it's best not to use them at all. Many of the deprecated elements and attributes, such as the frequently used center and font elements, are replaced by CSS rules that achieve similar results.

Some of the deprecated elements include applet, basefont, center, dir, font, isindex, menu, s, strike, and u. You can review a list of deprecated elements and attributes,[8] and access the current Index of Elements,[9] at the W3C web site.

☑ Mark up text using an HTML editor or W3C-compliant CMS.

Don't use word processing programs to convert your text to HTML or XHTML. Word processing and other software programs that convert text to HTML or XHTML are notorious for producing bloated, inappropriate markup. Instead of these packages, use an HTML editing program or CMS that's based on the W3C Recommendations, and always validate your pages prior to publishing them, to help ensure their proper rendering.

If you find yourself in the unfortunate position of having to deal with existing web pages that have been converted from a word processing program, consider using one of the tools available to help you eradicate the bloated markup, such as HTML Tidy, or the Clean Up HTML command in Macromedia Dreamweaver.[10]

☑ Optimize the markup generated by graphics programs.

Graphics software programs are notorious for placing sliced images in table cells. This approach creates incredibly messy and bloated markup—the designer can simply forget about separating content from presentation! So it's important to optimize the markup created by graphics programs, or better still, to write your own code that uses CSS for presentation, and reserves the table element for the purpose of displaying tabular data.

Staying Informed of the Recommendations

The W3C Recommendations for technologies such as HTML, XHTML, XML, CSS, and DOM provide enormous possibilities for designers and developers, and are increasingly being supported by browser makers and software companies. It's important to become

---

[8] http://www.w3.org/TR/REC-html40/appendix/changes.html#h-A.3.1.2
[9] http://www.w3.org/TR/REC-html40/index/elements.html
[10] For help in using these tools, see *Clean up your Web pages with HTML TIDY* [http://www.w3.org/People/Raggett/tidy/], on the W3C site, and Macromedia's tutorial, *Importing a Microsoft Word HTML File* [http://livedocs.macromedia.com/dreamweaver/mx2004/using/04_doc10.htm#90636;].

well-versed in the technologies that you plan to use, and to continue to stay informed of the latest changes and best practice approaches to their application.

Separating Content from Presentation

By separating content from its presentation we gain the flexibility to create device-independent sites, repurpose content, simplify content updates and web site maintenance, and increase our sites' performance. Use the checklists below to help ensure that your web sites separate content from presentation as much as possible.

Checklist 9.2

☑ **Use external CSS.**

Linking external CSS files to your web pages is an efficient and convenient way to handle your site's CSS. This way, you can make site-wide changes via your external style sheet, rather than having to make changes to every single web page. Not only does this approach ensure the true separation of content from presentation, it also saves bandwidth and reduces file size: the style sheet downloads directly to users' browser caches, and is used by every page of your site that those visitors request. The file is accessed through the link element in your page header:

```
<head>
<title>Your Page Title Here</title>
⋮
<link rel="stylesheet" href="/css/styles.css"
    type="text/css" media="all" />
</head>
```

☑ **Use absolute links, rather than relative links, with externally linked files**

Old browsers do not predictably or consistently recognize the location of a linked file or page relative to the web page that contains the link.[11] Play it safe by using the absolute path to the file from the domain root in your link. You can replicate absolute links on every page of your web site, regardless of the file locations, and absolute links look a lot nicer than relative links.

[11] Jeffrey Zeldman, *Designing with Web Standards* (Indianapolis: New Riders, 2004), 233.

For example, consider this relative link:

```
<link rel="stylesheet" href="../../css/styles.css"
    type="text/css" media="all" />
```

This would, ideally, be replaced with the following absolute link:

```
<link rel="stylesheet" href="/css/styles.css"
    type="text/css" media="all" />
```

The relative link instructs the system to jump back two directory levels, then select the `css` folder, in order to find the `styles.css` file. The absolute link is a much simpler command; it tells the computer to start at the root directory, then select the `css` folder. This line of HTML will work regardless of whether the file that contains it is one, two, or even ten directory levels away from the root directory.

☑ Avoid the use of embedded scripts and embedded or inline CSS.

Embedded scripts and CSS add to the file size of a web page, and can make the markup messy. It may be appropriate to use embedded or inline CSS and scripts if you have a style that's specific to a page, or to certain elements on a page; otherwise, try to avoid embedded and inline scripting as much as possible.

☑ Use CSS to control web page presentation and element styling.

Thankfully, modern browsers support more CSS than ever before, which means that developers can use CSS extensively for web page presentation purposes. In fact, you can use CSS to style almost all of the elements on your web page, including text, images, tabular data, horizontal rules, headers, and more. For instance, you might use CSS to:

❑ Alter the font, size, and color of text.

❑ Add borders, margins, and padding to your images or table cells.

❑ Change the alignment of text or content in table cells.

❑ Change background colors and apply background images.

Your web pages will no longer be bloated with FONT elements and inline styles, and the resulting improvements in file size can be dramatic! And, of course, the specification of style rules in your CSS makes web site maintenance and updates infinitely easier.

note

Look Out for Proprietary Markup

Be on the lookout for old, proprietary markup! Before decent browser support was provided for CSS, an old approach that many designers used to ensure that margins would display consistently across different browsers and platforms was the proprietary Four Horsemen of Non-Validation[12] approach:

```
<body leftmargin="0" topmargin="0" marginwidth="0"
    marginheight="0">
```

Around the time at which version 2 browsers were released, Internet Explorer created its proprietary `leftmargin` and `topmargin` attributes, while Netscape created its proprietary `marginwidth` and `marginheight` attributes. You'll still find these lurking about within the markup of many sites—you may even have a redesign project that's riddled with them.

By using external CSS to control margins, you can ensure that the markup for the web page **body** element is lean. You'll reduce bandwidth in the process, since the Four Horsemen aren't used on every web page, and the external CSS loads only once for the entire web site:

```
body {
  margin:0;
  padding:0;
}
```

So, if CSS is used to designate page margins and padding, what does the **body** element look like?

```
<body>
```

That's much leaner and cleaner, too!

---

[12] For more on the Four Horsemen, see Jeffrey Zeldman's article, *From Table Hacks to CSS Layout: A Web Designer's Journey* [http://www.alistapart.com/articles/journey/].

☑ **Use the `table` element to display tabular data only.**

The `table` element's actual purpose is to display tabular data, such as charts.[13] However, before browsers supported presentational CSS, designers resorted to using the `table` element to create web page layouts and presentation, especially with David Siegel's single-pixel GIF trick and invisible table trick.[14] Modern browsers have supported presentational CSS for a few years now, and best practice recommendations include using CSS—not the `table` element—for page presentation. Reserve your use of the `table` element for displaying tabular data, and use CSS for web page layouts.

Top CSS References

An increasing number of helpful, creative, and well-written books and references are available on the topic of CSS. A few highly recommended titles include *HTML Utopia: Designing Without Tables Using CSS, Second Edition*,[15] by Rachel Andrew and Dan Shafer (SitePoint, 2006), *The CSS Anthology*[16] by Rachel Andrew (SitePoint, 2005), *Cascading Style Sheets: Separating Content from Presentation, Second Edition*, by Owen Briggs, Steven Champeon, Eric Costello, and Matt Patterson (Berkeley: friends of ED, an Apress Company, 2004); *Designing with Web Standards*, by Jeffrey Zeldman (Indianapolis: New Riders, 2004); *More Eric Meyer on CSS*, by Eric Meyer; and *Web Standards Solutions: The Markup and Style Handbook*, by Dan Cederholm (Berkeley: friends of ED, an Apress Company, 2004). Two great web resources on the topic are the CSS area on A List Apart,[17] and the tutorials on the Project Seven site.[18]

Ensuring the Integrity of your Markup

As we've already discussed, well-executed structural markup is consistent and easily understood by anyone working on your web site. Your can style your

---

[13] W3C, *Tables: Introduction to Tables* in HTML 4.01 Specification (December 24, 1999) [http://www.w3.org/TR/REC-html40/struct/tables.html#h-11.1].

[14] David Siegel, *Creating Killer Web Sites: The Art of Third-Generation Site Design*, (Indianapolis: Hayden Books, 1996), 67–82; David Siegel, *The Single-Pixel GIF Trick*, Web Wonk: Tips for Writers and Designers (March 14, 1996) [http://www.dsiegel.com/tips/wonk5/single.html].

[15] http://www.sitepoint.com/books/css2/

[16] http://www.sitepoint.com/books/cssant1/

[17] http://www.alistapart.com/topics/code/css/

[18] http://www.projectseven.com/tutorials

markup using CSS to ensure easy-to-maintain site-wide consistency. Search engines and alternative devices also rely on structural markup. So it's a good idea not to "fake" your markup in any way, or to take shortcuts. Use markup as it was intended!

Checklist 9.3

☑ Use proper heading elements.

Do use the proper heading elements, not custom-styled classes for headings. Always begin each web page with the h1 element, then mark up subsequent headings sequentially:

```
<h1>Page Title</h1>
<h2>Article Heading</h2>
<p>Text</p>
<h3>Article Subhead</h3>
<p>Text</p>
<h3>Article Subhead</h3>
<p>Text</p>
```

Do not fake heading markup like this:

```
<p class="header">Heading Text</p>
<span class="header">Heading Text</span>
<div class="header">Heading Text</div>
```

Or, even worse, like this:

```
<p><font size="3"><bold>Heading Text</bold></font></p>
```

☑ Use ul, ol, and li elements to mark up lists.

As well as using unordered lists (ul) and ordered lists (ol) within text content, the use of list item (li) elements for navigation is very popular among designers and developers who understand the usefulness, flexibility, and semantic benefits of this technique. By using CSS to create your navigation, you can change its appearance dramatically—for instance, displaying the navigation list items horizontally across a page without bullets, and using background images to create visually appealing navigation—with a minimum of effort.

☑ Use definition list elements—**dl**, **dt**, and **dd**—for lists of definitions.[19]

☑ Use the **br** element for line breaks only.

Don't use the br element to define new paragraphs or list items, like this:

```
Paragraph text<br /><br />
Paragraph text<br /><br />
1. List item 1<br /><br />
2. List item 2<br /><br />
```

Instead, use the correct markup:

```
<p>Paragraph text</p>
<p>Paragraph text</p>
<ol>
  <li>List item 1</li>
  <li>List item 2</li>
</ol>
```

Tip

Styling Paragraphs and List Items

You can use CSS to style paragraphs and list items. For some excellent examples and tutorials, see Dan Cederholm's *Web Standards Solutions* (Berkeley: friends of ED, an Apress Company, 2004); Eric Meyer's *More Eric Meyer on CSS* (Indianapolis: New Riders, 2004), and the area of Russ Weakley's Listmatic web site that's devoted to styling lists with CSS.[20]

☑ Avoid using the **pre** element for general formatting.

The pre element forces preformatted text to display, which disables word wrapping. Additionally, unless you include specific styles in your CSS, text within the pre element uses the browser's default, fixed-width font and leaves white space intact. You'll find the pre element is sometimes used

---

[19] Dan Cederholm, *More Lists* in *Web Standards Solutions: The Markup and Style Handbook* (Berkeley: friends of ED, an Apress Company, 2004), 110–20; W3C, *Definition Lists: the DL, DT, and DD Elements* in HTML 4.01 Specification (December 24, 1999) [http://www.w3.org/TR/html401/struct/lists.html#h-10.3].
[20] http://css.maxdesign.com.au/listamatic/

for poetry, and is used frequently with code examples, since it shows the preformatted indentations and line breaks as they should appear.[21]

☑ **Use the span element sparingly.**

If more meaningful markup exists, use it. For example, instead of using `<span class="emphasis">emphasized text</span>`, use the proper element for emphasis: `<em>emphasized text</em>`. Use the span element only as a last resort.

Tip

Don't Fake your Markup!

There are numerous resources online that provide sound advice to help you ensure the integrity of your markup. I've written a couple of articles myself: *Don't Fake Your Markup: Accessibility Issues for CSS*,[22] and *Semantics, HTML, XHTML, and Structure*.[23]

Excellent XHTML

HTML is more forgiving than XHTML. If you're in the habit of validating your markup, the switch to XHTML will be a simple matter. If you're not big on closing elements, using quotations around attribute values, or paying attention to your elements' nesting, there's no time like the present to develop the habits that will enable you to improve your coding skills! This checklist will help you make the transition from HTML 4.01 to XHTML 1.0 Transitional, which still supports older browsers.

Checklist 9.4

☑ **Nest all elements properly.**

XHTML requires elements to be nested properly.[24]

Here's an example of poor nesting:

---

[21] W3C, *Preformatted Text: The PRE element* in HTML 4.01 Specification (December 24, 1999) [http://www.w3.org/TR/html401/struct/text.html#edef-PRE]; Shirley E. Kaiser, M.A., *Semantics, HTML, XHTML, and Structure*, Brainstorms & Raves (March 2, 2004) [http://brainstormsandraves.com/articles/semantics/structure/].
[22] http://brainstormsandraves.com/archives/2002/05/14/dont_fake_your_markup_accessibility_issues_for_css/
[23] http://brainstormsandraves.com/articles/semantics/structure/
[24] W3C, [Differences with HTML 4] in *XHTML 1.0: The Extensible HyperText Markup Language (Second Edition): A Reformulation of HTML 4 in XML 1.0* (August 1, 2002) [http://www.w3.org/TR/xhtml1/#diffs].

```
<p><strong>Text here</p></strong>
```

This constitutes proper nesting:

```
<p><strong>Text here</strong></p>
```

☑ **Use lowercase letters for all element and attribute names.**

☑ **Close all elements.**

We must use /> —note the space preceding the / character—to indicate the end of an empty element. This trailing space on the content of the tag is necessary for backward compatibility with older browsers. Table 9.2 provides a quick outline of some of the most commonly-used closing tags.

Table 9.2. Closing empty elements in XHTML

HTML 4	XHTML 1.0
` `	` `
`<hr>`	`<hr />`
`<img src="image.gif" height="150" width="40" alt="funny face">`	`<img src="image.gif" height="150" width="40" alt="funny face" />`
`<link rel="stylesheet" type="text/css" href="styles.css">`	`<link rel="stylesheet" type="text/css" href="styles.css" />`

Non-empty elements must also be closed with the appropriate tags.[25] For example, the p and li elements in the following example are correctly closed with </p> and </li> tags:

```
<p>Text here</p>
<ul>
  <li>Text for first list item</li>
  <li>Text for next list item</li>
</ul>
```

---

[25] W3C, [Differences with HTML 4] in *XHTML 1.0: The Extensible HyperText Markup Language (Second Edition): A Reformulation of HTML 4 in XML 1.0* (August 1, 2002) [http://www.w3.org/TR/xhtml1/#diffs].

In your work with HTML, you may have been able to get away without closing the `</p>` and `</li>` tags; however, if you're using XHTML, your file will not validate with unclosed tags.

☑ **Include a value for minimized attributes such as `selected` or `checked`.**[26]

For example, in your work with HTML 4, you'd have been able to use the following code to display a checkbox on a form:

```
<input type="checkbox" name="funbox" value="funvalue"
    checked>
```

To display the same checkbox legitimately in XHTML, you must add a value for `checked`:

```
<input type="checkbox" name="funbox" value="funvalue"
    checked="checked" />
```

☑ **Use the `id` and `name` attributes for fragment identifiers.**

For example, if you use `<a href="#top">top of page</a>` as an internal link to the top of the page, use `<a id="top" name="top"></a>` for the fragment identifier. Older browsers may not support the `id` attribute, but they do support the `name` attribute, so this approach covers both old and new browsers, and will pass W3C validation.[27]

☑ **Use the `alt` attribute with images.**

When you use the `alt` attribute, include helpful, concise, descriptive information about the image. XHTML 1.0 also requires us to include quotes around the attribute values, like this:

```
<img src="/images/johndoe.gif" height="150" width="100"
    alt="John Doe, company president" />
```

For extraneous or decorative images, we may leave the `alt` attribute empty, like so:

---

[26] W3C, *Attribute Minimization* in *XHTML 1.0: The Extensible HyperText Markup Language (Second Edition): A Reformulation of HTML 4 in XML 1.0* (August 1, 2002) [http://www.w3.org/TR/xhtml1/#h-4.5].
[27] W3C, *Fragment Identifiers* in *XHTML 1.0: The Extensible HyperText Markup Language (Second Edition): A Reformulation of HTML 4 in XML 1.0* (August 1, 2002) [http://www.w3.org/TR/xhtml1/#C_8].

```
<img src="/images/spacer.gif" height="1" width="200"
    alt="" />
```

☑ **Use & to express the ampersand (&).**

The ampersand is sometimes used in URLs—especially those created by a CGI script, or returned from a search function. Consider this URL:

http://mybyz.com/cgi-bin/myscript.pl?class=john&doe=member

In XHTML, we must express the ampersand in this URL like so:

```
<a href="http://mybyz.com/cgi-bin/myscript.pl?class=john&amp;
doe=member">
```

Table 9.1 details the encoding of the more common reserved HTML characters—the double quote ("), ampersand (&), less-than symbol (<), and greater-than symbol (>).

☑ **Avoid including line breaks and multiple white space characters within attribute values.**

Different browsers handle line breaks and multiple white space characters within attribute values inconsistently, so it's best to avoid using them.[28]

☑ **Format comments correctly.**

Double dashes within a comment are not permissible. For example, the following comments are correct:

```
<!-- A valid comment - one dash is okay -->
<!-- A valid comment - - space between dashes is okay -->
<!-- =============== -->
```

Both the comments below are invalid, as they contain double dashes (or more!):

```
<!-- An INVALID comment -- it contains double dashes -->
<!----------------------->
```

---

[28] W3C, *Line Breaks within Attribute Values* in *XHTML 1.0: The Extensible HyperText Markup Language (Second Edition): A Reformulation of HTML 4 in XML 1.0* (August 1, 2002) [http://www.w3.org/TR/xhtml1/#C_5].

☑ **Ensure that embedded CSS and scripts are uncommented.**

Although the following command syntax was used frequently in HTML 4 to hide CSS from older browsers, it can't be used in XHTML:[29]

```
<style type="text/css">
<!--
body {
  background-color: white;
  color: black;
}
-->
</style>
```

Create your embedded styles and scripts without the comment syntax, like so:

```
<style type="text/css">
body {
  background-color: white;
  color: black;
}
</style>
```

Spectacular CSS

☑ **Use CSS for decorative images.**

Instead of adding decorative images to your web page through its markup, use CSS to style backgrounds, list bullets, borders, and dividers. For references designed to help you achieve great-looking designs with CSS, see the tip earlier in this chapter, titled Top CSS References.

☑ **Use CSS to designate borders and whitespace, and achieve the visual alignment of images.**

The hspace, vspace, and border attribute definitions are deprecated, effective 1999, in favor of using CSS,[30] such as:

---

[29] Owen Briggs, Steven Champeon, Eric Costello, and Matt Patterson, *Cascading Style Sheets: Separating Content from Presentation, Second Edition* (Berkeley: friends of ED, an Apress Company, 2004), 33.
[30] W3C, *Objects, Images, and Applets: Visual Presentation of Images, Objects, and Applets* in HTML 4.01 Specification (December 24, 1999) [http://www.w3.org/TR/REC-html40/struct/objects.html#h-13.7].

```
#header img.logo {
  margin: 0 10px 0 0;
  padding: 0;
  border: 0 none;
  float: left;
}
```

☑ **Designate the anchor pseudo-class rules in order: `link`, `visited`, `focus`, `hover`, `active`.**

Since these states can occur simultaneously,[31] use their proper order to indicate which rule takes precedence:[32]

```
a:link, a:visited {
  text-decoration: underline;
  font-weight: bold;
  color: blue;
}

a:focus, a:hover {
  color: orange;
}

a:active {
  color: red;
}
```

Otherwise, you may find that they don't work as you wish.

Tip

A Helpful Mnemonic

If you have trouble remembering the order, you might try to remember the popular acronym, "LoVe-HAte." The only problem is that it excludes `focus`. Perhaps "LoVe-From-HAte" could work? Well, you get the idea!

---

[31] `link` and `visited` are mutually exclusive, but may each occur with any combination of `focus`, `hover`, and `active`.

[32] Briggs, Champeon, Costello, and Patterson, 88.

☑ **Minimize the use of CSS hacks and workarounds, and ensure that those you *do* use, validate.**

Develop a test page and its CSS rules without using any hacks or workarounds first. Then, only introduce hacks if they're the only method available to resolve specific issues. Remember that the rules you use must validate and render correctly in standards-based devices.

Using Appropriate CSS Naming Conventions

Checklist 9.6

☑ **Use the `id` attribute for core structural components.**

Structural components include, for example, your site's header, navigation, content, sidebar, footer, and search.

☑ **Assign helpful, descriptive names to describe the function or purpose of each CSS `class` and `id`.**

For example, don't use ambiguous names like `red` or `dave-likes-this`. Maybe you're using the color red in this iteration of the site—and perhaps Dave does indeed like it—but what will happen later, when you decide to use green, Dave's most loathed color? Be sure to use a name that describes the purpose or function of the item, such as `localnav` or `footer`.

☑ **Begin `id` attribute names with a letter, not a number.**[33]

It's better not to use numbers at all, just to avoid the potential for confusion.

☑ **Avoid using underscores in CSS `class` and `id` attributes.**

Underscores in CSS `class` and `id` values are problematic. Hyphens are acceptable but, once again, it might be better to avoid punctuation rather than to try to remember which punctuation items are and are not allowed.

---

[33] W3C, *Anchors with the id Attribute* in HTML 4.01 Specification (December 24, 1999) [http://www.w3.org/TR/1998/REC-html40-19980424/struct/links.html#anchors-with-id]; W3C, *Element Identifiers: the id and class Attributes* in HTML 4.01 Specification (December 24, 1999) [http://www.w3.org/TR/1998/REC-html40-19980424/struct/global.html#h-7.5.2].

☑ **Avoid names that describe location, such as "left" or "right."**

Those page elements could be relocated in your site's next design overhaul. So, for example, if your web site design includes a left-side local navigation column, instead of `leftcolumn`, consider calling it `sidebar` or `localnav`.

Beware of Browser Bugs and Problems

Checklist 9.7

☑ **Avoid using `a:active` to alleviate problems with Internet Explorer.**

When a link enters the "active" state in Internet Explorer 6, it can be difficult to deactivate! The `active` pseudo-class tends to behave unpredictably in this browser.[34]

☑ **For Netscape 4, specify bold text for the heading (h1, h2, h3, h4, h5, h6) and strong elements.**

Netscape 4 browsers are unpredictable in use of bold text for heading (h1, h2, h3, h4, h5, h6) and `strong` elements. Consider including rules to address Netscape 4, like this:

```
h1, h2, h3, h4, h5, h6, b, strong {
  font-weight:bold;
}
```

☑ **Use the `@import` rule with a separate external style sheet to hide CSS rules that Netscape 4 bungles.**

The `@import` statement imports rules from other style sheets. Browsers of version 4 and earlier—including Netscape 4—ignore any CSS within the `@import` rule. So you could create a separate style sheet to include style rules that render poorly in these browsers, and link to it in your web page, like so:[35]

```
<style type="text/css" media="all">
@import "/css/import.css";
</style>
```

---

[34] Jeffrey Zeldman, *Designing with Web Standards* (Indianapolis: New Riders, 2004), 242.
[35] W3C, *The @import Rule*, in Cascading Style Sheets, Level 2: CSS2 Specification (May 12, 1998) [http://www.w3.org/TR/REC-CSS2/cascade.html#at-import]; Briggs, Champeon, Costello, and Patterson, 104, 240–42.

Although this approach is technically a workaround, since it uses CSS for something other than its intended purpose, it's easy to add the CSS rules back into your main style sheet later. Although each web site varies, style rules that are commonly placed into the `@import` style sheet include those that deal with margins and padding, background transparency, some list-item styles, and positioning.

☑ **Test continually as you develop your pages and your CSS.**

Test as you develop the first page of your site, making corrections as you go. This is especially important for identifying potential browser problems and making changes early in the development process.

note

Squashing CSS Bugs

This section mentions just a few of the potential browser bugs that you may need to resolve for your web site. The good news is that there are incredibly helpful communities of web site designers and developers who share information, as well as books and other resources, that also provide helpful insight. Each resource is unique and offers something different, so be sure to check helpful CSS resources such as the css-discuss discussion list[36] and Wiki,[37] Big John's and Holly Bergevin's Position is Everything site,[38] Peter-Paul Koch's Quirksmode site,[39] SitePoint's Stylish Scripting blog on DHTML & CSS,[40] and *Cascading Style Sheets: Separating Content From Presentation, Second Edition*, by Owen Briggs, Steven Champeon, Eric Costello, and Matt Patterson (Berkeley: friends of ED, an Apress Company, 2004).

Using CSS for Print

Using a separate print media style sheet can help you avoid creating a separate web page for print use. Identify the information and elements that will be most helpful—and which items aren't necessary—on a printed page, and create your print style sheet accordingly. For example, a printed page doesn't need to include your site's navigation. Clickable hyperlinks won't work on a printed page, either, so printing the actual URL will be more helpful. Use the checklist below to help develop CSS for print purposes.

---

[36] http://www.css-discuss.org/
[37] http://css-discuss.incutio.com/
[38] http://www.positioniseverything.net/
[39] http://www.quirksmode.org/
[40] http://www.sitepoint.com/blog-view.php?blogid=5

☑ **Use a separate external style sheet to specify print rules.**

You might link to your external style sheet by specifying `print` as the `media` attribute in the `style` element, like so:

```
<style type="text/css" media="print">
@import "/css/print.css";
</style>
```

Alternatively, you could use the `@media print` rule in your main style sheet, as follows:

```
@media print {
  body {
    margin: 0;
    padding: 0;
  }

  #localnav {
    display: none;
  }
}
```

While it's better to use external style sheets, if you have specific print styles that apply to one particular web page, you could embed those page-specific styles using the `media` attribute in the `style` element within the `head` element of your markup, like this:

```
<head>
<style type="text/css" media="print">
body {…}
⋮
</style>
</head>
```

☑ **Specify print-only images, such as your logo, that have been optimized for print use.**

Some images—transparent `.gif`s, for example—don't print well, so, in your print styles, it's a great idea to specify images that have been optimized for print. For example, your print style sheet might hide the screen-only version of the image:

```
img.logo {
  display: none;
}

img.logoprint {
  border: 1px solid black;
}
```

Conversely, you might hide the print-only version in your screen style sheet:

```
img.logoprint {
  display: none;
}
```

Beware Bad Browser Support

Beware! If given the markup above, a browser that does not support CSS fully may render both the versions of the logo on-screen and in print! It's a good idea to find some statistics that identify the percentage of your visitors who use such browsers. You might consider hiding these CSS rules from problem browsers to avoid this possibility.

Prevent web site navigation from appearing when the page is printed.

To achieve this, you might use something like the following style rule:

```
#globalnav, #bottomnav {
  display: none;
}
```

Avoid forcing page margins and padding.

Printers set margins automatically. You could either decide not to specify page margins at all, or you could set them to zero, like so:

```
body {
  margin: 0;
  padding: 0;
}
```

Overriding Main Styles in Printed Layouts

If you specify 0 for margins and padding as above in your main style sheet without specifying a media type or with media set to all for that main style sheet, the printed version will use those values. To make certain the printed version prints as intended, set the appropriate values in your print style sheet, which will then override your main style sheet's values. Alternatively, identify your main style sheet as being specifically intended for screen media, like so:

```
<link rel="stylesheet" href="mainstyle.css"
    media="screen" type="text/css" />
```

By adding the `media` attribute, you should ensure that other media types—including print, handheld devices, and projectors, among others—will ignore the styles intended only for on-screen viewing.

☑ **Avoid forcing font sizing for text content.**

If it is necessary to specify font sizes, use points, not pixels.

☑ **If possible, make URLs for hyperlinks appear in printed versions of the page.**

CSS2 includes the `:before` and `:after` pseudo-elements that allow us to generate and style content to be located immediately before or after the element's content.[41] You can use the `:after` pseudo-element in your print style sheet to insert the URL of a link after the link's text, as is shown in the example below, which adds parentheses around the URL:

```
#content a:link:after, #content a:visited:after {
  content: " (" attr(href) ")";
}
```

CSS2-compliant browsers display the print page as shown in Figure 9.2.

Support for `:before` and `:after`

It's important to note that several recent browsers, such as Opera 7, Netscape 7, and Mozilla, support the `:before` and `:after` pseudo-elements, though Internet Explorer 7 does not. Hopefully, the next version of Internet Explorer will support these helpful and valuable pseudo-elements.

---

[41] Eric Meyer, *CSS Design: Going to Print* [http://www.alistapart.com/articles/goingtoprint], A List Apart (May 10, 2002); W3C, *The :before and :after Pseudo-elements* in Cascading Style Sheets, Level 2: CSS2 Specification, W3C Recommendation (May 12, 1998) [http://www.w3.org/TR/REC-CSS2/generate.html#before-after-content].

Figure 9.2. Print URL

Tips for Traveling with a Digital Camera

Meandering through the Naturescapes.net website mentioned in my previous post, Amazing New Shadow/Highlight Tool in Photoshop CS (http://brainstormsandraves.com/archives/2004/08/09/photoshop/) , I came across Lessons from the Field: Avoiding Some of the Perils of Digital Photography (http://www.naturescapes.net/102003/ea1003.htm) , by Ellen Anon, an insightful article about venturing out or traveling with a digital camera.

Summary

The checklists in this chapter address the questions of creating best-practice markup and implementing CSS to W3C Recommendations. We discussed the important task of structuring content using meaningful, semantic markup, which includes separating content from presentation, using consistent, semantic markup, and creating well-formed XHTML. We also discussed the intricacies of using CSS for presentation, which covered developing CSS naming conventions, watching for browser bugs and problems, and the creation and application of CSS print rules.

10

Creating Accessible Web Sites

Is there a correlation between greed and accessibility? Accessibility guru Joe Clark certainly thinks so: "The true reason to design for accessibility is greed. Quite simply, I want it all, and so should you."[1]

Joe's greedy about creating accessible *and* visually appealing web sites using features that aren't expensive or difficult to implement. Impossible? Not at all! Think about all the steps that are taken to make daily life situations accessible. Often, they're so subtle that we take them for granted, or don't notice them at all. Let me illustrate.

Think back to the last time you caught an elevator. Now, most elevators include a number of "accessibility" features: the button for each floor is supplemented by a Braille indicator, and the elevator controls are positioned fairly low on the wall, so that they may be used by those in wheelchairs. Many elevators also have a speaker system over which a voice identifies the different floors, which is of benefit to people with sight problems; they may also have a visual display that does the same job for those with hearing problems. The doors of elevators open wide, to allow people to pass in and out of the elevator easily, whether they're walking, in wheelchairs, carrying bags or parcels, and so on.

---

[1] Joe Clark, *Building Accessible Websites* (Indianapolis: New Riders, 2003), 1.

These accessibility features make a world of difference for those who need them, yet they're so subtle and well-executed that they're barely noticed by those who don't. Of course, it's glaringly obvious to users when the features they specifically need are not present. The same is true on the Web.

It's possible to create a web site that accommodates special needs without adversely affecting the experience for everyone else. The cost, especially if you plan for accessibility from the start, is quite small.

Consider the visitors you preclude from using your web site if you don't make it accessible. The number may seem small, but it's not good business to exclude even 5% of your potential customers, particularly if all it takes to accommodate them is a little planning. Also, a growing number of countries and local governments now require their own sites, as well as the sites of organizations with which they deal (with an emphasis on commercial and education sites), to provide access for all.

Obviously, accessibility is crucial. This chapter's checklists will help you ensure that your site's accessible to anyone who stops by!

The Bare Bones of Creating an Accessible Web Site

Checklist 10.1

☑ **Ensure that your web site conforms to W3C WCAG 1.0 Priority 1 or better.**

The Web Content Accessibility Guidelines (WCAG) are designed to help promote a degree of universal accessibility by providing advice for the creation of web sites that are accessible to everyone, regardless of their abilities or disabilities.

To conform to WCAG 1.0, your web site must comply with the WCAG 1.0 Priority 1 guidelines. It should also comply with WCAG 1.0 Priority 2 guidelines, and it may also comply with WCAG 1.0 Priority 3.

Recommended Repairs

Be sure to check the W3C web site for the latest information on recommended "repair techniques," as well as the W3C's Web Accessibility Initiative (WAI) section[2] for the latest news about the status of the WCAG 2.0.

Ensure that your web site conforms to your local laws, government guidelines, or company guidelines for accessibility.

Many company and government web site accessibility requirements include WCAG conformance, in addition to their own specific requirements.

Use valid, structured, semantic markup.

The successful use of adaptive and assistive technology, and the functionality of modifications that might be made to hardware or software specifically to help disabled users, depends upon valid, semantic, structural markup. Such technologies and modifications are invariably built to standards, so they need to receive valid, standards-compliant markup in order to interpret your document accurately.[3] Your web page markup can provide valuable "meaning" that's interpreted and used by adaptive technology, but only if you use the various markup elements for the specific purposes for which they were created.

Make sure that your code is valid by W3C standards, using the W3C markup validator.[4]

Separate content from presentation.

The WCAG requires that you separate your document's content—including structural content elements such as headings and lists—from its presentation, in the interests of improving accessibility. Separating content from presentation is easily achieved with CSS, and ensures that devices that are incapable of rendering the presentation aspects of your web site will still communicate the content of your pages.

Provide accessible navigation.

Ensure that your navigation system can be used by visitors who don't have or use a mouse. We'll discuss tips and checklists to achieve this later in the chapter.

---

[2] http://www.w3.org/WAI/
[3] Clark, 29.
[4] http://validator.w3.org/

☑ **Provide users the ability to adjust text size via the browser or a style switcher.**

Using relative font sizing instead of absolute font sizing will allow visitors to adjust the text on your site's pages to a comfortable size through their browser. If your layout does not provide ideal conditions for relative font sizing, use CSS to create a style switcher instead.

 Tip

Tell 'em About Text

Not all users know that they can change text sizes via their browser preferences, so it's helpful to include brief information about this functionality on your web site, or to provide a link to instructions located elsewhere online. In this way, you can help educate visitors about the functionality provided in their browser settings, which in turn improves their experience of all web sites—not just yours.

☑ **Use clear, simple language that's appropriate for your web site's content.**

All users—but especially those with cognitive, learning, and/or reading disabilities—can benefit from clearly stated content. Use simple sentence structure and words that your audience will understand. Provide definitions of terms wherever they may be helpful, and include summaries of information to help those who don't read well to understand the content.

☑ **Conduct tests to ensure that your web site makes sense without CSS.**

☑ **Avoid the use of frames.**

Sighted visitors using modern browsers can view two or more frames in the browser window simultaneously. However, adaptive technology reads frames one at a time, in a linear procedure, as if each frame was a separate window. A typical framed page configuration in which one frame contains navigation and another contains content is a veritable nightmare for visitors using adaptive technology. I, personally, can vouch for the difficulty of browsing frames using speech recognition software, which, like most adaptive technology, relies on keyboard commands.

If, for some reason, you are compelled to use frames, make them accessible: use the `name` attribute within the `frame` element to indicate the frame's basic function and the `title` attribute for a more complete explanation.

In addition, use the `noframes` element to the users' advantage, providing helpful content that includes a link to your web site's navigation, sitemap, or table of contents, and ensuring that your framed web site content is available without frames.

☑ **Avoid causing the screen to flicker.**

Flickering or flashing screens can cause seizures in some users, especially those with photosensitive epilepsy, so avoid using animations, effects, and so on that cause screen flicker.[5]

Creating Valid, Structured, Semantic Markup

Checklist 10.2

☑ **Use the correct DOCTYPE for every web page.**

Adaptive technologies use the DOCTYPE to render the web page properly. For more on DOCTYPE, see Chapter 9.

☑ **Specify a character encoding for every web page.**

Mainstream web browsers, adaptive technologies such as screen readers, and alternative devices such as PDAs can handle poorly- or incorrectly-specified character encoding unpredictably. Include correct character encoding within every web page, like so:

```
<head>
 :
<meta http-equiv="content-type"
    content="text/html; charset=iso-8859-1" />
</head>
```

☑ **Use the `lang` attribute to identify the primary language for each web page and to highlight a language change within a page.**

As well as helping speech synthesizers and Braille translators to use your page, language designation via the `lang` attribute is required by an increasing number of government agencies and other organizations. Language information can be of use to a wide range of applications, such as authoring

---

[5] W3C, *Screen Flicker* in Core Techniques for Web Content Accessibility Guidelines 1.0: W3C Note 6 November 2000 (November 6, 2000) [http://www.w3.org/TR/WCAG10-CORE-TECHS/#flicker].

tools, translation tools, search tools, and parsing tools—some or all of which might be used by visitors to your web site.

The xml:lang and/or lang[6] attributes are used to designate languages for XHTML 1.1 and HTML 4.0, respectively.

You can identify the primary language for a web page like this:

```
<html xmlns="http://www.w3.org/1999/xhtml"
    lang="en" xml:lang="en">
```

The markup below designates a language change within a web page, as a German quote appears in an English-specified page:

```
<blockquote lang="de"
    title="Faust: Der Tragödie erster Teil, by Johann
Wolfgang von Goethe"
    cite="http://gutenberg.org/catalog/world/readfile?fk_file
s=347&amp;offset=13356">
  Ihr naht euch wieder, schwankende Gestalten, Die früh sich
  einst dem trüben Blick gezeigt. Versuch ich wohl, euch
  diesmal festzuhalten? Fühl ich mein Herz noch jenem Wahn
  geneigt? Johann Wolfgang von Goethe, Faust: Der Tragödie
  erster Teil, http://gutenberg.org/catalog/world/readfile?fk
_files=347&amp;offset=13356.
</blockquote>
```

Designate a Primary Language

Designating the primary language of a web page is given Priority 3 in the WCAG 1.0; however, specifying a change to the primary language is a Priority 1 guideline. Since the primary language needs to be designated to specify a change, you are better off accommodating these guidelines right from the start.

---

[6] W3C, *Declaring the Language of a Page* in Authoring Techniques for XHTML & HTML Internationalization: Specifying the Language of Content 1.0, W3C Working Draft 15 October 2004 (October 15, 2004)
[http://www.w3.org/TR/2004/WD-i18n-html-tech-lang-20041015/#ri20030510.102829377]; W3C, *Specifying Language* in Authoring Techniques for XHTML & HTML Internationalization: Specifying the Language of Content 1.0, W3C Working Draft 15 October 2004 (October 15, 2004)
[http://www.w3.org/TR/2004/WD-i18n-html-tech-lang-20041015/#ri20030218.131140352].

☑ **Use heading elements (h1, h2, h3, h4, h5, h6) sequentially, beginning with h1.**

Adaptive technologies, such as screen readers and Braille displays, tab from item to item sequentially, primarily on the basis of the web page markup for headings, list items, and hyperlinks.[7]

☑ **Use correct markup for lists and list items.**

Use ul, ol, and dl appropriately for lists and li, dt, and dd for list items. Don't use other markup to create displays that look like lists, and don't use ul, ol, and dl simply to achieve layout indentation.

☑ **Use ordered lists to help provide context for non-visual users when appropriate.**

Using Recommended Markup in Content

Use these recommendations as you mark up your page content to put that information into context for users of adaptive technologies.

Checklist 10.3

☑ **Use blockquote to mark up quotations.**

You may have noticed that a few sites still use the blockquote element to indent text. Reserve the blockquote element for quotes and create indentations using CSS.

☑ **Use em instead of i for emphasis.**

It's important to differentiate between *structural* and *presentational* markup. Both the i and b elements are examples of presentational markup, their respective structural counterparts being em and strong.

Browsers will render the em element as italicized text by default. Adaptive technology will read text between the em element tags as emphasized text.

---

[7] W3C, *2. The User Agent Accessibility Guidelines: Guideline 9. Provide Navigation Mechanisms* in User Agent Accessibility Guidelines 1.0, 17 December 2004 (December 17, 2002) [http://www.w3.org/TR/WAI-USERAGENT/guidelines.html#gl-navigation].

☑️ **Use `strong` instead of `b` for stronger emphasis.**

Adaptive technology will read the text within the `strong` element as having strong emphasis, while browsers will render the text in a bold font.

☑️ **Use `cite` to mark up the citations of names, such as the titles of books, movies, plays, and television shows.**

☑️ **Use `dfn` to mark up definitions.**

The `dfn` element applies to the term that's being defined, not the definition text. Browsers will render the `dfn` element as italicized text by default; however, as with all elements, you can use CSS to give this content custom styling.

Tip

Using `title` with `dfn`

You can use the `title` attribute to include a definition or supplementary information about terms marked up as `dfn`. Sighted users who use a mouse will have access to the tooltip feature, so they'll see the definition when they hover the mouse over the term.

```
A <dfn>computer</dfn> is a programmable electronic
device that can store, retrieve, and process data.
Access to a <dfn title="a general-purpose
     computer equipped with a microprocessor and
     designed to run software, such as a word
     processor or Web browser, for an individual
     user">personal computer</dfn> is generally
required for a college student.
```

It's helpful to add `cursor: help` to your CSS style for elements such as `dfn`, as this provides added visual cues for users, as Figure 10.1 shows.

note

Take Care with Tooltips

Always consider your audience when using tooltips. While your site's more technology-savvy users will probably have no problems understanding the purpose of tooltips, other users may not be as familiar with the process of hovering the mouse over words to access more information, even if they're familiar with the concept that underlined words are clickable links in the online environment. If your usability tests show that users don't know how to use tooltips, you might

Figure 10.1. A styled `dfn` element with a `title` attribute and styled cursor

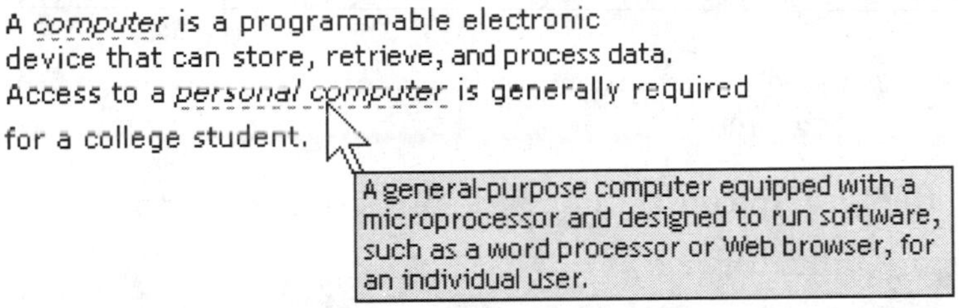

A *computer* is a programmable electronic
device that can store, retrieve, and process data.
Access to a *personal computer* is generally required
for a college student.

A general-purpose computer equipped with a
microprocessor and designed to run software,
such as a word processor or Web browser, for
an individual user.

consider spelling them out in parentheses instead of using the `title` attribute text. Always consider your users and identify an approach that they will understand most easily.

- ☑ Use **code** to denote program code.

- ☑ Use **var** to mark up variables within code.

- ☑ Use **kbd** to represent text typed at a computer keyboard.

- ☑ Use **samp** to mark up samples of computer program output.

- ☑ Use **acronym** and **abbr** (though these are not yet supported by Explorer) to mark up acronyms and abbreviations.

To assist those using adaptive technologies, as well as your site's more technology-savvy visitors, use the `acronym` element to mark up the first appearance of an acronym or abbreviation on a web page, like this:

```
I will take the <acronym title="North Atlantic Treaty
    Organization">NATO</acronym> document with me on my trip
to Victoria, <abbr title="British Columbia">BC</abbr>,
Canada.
```

Screen readers and other adaptive technologies can recognize these elements if the user turns on settings to read them. For example, when reading the symbol for sodium chloride, a screen reader would pronounce "NaCl," as "nackle." If you use the `acronym` element with the appropriate `title` attribute text, as shown below, the screen reader can instead say "sodium chloride."[8]

```
<acronym title="Sodium Chloride">NaCl</acronym>
```

You can use a method similar to that described for `dfn` to provide users with tooltips for abbreviated terms.[9]

 Use `address` to mark up contact information about the author.

Here's an example:

```
<address>This document was written by
  <a href="/contact/">John Doe</a></address>
```

Providing Accessible Navigation

Checklist 10.4

 Ensure that all parts of your navigation system are accessible without a mouse.

In addition to screen readers, quite a few other technologies—including alternative approaches that don't even use a keyboard!—rely on keyboard commands to access content. Technologies such as "puff and sip" devices, single-switch devices, and speech recognition software often mimic keyboard use though they don't actually require a keyboard to be connected.[10]

 Avoid making Flash or other plugins necessary for the use of navigation systems unless you provide accessible alternatives.

As well as being a potential barrier to site use for non-disabled visitors, the use of plugins for critical web site functionality can prevent visitors with adaptive technologies from using your web site altogether. If you do use Flash or other plugins for navigational purposes, be sure to include an accessible alternative such as a non-flash version of your web site.

---

[8] For more on the ways in which different technologies use the `<acronym>` and `<abbr>` tags, see Elizabeth J. Pyatt's article, *Creating Accessible Web Sites: Abbreviations* [http://tlt.its.psu.edu/suggestions/accessibility/abbreviations.html].
[9] For more on acronyms and abbreviations, see Ian Lloyd's article, *Why Use the acronym and abbr Tags* [http://www.accessify.com/tools-and-wizards/developer-tools/acrobot/why-use.php], and Joe Clark's book, *Building Accessible Websites* (Indianapolis: New Riders, 2003).
[10] *Keyboard Accessibility Techniques*, WebAIM (no date.) [http://www.webaim.org/techniques/keyboard/].

☑ **Consider specifying link focus with the CSS `focus` pseudo-class to provide helpful visual cues, especially for the mobility-impaired.**

Those who use adaptive technologies or have keyboard-only access won't benefit from visual cues generated by the CSS `hover` pseudo-class. Keyboard input (almost exclusively) distinguishes focus from the hover or active states.[11]

You can use the `focus` pseudo-class to provide a visual cue for keyboard users as links gain focus, like this:

```
a:link {
  color: #900;
}
a:visited {
  color: purple;
}
a:focus {
  color: red;
}
a:hover {
  background: #fffff0;
  color: #000080;
}
```

By default, many browsers display a border around links in focus.

Link States Matter

IMPORTANT

Note that the order in which the link states are listed in your style sheet *does* matter: you must list them in the order shown in the example above. For more on these anchor pseudo-classes, see Chapter 9.

Also note that the `active` pseudo-class is not included in the above example because it does not function as expected in Internet Explorer 6, as we discussed in Chapter 9.[12]

☑ **Provide several ways for users to navigate through your web site.**

For example, provide easy-to-use global navigation, local/section navigation, and internal navigation. In addition, include a sitemap and a web site

---

[11] Clark, 219–20.
[12] Jeffrey Zeldman, *Designing with Web Standards* (Indianapolis: New Riders, 2004), 242.

search feature, and consider including a site index if yours is a large web site. These features enhance both the accessibility and usability of your web site.

Use "skip" links when necessary, for example, before each navigation area (global, local/section, and internal) or block.

Including skip links to allow users to skip past blocks of navigation or other links in your web site's content helps keyboard-only and adaptive technology users tremendously. Navigating through a web site without a mouse can be incredibly tedious and troublesome if users must tab through every single link within the site's navigation, on every single page that they visit. Here's how you might create a skip link; this markup displays as shown in Figure 10.2:

```
<div id="globalnav">
  <a href="#skiptocontent">Skip navigation</a>
  <ul>
    <li>Home</li>
    <li><a href="/services/">Services</a></li>
    ⋮
  </ul>
</div>
<div id="content">
  <a name="skiptocontent" id="skiptocontent"></a>
```

You should also provide skip links to allow users to skip *past* content *to* the navigation when appropriate. Look at your site and its pages very closely—and, ideally, test the site with users—to determine the points at which skip links may be useful.

The decisions you make about where and when to use skip links will depend on your target audience. How likely are your visitors to have keyboard-only access to the Web? I've often seen people argue in discussion lists and forums that skip links are not required for navigation systems that contain only five or six links, but don't be fooled! If you were the person who had to tab through all of those links on every single page of a site, you'd probably wish the developer had included skip links.

Avoid skipping past web site functions, such as search boxes and login forms.

Figure 10.2. Providing skip links for each block within navigation

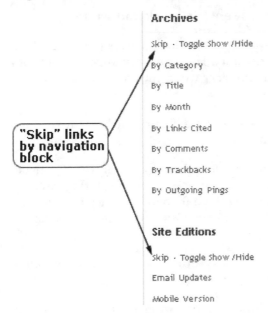

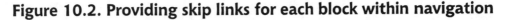

☑ Avoid skipping past navigational links such as **Next**, **Back**, or **Top of page** buttons or links.

☑ Avoid hiding skip links.

If you hide your skip links, keyboard-only visitors using mainstream web browsers won't be able to see them, so they won't be able to use them. Instead, plan to create a visually appealing web site design that includes visible skip links.

Color for the Masses

Part of the process of designing an accessible web site is giving consideration to people who have color interpretation or other vision deficiencies. This checklist will help you to ensure that your site employs typefaces and colors that can be perceived and used by all visitors.

☑ **Ensure that your web site makes sense in black and white.**

Color should not be the only visual cue that directs users to access or use important information and functionality. The context of important information and navigation should remain clear when the web site is viewed in black and white.

☑ **Specify colors for the browser to use as defaults for body text, page backgrounds, links, and so on.**

If you have defined a comprehensive color scheme for your web site, make sure you specify colors for the above-mentioned elements. Otherwise, the browser's default colors could clash with your color scheme which, as well as having the potential to look ugly, can also cause significant access problems.

☑ **Avoid using black text on red backgrounds or red text on black backgrounds.**

The color red appears dark for those with protanopia, a type of color perception deficiency, so if you use these color combinations, those users might have difficulty seeing the text, or may not perceive it at all.

☑ **Avoid using green text on red backgrounds or red text on green backgrounds.**

People with protanopia or deuteranopia, types of color perception deficiencies, have difficulty distinguishing between shades of red and green. In addition, since red and green are complementary colors, they will seem to sizzle on screen even for users without color perception issues.

☑ **Avoid mixing beige, yellow, or orange with red and green.**

Those with protanopia or deuteranopia may find these color mixes confusing and potentially indistinguishable.

A Thousand Words to Each Picture

 Provide a text equivalent for each image by specifying the alt attribute.

Writing helpful text for the img element's alt attribute is one of the most important—and easy—ways to make your images more accessible and WCAG-compliant.

Decorative images will still require an alt attribute; however, you can leave this blank, as shown below:

```
<img src="house.jpg" width="30" height="30" alt="" />
```

 ### Use longdesc

You can also use the longdesc attribute to provide a text alternative to images, but be aware that currently it is not well supported.

 Ensure that the alt attribute text makes sense out of context.

 Avoid animations, including blinking or scrolling text.

Moving text and animation can be very distracting for people with cognitive disabilities. Additionally, screen reader users and those who have visual or cognitive disabilities may have trouble reading moving text. Animations are also a nightmare for people who use screen magnification technologies.[13]

Avoid blink and marquee

You should *not* use the blink and marquee elements to make your text blink or scroll, as these are not considered valid markup by the W3C.

---

[13] Jim Thatcher et. al., *Constructing Accessible Websites*. (New York: glasshaus, an Apress Company, 2002), 108.

Accessible Image Maps

Contrary to popular opinion, it's not difficult to make image maps accessible. Like other images, you must provide text equivalents for image maps if your site is to conform to WCAG 1.0.

☑ **Use the `alt` and `title` attributes for all the graphical areas of your image map.**

In most graphical browsers, the `alt` attribute remains invisible unless the image is missing, and the `title` attribute text pops up as a tooltip. Be sure to identify link destinations in your tooltip text.

☑ **Reproduce graphical text in the appropriate `alt` or `title` attributes.**

☑ **If providing You are Here cues, include the You are Here information within the `alt` or `title` attributes.**

☑ **Use the `nohref` attribute within the `area` element to make sure the current location cannot be selected from the You are Here cues.**

To help avoid user confusion, don't include an active link to the current page either in image map or among other web site navigation links. Here's an example of the `nohref` attribute at work:

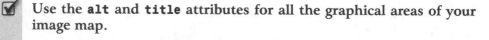

```
<area nohref="nohref" alt="YOU ARE HERE: Services"
    title="YOU ARE HERE: Services" shape="rect"
    coords="30,60,120,30">
```

Multi-purpose Multimedia

You might think it's financially unrealistic or impossible to provide accessible versions of your multimedia and plugin materials; however, a little research could reveal that the costs are more reasonable than you initially thought. The checklist below provides tips to make your multimedia content accessible without breaking the bank.

☑ **Implement the built-in accessibility features for all plugins and alternative content formats.**

☑ **Provide accessible alternatives if your content is not compatible with your users' accessibility requirements.**

You might choose, for example, to create a well structured HTML version of the content as an alternative.

Creating Accessible PDFs

To make the content in PDF files more accessible, you'll need to create tagged PDF files—PDF files that contain special tags to boost their accessibility. Just like HTML, if your PDF is to be accessible, it must be well-structured. If document formatting is too complex to be compatible with your users' accessibility requirements, you'll need to provide an accessible alternative, such as a well-structured HTML version.

Creating accessible PDF files is a big topic, so you might like to check out some web sites that explore this in detail. Information can be found on the Adobe[14] and W3C[15] web sites, and you'll find more useful references through a quick web search.

☑ **Provide text information for non-text content that conveys information, such as instructional animations or videos.**

☑ **Provide accurate text transcripts for audio and video files, including conversation and relevant sound elements.**

In Good Form

Like everything else on your web site, your web forms must be accessible to all users. Use the following checklists as guidelines to create accessible forms.

---

[14] http://www.adobe.com/
[15] http://www.w3.org/

☑ **Place prompts above, or to the left, of text fields and combo boxes on forms.**

Figure 10.3 shows an example.

Figure 10.3. Providing prompts for text fields and combo boxes

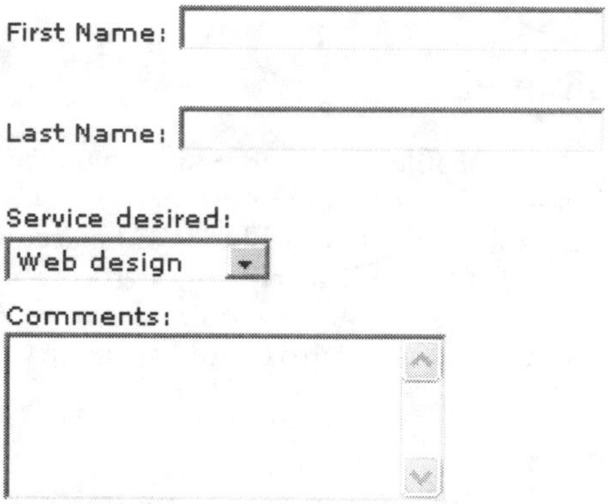

First Name: [   ]

Last Name: [   ]

Service desired:
[Web design ▼]

Comments:
[   ]

☑ **Place prompts to the right of checkboxes and radio buttons on forms.**

Figure 10.4 shows how such prompts should be placed.

Figure 10.4. Providing prompts for checkboxes and radio buttons

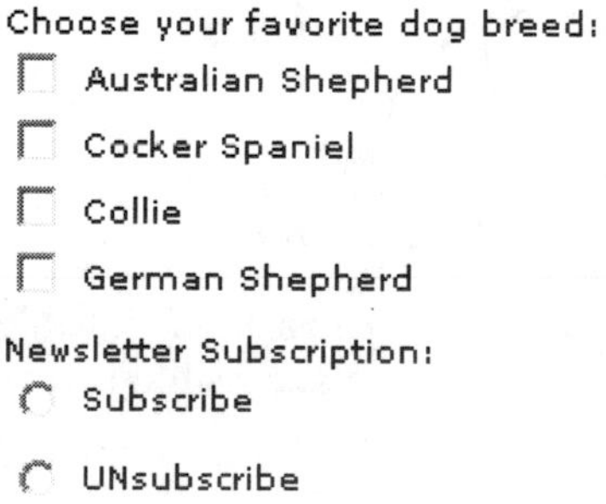

Choose your favorite dog breed:
☐ Australian Shepherd
☐ Cocker Spaniel
☐ Collie
☐ German Shepherd

Newsletter Subscription:
○ Subscribe
○ UNsubscribe

☑ **Wrap the `label` element around its related `input` element whenever possible.**

```
<label>First name: <input type="text" name="fname"
    value="firstname" /></label>
```

Use of the `label` element makes forms particularly accessible for those using adaptive or assistive technology. Wrapping the form control description and text input field in a `label` element, as shown in the example markup above, prevents these technologies from interpreting the control and its description as separate entities. You can use the `label` element with any form control element, including text inputs, buttons, checkboxes, radio buttons, and menus.

☑ **Use the `for` attribute with the `label` element to associate prompts with their respective controls when necessary, for instance, when they're in separate table cells.**

If you have an existing web site that uses tables for form layout, you'll most likely find that text is located in a different table cell from the form control with which it's associated. In such cases, you won't be able to wrap the `label` around the associated `input` element; however, you can make the necessary link using the `for` attribute with a corresponding `id` attribute, as shown in bold here:

```
<tr>
  <td><label for="fname">First name:</label></td>
  <td><input type="text" id="fname" name="fname"
        value="firstname" /></td>
</tr>
```

☑ **Group related form fields using `fieldset`.**

This technique makes forms clearer and more easily understood. For example, you may use the `fieldset` element to group:

❑ name information collected in separate fields for first name, middle name, and surname

❑ address details collected in fields for a street address, city, state/province, postal/zip code, and country

❑ telephone numbers

❑ email addresses and URLs

❑ credit card details

Here's an example of the code that groups related address form fields using the `fieldset` element. The resulting display is shown in Figure 10.5.

```
<fieldset>
  <legend>Address Information:</legend>
  <label>Street address: <input type="text" name="street"
       value="streetaddress" size="50" /></label>
    ⋮
  <label>Country: <input type="text" name="city" value="city"
       size="30" /></label>
    ⋮
</fieldset>
```

Figure 10.5. Grouping form fields

```
┌─ Address Information: ─────────────────────┐
│  Street address:                            │
│  [                                       ]  │
│                                             │
│  City:                                      │
│  [                                       ]  │
│                                             │
│  State, Province:                           │
│  [                                       ]  │
│                                             │
│  Postal / ZIP Code:                         │
│  [                           ]              │
│                                             │
│  Country:                                   │
│  [                                       ]  │
└─────────────────────────────────────────────┘
```

 Tip

Removing `fieldset` Borders

By default, browsers will add a border around form fields grouped using the `fieldset` element. You can remove this border using the following CSS:

```
fieldset {
  border: 0 none;
}
```

☑ **Use the `legend` element to assign a caption to each `fieldset` group.**

Although it's not considered necessary,[16] using the `legend` element will help to further clarify related form groups, as Figure 10.5 shows.

☑ **Use the `title` attribute to provide advisory information.**

☑ **When using an `img` within a `button` element to produce a graphical button, use the `alt`, `value`, and `title` attributes to provide a text alternative.**

☑ **Avoid using a `reset` button to prevent its accidental use.**

Years ago, I, like many others, used to include a `<input type="reset">` button in each of my forms. However, after realizing that the `reset` button rarely seems to serve a useful purpose, and that its presence can actually cause confusion among users, who often activate it accidentally, I quit using it. Only use the `reset` button if there's strong justification for doing so.

Sturdy Tables

Checklist 10.10

☑ **Reserve the `table` element for displaying tabular data.**

Early version browsers didn't support CSS positioning, so creative web site designers and developers started using invisible tables to create visually appealing, complex, reliable layouts similar to grid-based displays that had already been available in desktop publishing software for a long time. Fortunately for us, CSS positioning is now widely supported in modern browsers. To create accessible web sites, use CSS to develop your layouts—stay away from table-based design.

---

[16] According to the HTML 4 standard, every `fieldset` element must contain a `legend`. This requirement was removed in XHTML 1.0, however, and as such is considered obsolete by most developers.

☑ Make sure the content included in tables makes sense when linearized.

Screen readers linearize table cell content. In other words, they will read the contents of each cell much as we would read a page of this book: from left to right, and from top to bottom.

For example, the data in the table shown in Figure 10.6 would be read by a screen reader as: 1 2 3 4 5 6 7 8.

Figure 10.6. Linearizing a table as it is read

1	2	3	4
5	6	7	8

Testing Linearization

Tip

To ensure that your data tables make sense when linearized, try viewing your page with Lynx,[17] a free text-only browser, or Tablin, a free linearization-checking tool produced by the W3C.[18] Alternatively, use a screen reader.

Note also that content contained in a table can be difficult to make sense of when it's linearized. If that's the case for one or more of your data tables, consider providing a detailed text description, or an alternative format, such as a plain text document, to deliver the tabular data in a way that makes sense to users of screen readers and other adaptive technology.

☑ Avoid using nested tables.

Screen readers read nested tables continuously, as if all the cells were in one table. Also, with the verbosity function turned on (which, typically, is the default), screen readers will inform users of every step along the way: as well as reading the cell contents in a linear fashion, they will identify structural features, such as the number of columns and rows in each table,

---

[17] http://lynx.browser.org/
[18] http://www.w3.org/WAI/Resources/Tablin/

as those structural features of the document are encountered. Keeping your tables simple will help prevent users of these technologies becoming disoriented, confused, and frustrated.

☑ Use proportional sizing for table and cell dimensions.

Proportional sizing can be achieved by using percentages instead of pixels to set cell and table dimensions, and allows your tables to scale to the size of the user's browser window. For example, you could choose to style your table using CSS as follows:

```
table {
  width: 90%;
}
th, td {
  width: 33.3%;
}
```

You'd then use the following HTML to create the table:

```
<table>
  <tr><th>Header</th><th>Header</th><th>Header</th></tr>
  <tr><td>data</td><td>data</td><td>data</td></tr>
</table>
```

Styling Tables Using CSS

Note how clean and lean the markup is when CSS is used to style the table. No more messy, confusing code! Use CSS to style other aspects of your table, such as borders, backgrounds, text colors, fonts, and even structural elements.

☑ Use the `caption` element to provide table names or titles.

The `caption` element is a structural element that informs users of adaptive technology of the name or title of a data table. Here's how it looks in a page's markup:

```
<table>
  <caption>Michael's Dogs</caption>
  <tr><th></th><th></th></tr>
  <tr><td></td><td></td></tr>
</table>
```

☑ **Use the `summary` attribute within the `table` element to provide brief summaries of complex data.**

The content contained within the `summary` attribute is not rendered on the screen; however, it does help adaptive technology users, so it's important that you include a summary for tables of complex data. Here's an example:

```
<table summary="Michael's dogs as of May 2005">
```

☑ **Use the `th` element to mark up table headers within rows.**

☑ **Use the `td` element to mark up data columns within rows.**

☑ **Use the `scope` attribute within the `th` or `td` element to associate headers with table cells.**

In this example, `<th scope="col">Name</th>` informs browsers and screen readers that all information in the column following the header is related to "Name," and `<th scope="row">Spot</th>` indicates that all the information in the row following that header is related to "Spot:"

```
<table>
  <caption>Michael's Dogs</caption>
  <tr>
    <th scope="col">Name</th><th>Age</th><th>Birthday</th>
  </tr>
  <tr>
    <th scope="row">Spot</th><td>5</td><td>April 1</td>
  </tr>
  <tr>
    <th scope="row">Spotless</th><td>8</td><td>March 10</td>
  </tr>
</table>
```

☑ **Specify the `tbody` element if you use the `thead` element.**

The `thead` (table header) element, although intended for visual presentation, also provides cues for adaptive technology by indicating the group of labels that apply to the contents of the table, but are not actually part of the table data.

Here's an example of thead in action:

```
<table summary="Michael's dogs throughout his lifetime">
  <caption>Michael's Dogs</caption>
  <thead>
    <tr><th>Dog's Name</th><th>Breed</th><th>Years</th></tr>
  </thead>
  <tbody>
     ⋮
  </tbody>
</table>
```

For much more detail about accessible tables, I highly recommend two books: Joe Clark's *Building Accessible Websites* (Indianapolis: New Riders, 2003), and Jim Thatcher's *Constructing Accessible Web Sites* (New York: glasshaus, an Apress Company, 2002).

Summary

In this chapter, we reviewed checklists that will help you to create a more accessible web site. We started by exploring the bare bones of creating an accessible web site, and reviewed a checklist on following accessibility guidelines and laws. We then discussed the details of creating accessible web page structures, navigation, text, images, forms, and tables. We also discussed the considerations involved in coloring your web site to optimize its accessibility.

In addition to the checklists in this chapter, I recommend that you download and use the checkpoints provided in the Checklist of Checkpoints for Web Content Accessibility Guidelines 1.0[19] on the W3C web site.

Always remember that providing an accessible web site makes your online presence available to more visitors. And, when you plan for accessibility right from the start, you can keep the costs of making the site accessible to a minimum and stay within your budget.

---

[19] http://www.w3.org/TR/WAI-WEBCONTENT/full-checklist.html

Web Site Optimization

If you're like me, you don't like waiting for a web page to load. Don't worry: we're not alone! Surveys show that, generally, web site visitors don't want to wait long for pages to load.[1]

Think about how many times you've changed queues in a supermarket because you thought the queue you were in was moving too slowly. The same behavior applies to web sites: if your visitors feel that they're having to wait too long for a page to download, or the completion of a processing task, they'll leave.

This is reason enough to want to optimize your web site to load quickly, but consider also the money you'll save on server space and bandwidth! The checklists in this chapter will help you speed up your web pages to their optimum loading time.

Creating Clean, Lean Markup

You can reduce your page load times drastically by streamlining your code to reduce file sizes. This section's checklists will help you do exactly that!

---

[1] Andrew B. King, *Speed Up Your Site: Web Site Optimization*, (Indianapolis: New Riders Publishing, 2003), xxi.

☑ **Use external CSS rather than inline or embedded CSS.**

Your visitors' browsers cache external CSS: the browser saves a copy of the CSS file to the computer on which it's installed. Usually, once a CSS file is downloaded, it doesn't need to be downloaded again during the current visit to that site unless the cache is cleared manually by the user. As you might expect, when you manage your entire web site through a single external CSS file, you'll save tremendously on the overall bandwidth your site use, and you'll reduce the file sizes of individual web pages, as you won't need to embed your CSS code into each page.

```
<head>
<link rel="stylesheet" type="text/css" href="/css/main.css"
    />
<style type="text/css" media="screen">
@import "/css/screen.css";
</style>
</head>
```

In the example above, the files `/css/main.css` and `/css/screen.css` will be cached by the user's browser.

☑ **Use external JavaScript.**

Using external JavaScript, instead of including the script within each page, provides the same advantages as using external CSS.

☑ **For every web page, specify a DOCTYPE and create well-formed markup.**

Pages tend to render more quickly if you use a strict DOCTYPE and close all markup elements. Why? The browser uses a faster parsing algorithm, and has less work to do in terms of adding and matching closing elements. Keep this in mind as you consider which DOCTYPE is the most appropriate for your site. Also, be aware that improperly nested and unclosed elements can cause rendering problems.

☑ **Minimize HTTP requests by using CSS instead of images, and consolidating external CSS and JavaScript files whenever possible.**

When a web site visitor accesses a page, the browser sends a request to the server in the form of an HTTP (HyperText Transfer Protocol) request. As the page downloads to the browser, that browser sends out additional, individual HTTP requests for each object—an external CSS file, an image, and multimedia files, for example.

Each HTTP request adds time to the web page's total download speed. Fortunately, modern browsers are able to send between two and eight simultaneous HTTP requests, which speeds up downloads. However, each request takes an average of one-half to two seconds at 56kbps.[2]

If you use CSS as much as possible, rather than images, you reduce the number of HTTP requests required to download images. Similarly, consolidating your external CSS and JavaScript files reduces the number of HTTP requests needed for external files.

For example, let's say you have a navigation design that uses JavaScript for graphic rollovers. You'll have two images for each rollover: one for the normal state and one for the rollover or active state. Doing the math for six navigation links, that means you'd need to download twelve images plus an external JavaScript file just for your navigation. If you used CSS instead, you could eliminate the images and the JavaScript file, as you'd add navigation styles to your external CSS, and your web page's file size would be smaller, because you'd use less markup. Consider the difference between the following code snippets. The first represents the markup you'd use for one navigation link in your JavaScript-based navigation:[3]

```
<li><a onmouseover="document.image1.src=imageon1.src"
    onmouseout="document.image1.src=imageoff1.src" href="/"
    ><img name="image1" src="/images/nav/1homeoff.gif"
    width="80" height="18" alt="Home" border="0" /></a></li>
```

With CSS, you could have this instead:

```
<li><a href="/">Home</a></li>
```

Multiply that markup for all six navigation links and you'll save substantially on your web page's file size and HTTP requests.

Consolidating Markup Creates Efficiencies

It makes sense to consolidate the markup for items that are used site-wide, because then, users will only need to wait for that external file

[2] King, 47, 51.
[3] Granted, this markup is somewhat dramatized by the inclusion on the JavaScript code within the HTML markup, but similar code would need to be included in an external JavaScript file anyway, so the net effect is not unrealistic.

once. After that, they'll have the item cached. However, if you have some JavaScript that's used on only 10% (or less) of your site, you should probably place that code in its own external `.js` file and link to it only on pages that use it—especially if it contains a large amount of data.

☑ Use structural markup and avoid presentational elements.

Use CSS to control the appearance of your web pages: this approach will help to streamline your markup and reduce file sizes.

☑ Avoid using tables for layout purposes.

Using tables for layout can add significant bulk to your web pages, and adds presentational markup to your content—something that's better avoided. Nested tables, which are a typical feature of web pages whose layouts depend on tables, create accessibility problems, too. As we saw in Chapter 10, they can be confusing for visitors who use assistive technologies.

☑ Remove excess whitespace and carriage returns from your HTML markup.

On average, whitespace accounts for a staggering 20–30% of a web page.[4] Typically, we add whitespace and carriage returns to make our markup easier to manage; however, browsers don't need all the extra spacing that human eyes like to see in markup!

Try it Yourself!

You may not think that whitespace and carriage returns could make a big difference. Why not try it for yourself? Take one of your web pages, save it under a different name and remove all the excess whitespace and carriage returns. Now compare the file size of this document to your original document—you'll be surprised!

---

[4] Andrew B. King, *Remove Whitespace*, WebSiteOptimization.com (June 19, 2004) [http://www.websiteoptimization.com/speed/tweak/whitespace/].

☑ **Minimize or delete HTML comments.**

Does your Software Use Comments Extensively?

Note that some software makes extensive use of HTML comments for the purposes of managing template-driven web sites. Dreamweaver is one such package (HTML comments are used to mark editable areas of page content), but it is possible to export a web site without template information (and, hence, without HTML comments) prior to uploading the site to the Web.

☑ **Avoid using redundant elements and attributes.**

For example, in the markup of the unordered list items below, an unnecessary CSS `class` has been added to each of the ul, li, and a elements:

```html
<ul class="navigationlist">
  <li class="navigationlistitem"><a class="navigationlink"
      href="/first/">First item</a></li>
  <li class="navigationlistitem"><a class="navigationlink"
      href="/second/">Second item</a></li>
  <li class="navigationlistitem"><a class="navigationlink"
      href="/third/">Third item</a></li>
</ul>
```

Instead, you should use much leaner, cleaner markup, like this:

```html
<div id="nav">
  <ul>
    <li><a href="/first/">First item</a></li>
    <li><a href="/second/">Second item</a></li>
    <li><a href="/third/">Third item</a></li>
  </ul>
</div>
```

☑ **Ensure that all img element alt attribute text is short and concise (but not at the expense of meaning).**

☑ **Include the img element height and width attributes.**

The height and width attributes tell the browser how much space to allow for the graphic image, as the browser lays out the web page before the graphics load. This helps support the user's perception that the page is fast-loading, and allows users to interact with the page sooner, even though including the `height` and `width` attributes doesn't actually improve the total page load time.[5]

Minimizing URLs

Checklist 11.2

☑ **Use root relative paths for internal link markup whenever possible.**

Try to avoid using relative paths, like this:

```
<a href="../../../">Home</a>
<a href="../../../newsletter/">Newsletter</a>
```

Instead, use root relative paths, like this:

```
<a href="/">Home</a>
<a href="/newsletter/">Newsletter</a>
```

You can use the same markup regardless of the directory location.

☑ **Eliminate the directory default filename in links, where possible.**

Avoid including `index.html` like this:

```
<a href="/index.html">Home</a>
<a href="/newsletter/index.html">Newsletter</a>
```

Instead, streamline the link, eliminating the directory default filename, like so:

```
<a href="/">Home</a>
<a href="/newsletter/">Newsletter</a>
```

This advice applies to internal links and many, but not all, external links.

Do Links Work without Directory Default Names?

IMPORTANT

As you apply this approach to external links, you must make sure those links work without the directory default filename. Unfortunately, not all web sites will resolve to default filenames within directories,

---

[5] Patrick J. Lynch and Sarah Horton, HTML and Graphics, *Web Style Guide, 2nd ed*, (March 5, 2004) [http://www.webstyleguide.com/graphics/html.html]. Also available in print (New Haven, Connecticut: Yale University Press, March, 2002).

which means your users experience a broken link. It's best to check your links before finalizing these changes.

☑ **Remove "www" from links whenever possible.**

Do External Links Work without the WWW?

IMPORTANT

As per the above advice on removing default directory names from external links, make sure each external link still works without the "www." Unfortunately, some web sites will not resolve domain names without the "www," so their URLs will not work unless the "www" is included.

Optimizing CSS

Checklist 11.3

☑ **Minimize CSS comments.**

☑ **Remove excess whitespace and carriage returns from your CSS.**

Consider this sample CSS rule:

```
body {
  padding: 5px;
  background: #fff;
  color: #000080;
  font-size: small;
  font-family: Verdana, Geneva, Arial, Helvetica, sans-serif;
}
```

You can reduce the file size by removing the whitespace and carriage returns, which would produce code like this:

```
body{padding:5px;background:#fff;color:#000080;font-size:
small;font-family:Verdana,Geneva,Arial,Helvetica,sans-serif;}
```

Cleaning Up your CSS

CSS software programs, such as Bradsoft TopStyle,[6] give users the option to format style sheets in a variety of ways. You can also configure TopStyle's Style Sweeper to remove the whitespace and carriage

---

[6] http://www.bradsoft.com/

returns for you. Be careful if you've used any CSS "comment hacks" in your style sheet, though, as these can bamboozle style sweepers and cause some very nasty side effects.

Group selectors that share the same declaration whenever possible.

Perhaps you list selectors separately, as shown here:

```
body {
  font-size: small;
}
body {
  font-family: Verdana,Geneva,Arial,Helvetica,sans-serif;
}
body {
  line-height: 1.35;
}
p {
  font-size: small;
}
p {
  font-family: Verdana,Geneva,Arial,Helvetica,sans-serif;
}
p {
  line-height: 1.35;
}
ul {
  font-size: small;
}
ul {
  font-family: Verdana,Geneva,Arial,Helvetica,sans-serif;
}
ul {
  line-height: 1.35;
}
```

You can reduce file size by grouping them together, like this:

```
body,p,ul {
  font-size: small;
  font-family: Verdana,Geneva,Arial,Helvetica,sans-serif;
  line-height: 1.35;
}
```

You could use the `font` shorthand property to make this markup even leaner:

```
body, p, ul {
  font: small/1.35 Verdana,Geneva,Arial,Helvetica,sans-serif;
}
```

In addition, you can eliminate the space between elements and after the colon and commas:

```
body,p,ul{font:small/1.35 Verdana,Geneva,Arial,Helvetica,
sans-serif;}
```

Eliminating those spaces may seem insignificant; however, when you eliminate them throughout an entire style sheet, you'll notice the file size reduction. Every little bit helps!

☑ **Use CSS shorthand properties whenever possible for `font`, `background`, `margin`, `border`, `padding`, and `list`.**

For example, you might originally have coded four individual declarations for body:

```
body {
  margin-top: 10px;
}
body {
  margin-right: 10px;
}
body {
  margin-bottom: 10px;
}
body {
  margin-left: 10px;
}
```

Before you upload the file, combine all four declarations into one rule:

```
body {
  margin-top: 10px;
  margin-right: 10px;
  margin-bottom: 10px;
  margin-left: 10px;
}
```

You can shorten this rule even further, like so:

```
body {
  margin: 10px 10px 10px 10px;
}
```

The 10px values apply in a clockwise rotation, from top, to right, to bottom, to left. Guess what? You can shorten this rule even further! Since all four values are the same, you can combine them into a single property, like this:

```
body {
  margin: 10px;
}
```

Shorthand Syntax at a Glance

Tip

Use these shorthand property syntaxes as a guide to creating CSS shorthand:

```
font: weight style variant size/line-height family
background: color image repeat attachment position
margin: top right bottom left
padding: top right bottom left
border-style/width/color: top right bottom left
border-top/right/bottom/left: width style color
border: width style color
list-style: type position image
```

☑ **Use short `class` and `id` values.**

In addition to choosing short names, it's also important to name your class and ID selectors according to their functions. You'll find more on naming conventions in Chapter 9.

☑ **Use the highest-level parent possible for your CSS declarations.**

You can use CSS inheritance to reduce your CSS file's overall size. For example, you can declare at least some of your documents' CSS rules, such as the background and font colors and font families, with the body element, like so:

```
body {
  background: #fff;
  color: #000;
  font-family: Verdana,Geneva,Arial,Helvetica,sans-serif;
}
```

body element descendants will then inherit these style rules.

IMPORTANT

Supporting Netscape 4?

If you need to support Netscape 4, keep in mind that this older browser doesn't consistently inherit styles, especially within table cells. I'd suggest that you test your CSS with Netscape 4 after you've tested it in other browsers, adding CSS rules like the one below as required to cover the inheritance quirks:

```
body,div,h1,h2,h3,h4,h5,h6,p,ul,ol,li,blockquote,
table,tr,th,td {
  font-family: Verdana,Geneva,Arial,Helvetica,
sans-serif;
}
```

See Chapter 14 for more on testing.

Use separate external CSS files for each media type you need.

You can reduce your CSS file size by creating separate CSS files that target specific media types, such as print or screen, and loading only the CSS file that matches the output medium from which it is called. This approach saves bandwidth and page load times.

Tip

Mixing Main and Media-Specific Style Sheets

Consider using one main style sheet for all media in conjunction with specific media type style sheets that contain only the settings that are specific to each separate media type. For example, in your print styles, you'd typically hide the web site navigation and set a white background. So, instead of having three style sheets of 5kb each (a total of 15kb), which contain many duplications, you could have one main style sheet that was 5kb in size, and two others that were 0.5kb each (adding up to 6k). Consider this markup, which contains links to a number of style sheets:

```
<style type="text/css" media="all">
@import "/css/main.css";
</style>
<link rel="stylesheet" media="screen"
    href="/css/screen.css" type="text/css" />
<link rel="stylesheet" media="print"
    href="/css/print.css" type="text/css" />
```

If you used this approach for your print style sheet, for example, the main style sheet would load into your users' browser cache when they accessed the page with a browser. When those visitors decide they want to print a page, the print media style sheet would load.

Use shorthand hexadecimal color values, RGB color values, or color names—whichever is shortest—where possible.

For example, here are the hexadecimal color values for white background behind black text:

```
h1 {
  background: #ffffff;
  color: #000000;
}
```

Here are the shorthand hexadecimal color values for that display:

```
h1 {
  background: #fff;
  color: #000;
}
```

This markup uses their color names:

```
h1 {
  background: white;
  color: black;
}
```

And this snippet uses their RGB color values:

```
h1 {
  background: rgb(255,255,255);
  color: rgb(0,0,0);
}
```

For both white and black, the shorthand hexadecimal color values use the fewest characters: each has four characters, which compares favorably with their corresponding color names (five characters each), and RGB color values (white has 16 characters, black has ten). Choose whichever approach uses the least number of characters in each separate case.

Assign multiple CSS classes to a single element where appropriate.

Perhaps you've defined separate styles for photos, holiday photos, and wedding photos, like so:

```
.photo {
  border: 2px solid black;
  margin: 10px;
}
.holidayphoto {
  border: 2px dotted red;
  margin: 10px;
}
.weddingphoto {
  border: 2px dashed green;
  margin: 10px;
}
```

You could simplify this CSS as follows (note that the margin is declared only once in the photo class):

```
.photo {
  border: 2px solid black;
  margin: 10px;
}
.holiday {
  border: 2px dotted red;
}
.wedding {
  border: 2px dashed green;
}
```

You'd then assign multiple classes to individual images in your HTML:

```
<img class="photo" src="friends.jpg" … />
<img class="photo holiday" src="crete.jpg" … />
<img class="photo wedding" src="markjenny.jpg" … />
```

Multiple Classes Not Recognized

Note that Netscape 4.x and other older browsers won't recognize multiple CSS classes.

Optimizing JavaScript

☑ **Use JavaScript to enhance, rather than create, the user experience.**

Minimize the need for JavaScript by excluding unnecessary scripts and features. As we saw above, it's often possible to use CSS for rollover effects, rather than creating multiple images and using JavaScript rollovers.

☑ **Use external JavaScript when possible.**

Linking a single external JavaScript file to web pages on which it's needed is preferable to placing (redundant) JavaScript on each page, as this approach helps reduce your pages' file sizes and your bandwidth usage. As we discussed previously, the browser will cache the JavaScript (`.js`) file and use it repeatedly, saving even more bandwidth. This approach is also more search-engine friendly.

☑ **Use the `defer` attribute to defer or delay loading your JavaScript files if possible.**

If your script doesn't produce any output—for instance, it's a function or array definition—you can defer the script's execution until the rest of your web page loads, like so:

```
<head>
    ⋮
  <script src="/scripts/magic.js" defer="defer"
      type="text/javascript"></script>
</head>
```

This way, your web page will load before the JavaScript loads, supporting the perception that yours is a fast-loading web page.

☑ **Design or modify your JavaScript to encapsulate code into functions that execute at page load.**

This approach allows you to defer the JavaScript's execution, and still include links to external JavaScript files within the `head` element of your web pages. Here's how this could be done using the `onload` attribute of the `body` element:

```
<head>
    ⋮
```

```
    <script type="text/javascript" src="magic.js"></script>
</head>
<body onload="magic();">
```

Better yet, you could assign the function as an `onload` event handler within the `magic.js` file:

```
function magic() {
    ⋮
}

window.onload = magic;
```

☑ **Load external JavaScript conditionally whenever appropriate.**

If you have JavaScript whose implementation is dependent upon certain conditions, you can create separate JavaScript files that load only when those conditions are met (such as when a web site visitor is found to be using a certain browser). You can use JavaScript, XSSI, or PHP, for example, to create a script that will conditionally load the appropriate JavaScript file(s).

☑ **Abbreviate and map your JavaScript.**

You can name JavaScript variables, functions, and objects as you wish, so create short names to help keep your JavaScript file sizes small. Avoid using longer names like these:

```
function validateParseAndEmail() {
    ⋮
}
var firstButton;
```

You could shorten those names like this:[7]

```
function email() {
    ⋮
}
var button1;
```

---

[7] Of course, the shorter the names you use in your JavaScript code, the more likely they will be to clash with identical names in another script in use on the same page. If this becomes an issue for you, you should look into so-called **unobtrusive scripting** techniques, which enable you to wrap the names in your script within a namespace, so that they do not interfere with other scripts.

☑ **Rework your code to make it simpler and more efficient.**

Refactoring is the art of reworking code in a disciplined way so that it's simplified and more efficient. Refactoring code can clarify and refine your code, and often speeds it up.

☑ **Tune your expressions for speed.**

For example, simplify operations like multiplication, division, and modulus into expressions like addition, or, and and.

Supporting Speedy Server Responses

Checklist 11.5

☑ **Include trailing slashes on the URLs of directories.**

You can boost server response time by including the trailing slash on the URLs of directories. If you omit it, you force the server to try to figure out whether the user is seeking a file or a directory.

☑ **Ensure that your server resolves your domain name without the "www".**

Your URL will be more user-friendly if it doesn't require the "www". If your server isn't set up to resolve domain names without the "www", your URL won't work without it. In other words, when someone types **mybyz.com** into the address bar, an error page would appear, telling the user that the URL didn't exist. Not good! So, make sure your domain names can be accessed with or without the "www", via `mybyz.com` and `www.mybyz.com`.

☑ **Use HTML compression when possible.**

You can substantially reduce your bandwidth usage and page load times by compressing your HTML. For example, gzip compression, a public domain compression algorithm, can reduce HTML files by 80–85%, reducing overall web site bandwidth by 30–50%. HTML compression can be a valuable tool, especially on high-traffic web sites. Check with your server administrator or ISP to see if your server is set up for HTML compression. You can use tools such as mod_gzip or PipeBoost to compress your data on the fly, or you can create gzipped versions of your web pages and let these tools uncompress the data.[8]

Optimizing Images, Multimedia, and Alternative Formats

Checklist 11.6

☑ **Always reduce image dimensions with a graphics program, not via HTML.**

If you change an image's dimensions with HTML, you won't reduce the image file size—your web site visitors will load the larger file size, though it will probably be blurred, distorted, or both. It's critically important to change an image's dimensions with a graphics program, not through your HTML, as this not only makes sure the images display properly, but also reduces the files' size. This results in faster download times, and uses less bandwidth and server space.

☑ **Crop each image to the smallest acceptable size, retaining only its most important areas.**

Smaller overall image dimensions can help reduce the file size. Cropping can also reduce image file size, improving page load time and reducing bandwidth. For example, you could crop out any extraneous background space, then reduce the (cropped) dimensions from 1200px x 860px to 350px x 251px.

☑ **Use the highest possible image compression without degrading image quality.**

In graphics programs, check images in the preview window prior to saving them for the Web, making sure each image is clean and noise-free before you compress it.

---

[8] Jeffrey Zeldman, *Designing with Web Standards* (Indianapolis: New Riders Publishing, 2003), 33.

☑ **In JPEG format files that have a prominent foreground and a less-important background, blur the background.**

JPEG image compression will be more efficient if the image has fewer hard edges, so if you can blur the background a little without degrading the image quality, you'll help the compression process.

☑ **For larger images, create thumbnail versions for display on web pages.**

The use of thumbnails improves web page download times and saves bandwidth. It's also a common approach that's already familiar to most web site visitors. You'll find examples of thumbnails in Chapter 3.

☑ **Use HTML text captions whenever possible.**

Avoid embedding captions within your image file using graphics programs. Artifacts often surround text included in a JPEG file, unless you turn off or minimize compression, which can potentially double the file size—not exactly a practical approach for web site images!

To help reduce your JPEG file sizes for use online, don't embed text captions into JPEG files at all. The same rule applies to other image file formats such as GIF and PNG.

Instead, regardless of the image file format, create a text caption using HTML within your web page markup, and format the text as you wish using CSS. An example of this approach is shown in Figure 11.1.

Figure 11.1. A JPEG photo with HTML text caption

Spot

☑ **Optimize alternative format files, including multimedia files.**

Use your software program's built-in web optimization tools to reduce the size of files such as Macromedia Flash, Apple QuickTime, Windows Media, RealMedia, and Adobe Acrobat. Acrobat's web optimizing tool, for example, will remove duplicate objects, streamline embedded fonts, and remove old or unnecessary versions of objects to create leaner, faster-loading PDF files. If your PDF file includes images, use vector-based images wherever possible, and optimize images separately for the Web before you create your PDF files.

Summary

This chapter presented checklists to help you ensure that your web pages load as fast as possible, use a minimum of bandwidth and server space.

We started with some tips for optimizing your code to create clean, lean markup. This discussion included checklists on minimizing URLs, and optimizing CSS and JavaScript. Next, we reviewed checklists that addressed the questions of speeding up your server, and optimizing images and alternative file formats.

The next chapter, Chapter 12, provides checklists that will show you how to optimize your web site for good listings and high rankings in search engines and web directories.

Search Engine Optimization

Optimizing your web site for search engines should be an integral part of your web site project, from the very beginning to the very end. Search engine optimization (**SEO**) should be considered, and if possible, implemented, throughout the planning, design, development, and maintenance stages of your web site.

The checklists in this chapter can be used as a guide to optimize your web site for search engines. However, it will definitely pay you to subscribe to some helpful SEO newsletters, visit web sites that cover the latest on SEO, and consider purchasing books by highly regarded SEO/SEM experts, such as *The Search Engine Marketing Kit*, by Dan Thies.[1]

You will *see* the results of your work first-hand if you consider SEO right from the start. For example, at the time of this book's publication, my own site is the number one listing on Google for its keywords, and has consistently remained within the top three (unsponsored) listings on the first page of Google and other search engines for several years. Yes, SEO is important, but more than that, it's rewarding! Let's get started.

---

[1] Dan Thies, *The Search Engine Marketing Kit* (Melbourne: SitePoint Pty. Ltd., 2005) [http://www.sitepoint.com/books/sem1/].

Successful SEO in a Nutshell

☑ **Plan your web site's SEO before you create the site.**

It's important to create your web site with SEO in mind. Changing a web site, or potentially even redesigning your web site, to optimize it for search engines can end up being an expensive proposition. Plan to create a search engine-friendly web site from the start.

☑ **Ensure that every page includes text, links and popularity components[2] that will help boost your search engine rankings.**

☑ **Employ other means to market your web site.**

In addition to SEO, consider paid submission programs, PPC (pay-per-click) advertising, reciprocal links campaigns, and advertising your site on others. Depending on your budget, you might consider advertising through traditional media, such as newspapers, magazines, radio, and television.

Working with Keywords and Keyphrases

☑ **Research keywords and keyphrases (multi-word phrases) before you create your web site.**

It's important to create your web site with keywords and keyphrases in mind *and* to put them in place as you develop the pages and content.

☑ **Target keyphrases rather than single keywords.**

Single keywords are much more commonly entered by web users, which makes them more difficult to target effectively than multi-word keyphrases. Unless the single keywords are highly unique, your best results will be achieved using keyphrases.

---

[2] Shari Thurow, [*Before You Build*] in *Search Engine Visibility* (Indianapolis: New Riders Publishing, 2002), 20.

☑ **Use longer words and plurals.**

If you target plural versions of your keywords or phrases, you'll get hits from people searching for the singular and plural versions of those words.

 Tip

Use that Thesaurus!

As part of your brainstorming for appropriate keywords and keyphrases, try using a thesaurus to find similar words. There are helpful thesauri online (you might start at Thesaurus.com[3]), but see also the Search Term Suggestion Tool[4], and Wordtracker.[5]

☑ **Focus on a few specific keyphrases for each web page.**

Pages that rank well in search engines tend to focus on specific keyphrases that usually appear in the HTML `title` element, heading elements, breadcrumb navigation links, product names and descriptions, and cross-links.[6]

☑ **Create keyphrase-rich text content, especially for your homepage.**

Identify the top two or three keyword phrases that potential visitors would use to find your web site, then write 200–250 words of homepage text that utilizes those keyword phrases—not the other way around. Follow this approach as you create content for other web pages, too. As noted above, keep in mind that titles and headings are considered more important than other content by some search engines, so consider this as you optimize your content. We'll discuss the topic of optimizing your markup for search engines in just a moment.

☑ **Include keyword and keyphrase research in your ongoing web site SEO maintenance plan.**

---

[3] http://thesaurus.com/
[4] http://inventory.overture.com/d/searchinventory/suggestion
[5] http://wordtracker.com/
[6] Shari Thurow, *Top Five SEO Design Mistakes*, ClickZ (September 27, 2004)
[http://www.clickz.com/experts/search/results/article.php/3412591].

Using Keywords and Keyphrases in your Markup

Search engines use a page's structural markup as a guide to rank the relative importance of its content. It's important to include keywords and keyphrases within your web pages—especially your homepage—and to place them within certain markup elements. Providing content that is relevant to your target audience will, naturally, help your search engine rankings, especially if you intentionally make strategic use of appropriate keywords and keyphrases. Use the checklist below to help.

Checklist 12.3

☑ **Include keywords and keyphrases in your site's information architecture.**

Keyword and keyphrase research results can play an important role in the words and phrases you use within your web site's information architecture. For instance, you might use keywords and keyphrases in your global and local navigation, your category labels, page `title` element text, heading element text, and internal links.

Using these terms in conjunction with the checklists from Chapter 5 and Chapter 7 not only helps your web site visitors find information more readily—it helps your site achieve good search engine ranking, too!

☑ **Use focused keyphrases within each web page's `title` element.**

Currently, creating keyphrase-rich text for your web page `title` element is critically important, because nearly all search engines give the `title` element's text a lot of weight. Create each page's `title` element text to reflect the specific content of that page, using keyphrases that people might type into search engines to find your web site.

☑ **Use your keyphrases within each web page's `description meta` element.**

Note that many search engines, including Google, Yahoo!, Inktomi, and others, index and use the text within the `<meta name="description">` tag; for instance, some use it as description text for display in search results. However, they don't use the text for search engine rankings at this point. Also, they largely ignore other `meta` elements, including the `keyword meta` element. While there's no guarantee that it will help improve your rankings, it's still worthwhile to include the `description meta` element in your web pages as shown below.[7]

```
<head>
  ⋮
  <meta name="description"
      content="Add your descriptive sentence or two here." />
  ⋮
</head>
```

☑ **Use your focused keyphrases within the page's heading elements, beginning with the h1 element.**

Keep h1 Close to body

Tip

The closer that you can locate your keyphrase-loaded `h1` element content to the opening `<body>` tag, the better. Some search engines will give a close proximity between the two a higher rating—it appears to the search bot that the content is important enough to earn itself a high-level heading, and that content appears early in the document. In addition, content that's placed closer to the top of the page is also considered more important by many search engines, so make sure your top 200–250 words are packed with keyphrase-rich content.

☑ **Use your focused keyphrases within link URLs and corresponding `title` attributes.**

Here's an example:

```
<a href="/design/checklists/"
    title="Deliver First Class Web Sites">Deliver
  First Class Web Sites: 101 Essential Checklists</a>
```

Keywords and Domain Names

note

Although some Search Engine Marketers believe that placing keywords in domain names can provide a significant boost to sites, others feel it doesn't really do much. According to SEO expert Jill Whalen, keywords in domain names might be afforded a small amount of weight by the search engines, but only when other site owners link to the web site using its domain name, rather than the web site title. The result is similar to having keyword- or keyphrase-rich links, which

---

[7] Jill Whalen, *The Meta Description Tag*, High Rankings (updated October, 2004) [http://www.highrankings.com/metadescription.htm].

is indeed helpful. Another SEO expert, Shari Thurow, also feels that other factors have much more impact than the inclusion of keywords in a domain name, such as keyphrase-rich content, links, and the site's popularity.[8]

☑ **Use relevant keyphrases within your img elements' alt attributes.**

Here's an example:

```
<img src="/images/checklists.jpg" alt="Deliver First Class
    Web Sites: 101 Essential Checklists, my kit with
    essential, helpful checklists for web site designers and
    web site owners" />
```

Being Search Engine-Friendly

Great keywords, keyphrases, terrific content, and having other web sites linking to yours does nothing for your search ranking if the search engines can't access your web pages to index them. Use this checklist to help ensure that your web site is based on search crawler-friendly design and markup.

Checklist 12.4

☑ **Avoid the use of splash pages.**

A splash page is a main entry page that displays either a large graphic image or a Flash animation, usually with a link to Enter a web site or Skip Intro (skip the animated introduction page). Splash pages usually redirect to a new web page after the animation has completed. As you might expect, splash pages typically lack keyword- or keyphrase-rich content, as they contain little or no visible body text other than Enter or Skip Intro links. Given little or no text content, the search crawlers have nothing to index.

Typically, splash pages use redirects to automatically advance the user to the web site's actual homepage. Currently, search engines tend not to index web sites that use redirects, and they'll ban web sites that create artificial redirects in an attempt to achieve higher rankings.[9]

---

[8] Jill Whalen, *Search Engine Marketing Q&A*, High Rankings Advisor, Issue 091 (March 24, 2004) [http://www.highrankings.com/issue091.htm]; Shari Thurow, *Search Engine Visibility* (Indianapolis: New Riders Publishers, 2002), 20.
[9] Shari Thurow, *Top Five SEO Design Mistakes*, ClickZ (September 27, 2004) [http://www.clickz.com/experts/search/results/article.php/3412591].

So, by using a splash page that contains little or no text content, and uses redirects, you'll likely have ruined your chances of having your web site indexed—let alone ranked—by search engines.

☑ Balance HTML text and graphics.

Professional, high-quality graphics can help support your credibility, as we discussed in Chapter 3. It's also critically important to provide plenty of keyword- and keyphrase-rich text content for search engine crawlers. There's no need to avoid using graphics; in fact, avoiding graphics could be detrimental to your web site's search engine success. Instead, plan your web site design to use graphics that have a purpose, insert meaningful text within each `img` element's `alt` attribute, and provide plenty of keyphrase-rich content that will help your search engine rankings, and benefit site visitors who read them.

☑ Create search-engine friendly HTML text navigation and cross-links.

Search engine crawlers follow HTML text links. If you provide good, search engine-friendly internal HTML text links within your site, crawlers will likely follow those links.

☑ If any of your web pages' URLs change, use server-side redirects to send search bots using the old link to the new URL.

Instead of allowing search engine crawlers (or web site visitors!) to find dead links, create server-side redirects, perhaps using `.htacess` and mod_rewrite techniques, that will automatically take search engines to the new URLs. On the server side, use a 301 code for permanently moved files and a 302 code for temporarily moved files (assuming that your host allows you access to such settings; many do not).

If you're not able to use server-side redirects, create a web page for each changed URL to inform search engine crawlers and visitors that the web page has moved temporarily or permanently, and provide a link to the new page. If there is no new URL, then be sure to provide a link to your homepage, sitemap, and local search to help your visitors and search engine crawlers (this is especially important in ensuring that the crawlers continue indexing your web site via these links). Don't use JavaScript redirects on these pages!

Rules for Using Static Redirect Pages

If you're forced to use static pages to inform people and search engines that a page has moved, be sure to have an inventory—a spreadsheet, perhaps—that you can refer to six to 12 months later. This should be enough time for the search engine crawlers to index the new locations, at which point you can check your search engine listings and consider removing these old holding files if the search engines are listing the new pages. You might consider leaving these static pages longer, though, especially for use by visitors who've bookmarked your moved pages.[10]

☑ **Use external CSS and JavaScript whenever possible, to maximize relevance.**

Search engines will read your markup, beginning at the top of your web page, but they'll also review embedded CSS and JavaScript within head elements. Generally, search engines tend to give more weight to the text that appears at the top of web pages than to text published further down the page.[11]

☑ **Use structural markup, and separate content from presentation as much as possible.**

Search engine crawlers use structural markup to understand what your web page content is about, and they give more weight to text within heading elements (h1, h2, h3, etc.).

Content Stuffers will be Penalized!

Don't try to fool search crawlers by stuffing content into heading elements or elsewhere, as they know about such trickery, and you could be banned from the search engine listings for trying to artificially improve your rankings. Honesty is always the best policy. Creating keyphrase-rich content that visitors will love to read is the best way to go. Other web sites will also link to it, which only helps boost your search engine rankings further.

---

[10] Ian Lloyd, *The Perfect 404*, A List Apart (January 16, 2004) [http://www.alistapart.com/articles/perfect404/].

[11] Danny Sullivan, *Search Engine Placement Tips*, Search Engine Watch (October 14, 2002) [http://searchenginewatch.com/webmasters/article.php/2168021]; Danny Sullivan, *Hiding JavaScript*, Search Engine Watch (June 10, 2003) [http://searchenginewatch.com/_subscribers/more/article.php/2153181] (subscribers-only area).

☑ **Provide a web site sitemap, and link to it from your homepage as well as all your other web pages.**

Providing a sitemap that links to your main pages will help search engines find your content, as well as being helpful to web site visitors. If your sitemap contains more than about one hundred links, though, break it logically into pages of no more than one hundred links each.

☑ **If you use JavaScript links, include fallback href attribute links within the <a> tags.**

For example, at my web site, I use DHTML for a show/hide toggle menu, which includes a crawler-friendly JavaScript link with an a element with an href attribute that looks like this:

```
<a href="/inc/arch.shtml" onclick="return toggleMenu('arch');
    return false;" onkeypress="return toggleMenu('arch');
    return false;">Toggle Show/Hide</a>
```

Here, href="/inc/arch.shtml" provides an alternative to the JavaScript event handlers. Since it's an HTML text link, search engine crawlers can read it and continue on to index the /inc/arch.shtml page. I had accessibility in mind when I decided on this particular approach, but it helps search engine crawlers, too.

JavaScript and Popups

Tip

Popup windows are another popular way to use JavaScript links. Ian Lloyd of Accessify.com fame wrote an excellent article for SitePoint, titled, *The Perfect Pop-Up*.[12] Check it out for a helpful approach that's accessibility-friendly and search-crawler friendly, too.

☑ **Avoid dynamic URLs that contain ?, &, $, =, +, and % characters, cgi-bin, session IDs, or cookies.**

These URLs are usually the result of query strings on dynamic pages. Some search engine crawlers are wary of such URLs because they could potentially be infinite links that would overload the crawler. As a result, they may not index pages that use these URLs, especially when three or more of these characters are included in the address. As Eytan Seidman, MSN Search Program Manager, states, "The algorithm starts to wonder whether it is

---

[12] http://www.sitepoint.com/article/perfect-pop-up/

going to get stuck in a loop endlessly crawling every single permutation of the query parameters. Thus, URLs with many (definitely more than 5) query parameters have a very low chance of ever being crawled."[13] Here's an example of the kind of URL Mr Seidman's talking about:

```
http://mybyz.com/products/page.aspx?view=14&tab=6&pcid=24B8-
1000849@@@@&section=586&origin=mybyzsearch&cookie=false
```

☑ **Use text alternatives to Flash content.**

If your site uses Flash to present content that you really want or need search engine crawlers to index, provide text alternatives that they can index. If you use Flash for your entire web site without providing text alternatives, don't expect search engine crawlers to index your site.

☑ **Provide metadata and text alternatives for audio and other rich media files.**

Typical metadata information includes the title, author, copyright, and a description of the content. Specialty search tools, such as Singingfish,[14] use this metadata to help users find rich media, including MP3 files. Be sure to include helpful text information about your rich media content within your web pages, too.

Avoiding Being Banned by Search Engines

Search engines will ban web sites that try to improve their rankings artificially, so it's important not to do anything accidentally that even hints at trying to fool them. Use the checklist below to help you avoid any misunderstandings between your web site and the search engines.

---

[13] Eytan Seidman, *Crawling the Internet...*, msnsearch's WebLog (November 18, 2004) [http://blogs.msdn.com/msnsearch/archive/2004/11/18/266087.aspx].
[14] http://singingfish.com/

☑ **Use genuine SEO methods.**

Don't even think about trying to play tricks on the search engines to improve your rankings! You run a good chance of having your web sites banned from their search results.

☑ **Avoid cloaking.**

Cloaking is an artificial technique that malicious users employ to deliver to search engines content that's not delivered to web site visitors.[15] Some web sites try to trick search engines by delivering specific content that only the search engines will see. There are many debates around the Web about what the term "cloaking" does or doesn't cover; for instance, some question whether or not using CSS to hide content from web site visitors, or using JavaScript sniffing to serve different content to specific search engines than is served to web site visitors, is cloaking.

☑ **Avoid using doorway pages or domain names used for doorways.**

Doorway pages, or domain names used for doorways, are web pages or domain names that are stuffed with keyphrases and submitted to search engines.

☑ **Avoid stuffing keywords into comments or `title` or `alt` attributes.**

Content in comment tags offers no benefit at all, and the image `alt` and `title` attributes should only be used as a text alternatives for an image.

☑ **Avoid using JavaScript or `meta refresh` redirects to try to trick search engines.**

Often, search engines won't index pages that use JavaScript or `meta` redirects because, historically, so many web sites used them to trick search engines. So even if you want to use these techniques without trickery in mind, avoid doing so! Otherwise, your web site may be banned from search engines by mistake. Some argue that these techniques fall under the definition of cloaking, but regardless of whether or not you agree with that opinion, it's better to avoid using JavaScript or `meta` redirects.

---

[15] "What is cloaking?" in *Google Information for Webmasters*, Google.com (no date) [http://www.google.com/webmasters/faq.html#cloaking].

Getting Listed

Getting your web site listed on search engines, other web sites, and directories is an important goal, but even more important is identifying the right time to do so, to which engines you should submit your site, and which pages you should submit. Doing some careful research and preparation will help make the submission process smoother and more efficient, and will help you achieve better results in the long run. Use this checklist as your guide.

Checklist 12.6

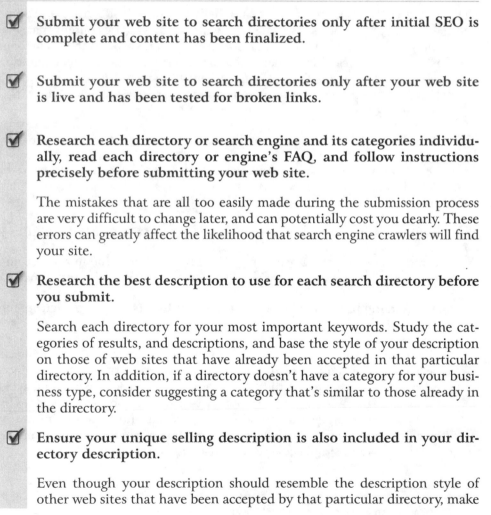

☑ **Submit your web site to search directories only after initial SEO is complete and content has been finalized.**

☑ **Submit your web site to search directories only after your web site is live and has been tested for broken links.**

☑ **Research each directory or search engine and its categories individually, read each directory or engine's FAQ, and follow instructions precisely before submitting your web site.**

The mistakes that are all too easily made during the submission process are very difficult to change later, and can potentially cost you dearly. These errors can greatly affect the likelihood that search engine crawlers will find your site.

☑ **Research the best description to use for each search directory before you submit.**

Search each directory for your most important keywords. Study the categories of results, and descriptions, and base the style of your description on those of web sites that have already been accepted in that particular directory. In addition, if a directory doesn't have a category for your business type, consider suggesting a category that's similar to those already in the directory.

☑ **Ensure your unique selling description is also included in your directory description.**

Even though your description should resemble the description style of other web sites that have been accepted by that particular directory, make sure your description is unique. For example, include specific services or products that you offer, and mention your target audience.

☑ **Write several descriptions of varying lengths to copy/paste into submission forms.**

Each directory has different requirements in the number of words allowed in a web site description. Write several descriptions within a plain text file that you can copy/paste into the submission forms as appropriate. Include descriptions with seven, ten, 15, 20, 25, 30 and 50 words.

☑ **Ensure your most important keywords are in every description, but avoid keyword stuffing.**

Make sure your web site's most important keywords are in every description, but don't stuff too many keywords into it! Directory editors don't like descriptions that basically read like a list of keywords.

☑ **Consider paid or expedited submissions as a way to have your web site listed more quickly.**

The sooner you can have your web site listed in search directories, the sooner your web site can receive referrals from those search engines. Using paid or expedited submissions is one way to help speed up the process of having your web site listed, and can sometimes make the wait as short as a day or two. It's important to note that paid inclusion doesn't typically guarantee high placement. Be sure to do your homework, and be sure to read quality SEO/SEM web sites and helpful books, such as Dan Thies's *The Search Engine Marketing Kit*, cited earlier.[16]

☑ **Submit your homepage to search directories before submitting other web pages.**

☑ **Submit other pages, particularly those on specialized topics, once your homepage is listed.**

You'll have a better chance of having your other web pages, particularly those on specialized topics, accepted for different categories once your web site's homepage is listed at that directory.

---

[16] See also Danny Sullivan, *Buying Your Way In: Search Engine Advertising Chart*, Search Engine Watch (November 22, 2004) [http://searchenginewatch.com/webmasters/article.php/2167941].

☑ **Submit your web site manually to search directories, rather than using automated submission software.**

Search engine crawlers, including Google, advise against using automated submission software.[17]

Automated Software Violates some Terms of Service

Note that some automated software violates the terms of service of many search engines and directories, so before you consider using any automated software for your search submissions, to check link popularity, or to check rankings, read the terms of service for each search engine and directory to ensure that you don't violate the rules.

☑ **Submit your web site to search directories such as Yahoo!, DMOZ, JoeAnt, and Gimpsy.**

Listings with major directories are critically important to the success of crawlers from search engines such as Google finding your web site.

☑ **Avoid over-submitting.**

Check to see if your web site is already listed on the search engine, and don't submit it again if it is listed. It's important to follow up and keep good records of your submissions, acceptance, listings, and rankings.

☑ **Use a `robots.txt` file and `meta robots` tags to denote content that you don't want indexed.**

You might have web pages, images, sound files, or other content that you don't want to have indexed. If so, you can specify that those files should be ignored in a `robots.txt` file that is saved to your server's root directory. Here's an example of a `robots.txt` file that instructs Google not to index images, and tells all search crawlers not to index the `procedures` directory, on the MyByz.com web site:

```
# robots.txt for http://mybyz.com/
# exclude images from Google
# see http://www.google.com/remove.html#images
User-agent: Googlebot-Image
```

---

[17] *Google Information for Webmasters* Google (2005) [http://www.google.com/webmasters/guidelines.html].

```
Disallow: /images
# exclude specific areas from all search engine crawlers
# (in this case, a directory containing procedural files
User-agent: *
Disallow: /procedures
```

You can also include the `meta robots` element on specific pages. For example, if you had a page that you didn't want to have indexed, but you did want the spider to follow the links on that page to other pages, you'd add the following instruction to your page's markup:

```
<meta name="robots" content="noindex,follow" />
```

Ignoring `meta robots` and `robots.txt` Files

Note that not all search crawlers will honor `meta robots` attributes or `robots.txt` files, but many will (including the most-used engine of all, Google), so these techniques are definitely worth using, if needed.

Creating an Ongoing Links Campaign

All major search engines place a lot of importance on a web site's overall link popularity. Highly-ranked web sites that link to yours can help boost your own site's ranking. Use the checklist below to help you plan and manage your web site's incoming and outgoing links.

Checklist 12.7

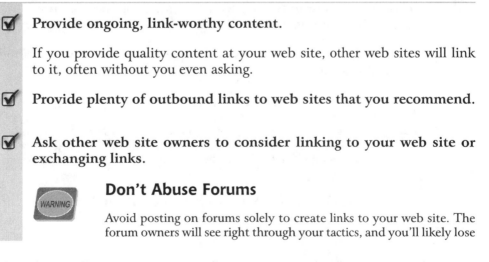

☑ **Provide ongoing, link-worthy content.**

If you provide quality content at your web site, other web sites will link to it, often without you even asking.

☑ **Provide plenty of outbound links to web sites that you recommend.**

☑ **Ask other web site owners to consider linking to your web site or exchanging links.**

Don't Abuse Forums

Avoid posting on forums solely to create links to your web site. The forum owners will see right through your tactics, and you'll likely lose all credibility. Such tactics would probably also cause other site owners to avoid linking to your web site legitimately. If you're serious about building links to your web site, create great content that others will want to link to, and don't hesitate to email other web site owners to ask if they'd be willing to link to your site.

 If any URLs change at your web site, be sure to inform those who link to it.

Keeping these other sites and site owners informed will help them, as well as your web site, to find and link to your current, live web pages, rather than maintaining old, dead links. Remember that it's important to use server-side redirects to the new URLs, as noted above.

SEO Takes Work

When it comes to optimizing your web site for search engines, there is no one single, magic solution. It takes time and patience to achieve high rankings, but you can work to boost your search engine rankings by following tips from SEO industry experts, using the checklists above, and remaining diligent about optimizing and promoting your web site. Don't use artificial techniques.

Planning for Ongoing Maintenance

Checklist 12.8

 Follow-up every four to five weeks with search engines and directories to ensure that your web site is listed.

If you don't find your web site listed at a particular directory within four to five weeks, go ahead and resubmit.

Track your Submissions

It's critically important to keep track of the dates of your submissions to each directory, along with the details of the categories to which you've submitted, and the descriptions and title content you used.

 Contact a directory representative if you don't find your web site listed at a directory after three submissions.

☑ **Check your server logs regularly to see how visitors find your web site and adjust your web site accordingly.**

You might need to do some tweaking to improve your rankings. You might also write new content with new keywords and keyphrases to support, or shift, your search rankings.

☑ **Add announcements about, and links to, new content from your homepage, to help web site visitors and search crawlers find it.**

☑ **Add new keywords and keyphrases to your SEO strategies when you add new content or make other changes to your site.**

If you've already optimized your web site, search crawlers will find your new content, especially if you link to that content from your homepage, as noted above.

☑ **Consider using analytics software to review keyphrases, search engine rankings, and listings status.**

Web analytics software, such as Web Position Gold, can help track top entry pages, top referring sites, top referring URLs, top search engines, top search keywords and keyphrases. You don't necessarily have to pay for expensive statistics software, though: free services, such as Extreme Stats,[18] provide much of this information, although in using many of these services you are obliged to display on your site a graphical links to the stats, which makes them available to all your site visitors.

☑ **Use the results of keyphrase analysis to add to your web site content that visitors seek.**

☑ **Avoid making changes to your site's SEO tactics for at least three months after you optimize the site and submit it to search directories.**

It takes time for your web site submissions to begin to appear at search engines and directories—it can often take two to three months or more, especially if you have a new site.[19] Try to be patient! Consistently high rankings take time.

[18] http://www.extreme-dm.com/tracking/
[19] Jill Whalen, *Robots Meta Tag – Changing Domain Names*, High Rankings Advisor Issue 137 (April 20, 2005) [http://www.highrankings.com/issue137.htm].

☑ **Avoid constantly tweaking your web site in an attempt to improve your search engine rankings.**

As I mentioned above, it takes time for your tweaked pages to show up at the search engines, so you'll need to wait to see how your pages are doing. After you've given your rankings plenty of time to filter through, if you decide you need to tweak any pages, wait to see what impact those tweaks have before making more changes. Time and patience are an important part of SEO success.

☑ **Check your link popularity at search engines regularly.**

Many web sites will link to yours without letting you know, and in addition to checking your referral logs, using search engines to find web sites that link to yours can be an easy way to find such sites. This information can help you ascertain and follow the efficacy of your reciprocal links campaign.

Tip

Checking Incoming Links

You can enter special queries at each search engine to check for web sites that link to yours. For example, at Google's search box, type:

```
link:www.domainname.com
```

At AltaVista's search box, type:

```
link:domainname.com
```

Keep in mind that only those web sites listed at a particular search engine will appear in that search engine's query results.

☑ **Depending on the industry, consider creating a calendar of keywords and keyphrases for future reference.**

In some industries, the popularity of given keywords can fluctuate throughout the year. Site owners operating in such industries might find it worthwhile to keep a calendar that lists which keywords and keyphrases are popular at different times of year.

Summary

This chapter covered the steps involved in optimizing your web site for search engines. The basic principles of successful search engine optimization (SEO) were explained in a nutshell, and were followed by checklists that showed how to research, prepare, and use keywords and keyphrases within your content and markup.

We also discussed checklists that showed how to create crawler-friendly markup, and how to avoid tricking crawlers. We highlighted in general terms the techniques that could see your web site banned from search engines and directories.

Finally, we stepped through checklists that addressed the important questions of creating and managing an ongoing links campaign, and maintaining your web site's SEO over time.

13 Design

First impressions last. When you go out for a meal in an expensive restaurant, the presentation of your meal makes an immediate first impact. It will only take one bite for you to decide whether or not you will return to the restaurant, and recommend it to your friends.

In a similar way, the visual appearance of your web site is the first thing your visitors will notice, and within only a few seconds of using the site, they'll have made up their minds as to whether it's worthy of their time, or a waste of their time.

Obviously, it's critically important that your site makes a strong positive impression. Just as a chef takes great care to present his culinary masterpieces, you must present your site in such a way that not only does it compel visitors to stay, but inspires them to use the site in the future, and tell their friends about it.

For many web site designers, the creation of a site's look and feel is a particularly fun part of any web project. Web site design is about creativity as well as problem solving—your design must encompass and reflect the site's overall goals and enhance its functionality. This chapter provides checklists to help you achieve these aims.

Basic Design Principles

Four basic design principles underlie any visually appealing web site design.

contrast	Using elements that differ somehow in the same space provides contrast. For instance, you might use the colors black and white, or set a serif font for headings and a sans-serif font for text content. The effective use of contrast adds visual interest to your design.
repetition	Repeating design elements throughout a web page—and a web site—provides visual cues that unify and give visual stability to your site's design. For example, you could decide to use the same font and styling for headings on each page of your site.
alignment	Alignment refers to lining up the top, bottom, sides, or middle of certain graphic elements on a page. Aligning elements, for example, left-aligning your headings, subheadings, and text content on each page of a site, helps to create cohesion and a more logical user experience.
proximity	Proximity helps to show relationships between elements. Placing your global navigation links next to each other, and providing whitespace to separate them from nearby page headings, is one example of proximity at work.

The following checklist provides tips to help you use these principles to create a visually appealing site design.

Checklist 13.1

☑ **Ensure contrasts are obvious in type, color, shape, whitespace, and lines.**

For example, contrast large type with small type, contrast typefaces (i.e., serif and sans-serif fonts), contrast colors, contrast textures, contrast spaces, and contrast large graphics with small graphics.

Tip

Crank Up the Contrast

Feel free to crank things up more than a notch or two. Don't try to contrast black and brown. Strong contrasts are much bolder—try black and white instead.

Use strong contrast to attract reader attention.

In Figure 13.1, a box with a single-pixel border and a shaded background color highlights a Latest News title in a large bold, serif font—a contrast that helps to draw attention to the heading. Article titles use a bold serif font, and they're underlined (since they're hyperlinks to the full news article page). This provides a strong contrast with the article descriptions, which use a smaller, sans-serif font. In addition, whitespace between each article listing helps to provide further contrast, which allows each article to stand out. The design of this Latest News area provides a strong visual contrast with the main content area, which uses a white background and a sans-serif, normal weight font.

Figure 13.1. A strong contrast attracts user attention

In Figure 13.2, the same content is shown without the contrasts. Photos were removed from this example, as they also provide a visual contrast that distinguishes them from the surrounding text. As you can see, the design shown in Figure 13.1 draws our attention more effectively.

Figure 13.2. Lack of contrast fails to attract reader attention

Latest News
Duis Autem vel eum Iriure
Stet clita kasd gubergren, no sea takimata
sanctus est Lorem ipsum dolor sit amet.
Sed diam Nonumy eirmod Tempor
At vero eos et accusam et justo duo dolores et ea
rebum. Stet clita kasd gubergren.
Consetetur sadipscing Elitr
Duis autem vel eum iriure dolor in hendrerit in
vulputate velit esse molestie consequat, vel illum
dolore eu feugiat nulla facilisis at vero eros et
accumsan et iusto odio dignissim.
Main content area. Ut wisi enim ad minim veniam, quis
nostrud exerci tation ullamcorper suscipit lobortis nisl
ut aliquip ex ea commodo consequat.

☑ **Balance page weight using contrast.**

Each element on a page has **weight**. When used effectively, the size, color intensity, and placement of objects can create balance. For example, graphics that contain areas of solid color typically have more weight than multi-tone photographs. Large type has more weight than small type, and bold type has more weight than normal type.

☑ **Create a strong, unifying visual identity using repetition.**

For example, if your web site provides information on beach vacations, your design might use small seashell graphics as list item bullets, a beach scene photo across the top header area, and a beachy color scheme of blues, greens, and yellows. Repeating a theme across all of the site's visual elements like this helps to strengthen the site's message.

☑ **Use repetition consistently throughout your web site.**

The consistent repetition of design elements gives your site a strong, unified visual identity.

Elements that work well to communicate a consistent message when repeated include colors, shapes, fonts, line thickness, sizes of various elements, and graphic concepts.

Research your Favorite Sites

Tip

Have a look at some of your favorite web sites, and make note of which elements they have repeated consistently to create a strong visual identity.

☑ **Create a clean, professional look by providing visual connections between elements.**

For example, when you add images within your text content, align at least one edge of the images with the edge of the text, as shown in Figure 13.3.

Figure 13.3. Aligning text and images to create a visual connection

Note also that aligning the top-of-page area or header (which typically contains a logo, global navigation, and possibly local/section navigation) with the bottom-of-page area or footer (which usually displays bottom-of-page navigation and copyright and other legal information) helps to provide a visual connection between these elements, too.

☑ **Use alignment consistently.**

A lack of alignment, or mixed element alignments, can create a sloppy, unorganized look that undermines readability, so it's best to create layouts that are carefully aligned, like the one in Figure 13.4.

Tip 💡 **Creating Clean Edges**

To create clean edges, left-align all of the headings in your content, across every page of your site. In addition, left-align your text content.

Figure 13.4. Aligning key elements in the design concept sketch

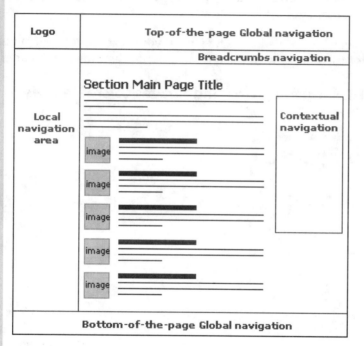

If you mix the alignment of elements, the page can appear messy and unprofessional, like the one shown in Figure 13.5. As Lynch and Horton state in their *Web Style Guide*, "Haphazardly mixed graphics and text decrease usability and legibility, just as they do in paper pages. A balanced and consistently implemented design scheme will increase readers' confidence in your site."[1]

---

[1] Patrick J. Lynch and Sarah Horton, [Design Grids for Web Pages], *Web Style Guide, 2nd ed.* (March 5, 2004) [http://www.webstyleguide.com/page/grids.html]. Also available in print (New Haven, Connecticut: Yale University Press, March 2002).

Figure 13.5. Sketch of design concept in which key elements display mixed alignments

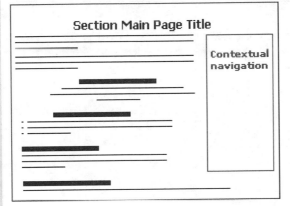

☑ **Avoid using justified text.**

While justified text can create clean left and right alignments, unfortunately, justified text displays poorly on the Web at this point, as it uses crude word-spacing adjustments to create the alignment. Even with sophisticated software, justified text often suffers from poor spacing, excessive hyphenation, and can require plenty of manual adjustments. For the best readability and visual appearance, stick with left-aligned text content for now.[2]

☑ **Group related items together.**

Grouping items together conveys to users the fact that they're related. For example, group navigation links together.

☑ **Visually separate unrelated items.**

☑ **Draw attention with isolated objects.**

Isolated objects draw attention. The more isolated an object, the more power it has to grab users' attention. Consider the example in Figure 13.6. Where does your eye go when you look at that layout?

---

[2] Patrick J. Lynch and Sarah Horton, [Alignment], *Web Style Guide, 2nd ed.* (March 5, 2004) [http://www.webstyleguide.com/type/align.html]. Also available in print (New Haven, Connecticut: Yale University Press, March 2002).

Figure 13.6. Using whitespace to great effect

Effective Typography

Type is a powerful design tool that can help create mood and even provide the entire look and feel for a web site.

Checklist 13.2

☑ **Apply the fonts you've used in your logo to other design elements.**

Your logo's main font might work well for heading text on your site. If it works well in your logo, but isn't appropriate for headings, choose a heading font that contrasts with that of your logo. If you choose to use HTML-rendered text for your headings, be sure to choose fonts that are common to your visitors' computers, so that they will be able to see your intended font.

Use HTML markup and CSS for your typography needs, and use graphic images for typographic purposes, such as headings, only when absolutely necessary. By relying on CSS and HTML, rather than graphics, you'll help to reduce page load times, reduce your site's update overheads, and improve accessibility. Consider using graphics for type only when you require a specific font that can't be created using HTML and CSS.

Use highly stylized novelty fonts sparingly, if at all.

When choosing a highly stylized novelty font, like the one in Figure 13.7, test it on all the words to which you want to apply it. Ensure their legibility, and assess the mood and look and feel of the resulting display.

 ### Use Novelty Fonts in Images Only

Not all fonts are present on all computers; as such, you should restrict novelty fonts for use in images only.

Figure 13.7. Stylized novelty fonts

Use fonts consistently throughout your site.

For example, if you decide to style headlines on your homepage in a serif font, use the same serif font for the headlines on all of your web pages. In addition, it's a good idea to use that same serif font for all your headings and subheadings. To achieve this, you'll need to apply the same serif font to h1, h2, h3, and other heading elements within your site's markup. Sub-headings typically use a smaller font size than headings, and are of a different color.

Specifying Fonts with Mac in Mind

As you designate fonts to be used with various design elements, such as headings and text content, specify in your CSS that the browser should try to render these elements in Geneva before Helvetica, and New York before or instead of Times or Times New Roman. This will make the text cleaner and easier to read for Macintosh users.[3] For example, you could specify the following CSS rules for your site:

```
body {
  font-family: Geneva,Helvetica,sans-serif;
}
h1,h2,h3,h4,h5,h6 {
  font-family: "New York","Times New Roman",Times,
serif;
}
```

The sans-serif font, Verdana, and the serif font, Georgia, were designed specifically for on-screen reading and work well on web sites. So, to make these your first choice, you could use the following rules, which place these fonts in the first position:

```
body {
  font-family: Verdana,Geneva,Helvetica,sans-serif;
}
h1,h2,h3,h4,h5,h6 {
  font-family: Georgia,"New York",
"Times New Roman",Times,serif;
}
```

Note also that type displays at a different size on PC than it does on Macintosh. PCs display type at 96ppi (pixels per inch), while type displays on Mac at 72ppi. Overall, text appears smaller on Macintosh displays.

For more on choosing fonts and cross-platform fonts, see Philip Shaw's Code Style[4] web site and Joe Gillespie's excellent article, *All you wanted to know about Web type but were afraid to ask.*[5]

✓ **Avoid using more than two font families on a page.**

A font family is a collection of font faces that are designed and intended to be used together. A font face is the style of one font within a font family. For example, the Goudy Old Style Regular, Goudy Old Style Italic, and Goudy Old Style Bold font faces are all part of the Goudy Old Style font family. Figure 13.8 shows the similarities in the letter shapes between these different fonts, revealing that they do indeed appear to be related.

---

[3] Robin Williams, *The Non-Designer's Design Book: Design and Typographic Principles for the Visual Novice, 2nd ed.* (Berkeley: Peachpit Press, 2004), 120.
[4] http://www.codestyle.org/
[5] http://www.wpdfd.com/editorial/wpd0704news.htm#feature

Figure 13.8. The Goudy Old Style font family

Goudy Old Style

Goudy Old Style Italic

Goudy Old Style Bold

 Use contrasting typefaces when using two or more fonts.

In keeping with the basic design principle of contrast, it's best to avoid using two similar typefaces on a page. As Figure 13.9 shows, the results are less than impressive.

Figure 13.9. Using similar fonts together

Palatino Linotype

Times New Roman

Instead, use two contrasting fonts. This approach provides greater visual impact, as Figure 13.10 illustrates.

Figure 13.10. Using contrasting fonts together

Edwardian Script

Arrus BT

 Capitalize only the first word and any proper nouns in headings and titles.

Since we read by primarily scanning the tops of letters and recognizing the overall shapes of words, capitalizing only the first word and any proper nouns in headings and titles boost their readability online. Figure 13.11 illustrates this point.[6]

Figure 13.11. Using capitalization to boost readability

New York hopes for 2012 Olympics

NEW YORK HOPES FOR 2012 OLYMPICS

☑ **Use boldface type only for strong emphasis.**

Boldface type provides a visual cue that the text is especially important. In terms of design, boldface type carries more weight than normal fonts.

 Avoid All-bold and All-caps

IMPORTANT

Don't use all boldface type or all caps for text content. A full page in bold type is quite difficult to read. Save boldface type for judicious emphasis.

☑ **Avoid using huge type.**

While you don't want your visitors to miss your message, you don't want to intimidate them by making them feel that your site's shouting at them! Essentially, this is what using huge type, or all-caps, will do.

Brainstorming

Now that you're aware of the basic design principles, it's time to take ideas, concepts, text, and research, and begin to explore design possibilities for your web site. Don't expect to come up with your final design concepts overnight; instead, give this part of your web design project the time it deserves. Bear in mind the functional aspects of your web site as you move through the design process.

---

[6] Lynch and Horton, [Case], *Web Style Guide, 2nd ed.*, (March 5, 2004) [http://www.webstyleguide.com/type/case.html]. Also available in print (New Haven, Connecticut: Yale University Press, March, 2002).

☑ **Develop paper prototypes.**

Research shows that designers who work out ideas on paper tend to explore ideas and concepts more broadly, and create more iterations of those ideas, than designers who use computer-based tools. Those using computer-based tools tend to take fewer ideas, and work them out in detail, rather than exploring more broadly first.[7]

You might use paper to sketch several different layouts—in grid or "wireframe" formats, which include only boxes (not graphics) to denote different areas—that combine all the basic elements of your web site. An example is shown in Figure 13.12. Create these kinds of layouts for your homepage, main section pages, information content pages, form pages, shopping cart pages, and so on. Essential elements that will probably be common to most of your pages might include your logo, navigation (global, local/section, breadcrumb), a search box, footer, and content areas.

Figure 13.12. A sketch of the design concept shows the key page elements

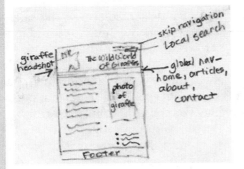

Try Sketch Designing Today

Tip

Some designers might resist sketching out design ideas on paper first. If you're one of them, I hope you'll at least try it with an open mind. You could be pleasantly surprised at how helpful it can be to try this approach.

---

[7] Douglas K. van Duyne, James A. Landay, and Jason I. Hong, *The Design of Sites: Patterns, Principles, and Processes for Crafting a Customer-centered Web Experience* (Boston: Addison-Wesley, 2003), 77.

☑ **Base the look and feel of your web site on your logo design and company colors.**

If it was designed well, your logo will have a unique appearance that conveys an impression about you or your company instantly. Logos typically use one or two fonts, and at least one or two colors. You might also have in place strict guidelines that control the use of the logo and company colors in your collateral—including your web site's design.

Among the early stages of the site's planning, you'll need to determine what you envisage the site will look like. Often, a designer will ask you to choose adjectives, such as strong, clean, peaceful, cheerful, professional, or casual, to identify the "feel" you want the site to convey. While these terms should agree with the mood or tone that your logo communicates, your web site should provide the opportunity to expand on that mood.

Even if you don't have a logo, it's still important to base the look and feel of the site on a unifying concept that's articulated by the terms you select.

☑ **Base design concepts on your web site's purpose, requirements, and visitor needs.**

It might be tempting to start to create a design solely for the sake of its look and feel. After all, creative brainstorming is exhilarating and fun—it's easy to get a little carried away! However, by necessity, your site's visual design must address a number of considerations, including the site's purpose, its target market or audience, information architecture, usability needs, accessibility requirements, content types, and search engine optimization goals. The design process gives you the opportunity to bring together all these considerations to create a visually appealing, interactive, functional, and user-friendly web site. Channel your creative brainstorming wisely by basing your visual design on these important elements.

☑ **Design for content.**

Your web site's content is the reason why people will visit your site. The site's visual design needs to emphasize your content's best qualities and features, so create your design around it, rather than trying to force your content into a design.

☑ Provide a flexible design.

Unlike print publications that have fixed designs—fixed widths, font sizes, and colors—web browsing software provides for flexible viewing. Users can expand and contract their browser windows and change font sizes. Many computer operating systems and software programs provide similar flexibility.

It's important that web sites embrace the flexibility of web browsing software and alternative devices, and take advantage of these capabilities. Try to avoid creating fixed designs: they can block many of these flexibility features, cause usability problems, and often reduce accessibility. Understanding web browsers and how your site visitors interact with them to browse the Web can help you create a design that leverages, rather than works against, these truly remarkable capabilities.

☑ Keep it simple.

Aim to keep your visual design simple. Ensure that each and every design element has a purpose, be it functional, business-related, or visual. If your web site design works without certain elements, remove them.

Finalizing the Design

Checklist 13.4

☑ Develop and refine paper prototypes into digital graphic prototypes.

Plan to work through a number of iterations as you tweak, refine, and test your graphic prototypes before final approval (whether that approval is your own or that of a committee). As Figure 13.13 shows, it's important to incorporate your logo and company branding into your graphic prototypes.

☑ Create an interactive prototype.

Once your visual design has been finalized and your graphic prototype is approved, create a working, interactive prototype of your homepage and important inner pages. This technique gives you the chance to see how the site will work on popular browsers.

Figure 13.13. Creating a preliminary graphic prototype

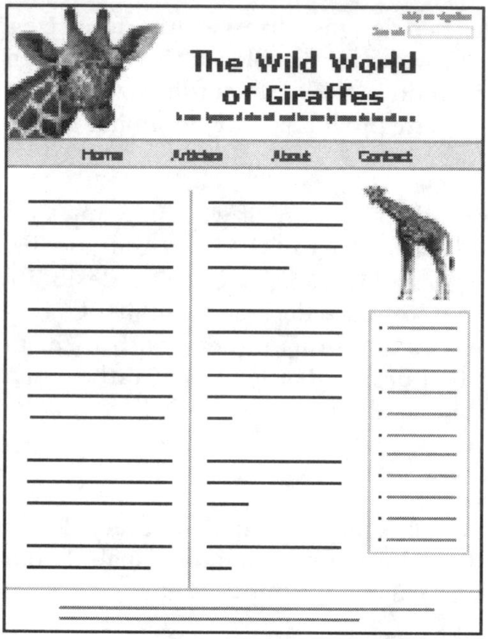

It's not necessary to include all the finalized site content in this proto-type—you could use "dummy" content like the popular "Lorem Ipsum" text used by many designers.[8]

☑ **Test the basic functionality of your interactive prototype.**

Test your interactive prototype to ensure that it accommodates all your web site's basic functional needs. And be sure to test the functionality and usability of the site's navigation. If you find that your web site's design doesn't really work in some places, brainstorm, revise, and remake your prototype.

Once you're happy with the way your design appears and functions, you can add real content and complete thorough testing as explained in Chapter 14.

---

[8] http://www.loremipsum.net/

Summary

This chapter covered what many designers consider the most fun part of a web site design project—creating a web site's visual design. This chapter identified the four basic design principles, and provided tips on how to use them to achieve a visually appealing web site design. It also explored the ways in which you can enhance your web site design using typography, and investigated the considerations that are of key importance during the brainstorming process for the initial design. The chapter concluded with a checklist that explained how to finalize your web site design by creating and testing interactive prototypes.

14 Testing

Testing plays a critical role in the development of your web site and its long-term maintenance. While smaller web sites—especially those with more limited budgets—may not need to follow the formal testing procedures that are required for large-scale, commercial web sites, every site needs to be thoroughly tested to ensure that it's error-free, user-friendly, accessible, and standards compliant.

Testing should be completed during each phase of a site's development. Two of the most costly web project mistakes are to delay testing until just before launch, or not to test at all. Testing *during* production makes it easier to locate and resolve errors, and minimizes the chance of existing bugs being replicated throughout later stages of development. Early and continued testing can eliminate the need for the costly redesigns and other major fixes that can result from overlooked errors.

This chapter's checklists will help you test your site both during development, and after.

Getting Started

☑ **Document your baseline web site testing requirements.**

Make use of the preliminary data you collected in Chapter 2 to help determine and document your baseline site testing requirements. For instance, the information you collected on the browsers and connection speeds that your visitors will use, and those visitors' skills and age groups, can be used as a basis for your testing plan.

☑ **Source and install all necessary tools.**

You can conduct tests very cheaply using free and low-cost testing tools. Most browsers are free or offer conditionally free versions, and you can download and install multiple browsers—including several versions of Internet Explorer for Windows—on one computer. Alternative device simulators and emulators, such as those for cell phones and PDAs, can also be downloaded and used for free, and most shareware and commercial software creators allow a 30-day trial of their products for testing purposes. Some web design-related discussion lists, as well as the SitePoint Forums, welcome testing requests and posts that solicit bug reports and feedback.

☑ **Provide acceptable testing protocols.**

Ultimately, the design and layout for each page of the site must be both aesthetically pleasing and functional across multiple platforms and browsers.

One of the difficulties associated with testing design elements on different platforms is that the test results can be subjective. For example, a designer may create a CSS-driven site that works perfectly on newer browsers, but doesn't look that hot in older browsers such as Netscape 4. The tester may interpret this as a failure point rather than acceptable "design degradation."

To avoid the time and effort involved in re-submitting pages for testing, spell out acceptable cross-browser, cross-platform differences in advance—including protocols for supporting old browsers.

Use Annotated Screenshots to Determine Display Protocols

At the end of the final prototyping stage, ask the designer to provide a series of screenshots that have been annotated to identify the differences in the ways the site displays on different browsers and platforms. These screenshots can be used in later testing to identify the displays that are deemed acceptable on each platform. Testers can then compare the protocols and screenshots with their findings.

☑ Set up a staging server.

A staging or test server that's identical to your web site's live server environment should be used for testing and development purposes prior to your site's launch.

Automated Programs for Larger Sites

Larger web sites typically require more robust testing procedures that test large sets of records, values, and content. You might consider using an automated program, such as Badboy,[1] eValid,[2] or TestComplete[3] for such purposes.

Good Testing Practice

Checklist 14.2

☑ Systematically test individual pages.

Thoroughly test your site one page at a time, making sure each page is solid before proceeding. Carry out a comprehensive test of the final version of the site in the same way.

☑ Track bugs and confirm fixes.

Document the details of discovered bugs and their resolutions.

---

[1] http://www.badboy.com.au/
[2] http://www.soft.com/eValid/
[3] http://www.automatedqa.com/products/testcomplete/

Regression test, especially when fixing bugs.

Regression testing, which is also known as verification testing, is the process of retesting pages or sections of a site to make sure that a recent bug fix hasn't broken some other aspect of the site, or reinstated bugs that were fixed previously. Conducting and documenting regression tests will allow you to identify any parts of the site that break, and document the causes of those errors and how you resolved them. If a bug resurfaces at some point, it will be spotted immediately and resolved quickly.[4]

Validate the markup for each individual web page.

Validate the markup for all your web pages to ensure that each uses structural, compliant markup. This will allow you to confirm that you've used the correct markup for the specified DOCTYPE, fix any typos you may have made, and resolve any syntax errors. Validating your markup as you build a page, rather than waiting until you've created an entire page (or worse, an entire web site), makes it easier to isolate, find, and correct markup problems.

Tip

Using Markup Validators

Some HTML editors integrate validation tools such as W3C's HTML and CSS validators, the WDG HTML Validator, and the CSE HTML Validator (an HTML/XHTML syntax checker and validator), which allow you to validate your markup conveniently while you work.

The CSE and WDG HTML Validators also include helpful batch processing features. So, for example, although I validate each page with the CSE HTML Validator and the W3C's validators as I work, I use CSE HTML Validator's batch processing to recheck multiple pages simultaneously. I also use batch processing as a final check when I've finished developing all the pages of the site.

Ensure that the validation tool you use is based on W3C Recommendations.

Validate all CSS.

Validate all the CSS you use on the site, including each external style sheet, plus all embedded and inline CSS.

---

[4] *Regression Testing*, Webopedia Computer Dictionary (no date) [http://www.webopedia.com/TERM/R/regression_testing.html].

☑ **Conduct load testing to stress-test programming technologies and server hardware capacities.**

You need to make sure that the programming technologies you've used, and the capacities of your server hardware, can cater to higher levels of traffic than you expect the site to receive. Taking this approach will help you ensure that your site remains online and fully functional at all times. Load testing procedures should include a trial run—tests that usually involve the use of automated scripts that emulate multiple simultaneous user sessions. The trial run will reveal how the programming technologies and server hardware you've used will cope with traffic spikes.

Matching Hosting with Projected Server Loads

Your ISP should match your hosting package with your projected server loads if you're using a web hosting service, so you should let them know what your loads will be. Your web host might recommend a different web hosting package that offers greater capacity if your load testing reveals that your existing setup has the potential for problems as traffic levels increase.

If you're managing your own server(s), check whether your server software provider offers free load testing software—many do. You might also consider using dedicated load-testing software products, such as those offered by WebPerformance[5] and NetMechanic.[6] In addition, numerous open-source performance analysis software tools[7] are available to help you assess, monitor, and manage your web site's performance.[8]

General Testing

Checklist 14.3

☑ **Test your web site on multiple browsers and platforms.**

The fact that your web site looks good and works well in one browser doesn't mean it will look as good or function as well on other browsers and/or platforms. Even if you're developing an intranet web site for an or-

---

[5] http://www.webperformanceinc.com/
[6] http://netmechanic.com/monitor.htm
[7] http://www.opensourcetesting.org/performance.php
[8] See also *Stress Tools to Test your Web Server*, Microsoft.com [http://support.microsoft.com/kb/231282/en-us].

ganization whose employees use the same browser and operating system, the hardware and software used by those employees can and will vary. In the long run, it's better to develop your web site on the basis of the W3C recommendations, then to follow up with extensive cross-browser, cross-platform testing. Stay informed of the release of new or updated browsers and operating systems so that you can keep your cross-browser, cross-platform tests current.

Which Browsers and Platforms to Test?

Tip

Check your server logs—as well as other on- and offline re-sources—that cover browser statistics, operating systems, and emerging Web use trends, so that you know which browsers, versions, and operating systems your web site visitors use now, and are likely to use in future. As part of your approach to site maintenance in the long term, plan to check your server logs weekly (monthly checks might be fine if you run a smaller web site with low traffic volumes) to follow changes and trends in your browser statistics. Take this data into account as your hone you your cross-browser, cross-platform testing procedures, to ensure that you're testing all of the browsers and operating systems that your visitors use. Here is a list of popular operating systems and browsers on which you might test your site:

Operating systems
Macintosh OS X, Macintosh OS 9, Windows XP SP1 and SP2, Windows 2000, Windows 98, Linux

Browsers for Macintosh OS X
Safari 1.2, Mozilla 1.6, Firefox 1.0, Opera 8, Opera 7, Internet Explorer 5.2

Browsers for Macintosh OS 9
iCab, Internet Explorer 5

Browsers for Windows XP
Opera 8, Opera 7, Mozilla 1.7, Firefox 1.0, Netscape 7.1, Internet Explorer 6.0, Lynx browser

Browsers for Windows 2000
Opera 8, Opera 7, Mozilla 1.7.3, Firefox 1.0, Netscape 7.1, Netscape 7.0, Netscape 6.2, Netscape 4.78, Internet Explorer 6, Internet Explorer 5.5, Internet Explorer 5.0, Lynx browser

Browsers for Windows 98
Internet Explorer 4.0, Lynx browser

Browsers for Linux
　　Konqueror 3.0.5, Mozilla 1.6, Opera 8, Opera 7, Emacs/W3, Netscape 7, Netscape 4.8

☑ **Test page optimization with every update.**

Optimizing your pages right from the start can help ensure that your site design and images support fast page load times, and that the site's development is smooth and efficient. Whenever you add anything to your web site—new content, new images, or new web pages—check that content's optimization to help keep the site streamlined. If you're not yet familiar with web site optimization, see Chapter 11.

Tip

Document Weight and Load Time Tools

Some HTML editors include features that tell you a document's weight, or a page's load time at various connection speeds, and most image editing software products indicate file size load times at various connection speeds.

There are also free online tools that calculate document weight, composition, and page load times, and even offer recommendations for optimizing web documents. Siteoptimization.com's helpful Web Page Analyzer[9] is one such tool.

☑ **View pages on a variety of displays.**

You may find that your beautiful design, which is wonderfully contrasted on an LCD monitor, is impossible to read on a CRT monitor, and completely unusable on alternative devices. Different displays will not always interpret your site's design and colors consistently, so it's worth testing your initial design, as well as the site's ongoing development, in a variety of displays.

☑ **View pages on different screen resolutions and with various color settings.**

Some HTML editors provide a feature that allows you to check your pages at various screen resolutions and with a range of color settings. Similar tools can also be downloaded as plug-ins for some browsers. For example, the highly recommended Web Developer Toolbar extension for Firefox

---

[9] http://www.webpageanalyzer.com/

includes a customizable window resizing tool, among many other useful features.[10]

Consider Nonstandard Resolutions

Screen display sizes may or may not reflect the actual dimensions of the viewable web page. Many users don't expand browser windows to fill the entire screen (especially on larger monitors), and various toolbars and side panels can take up portions of the screen width and height. For example, on an 800x600 display, a browser that has a side panel and a couple of custom toolbars across its top would display only 500x400 pixels of a web page—less if the browser window isn't maximized. Be sure to conduct testing that accounts for this wide range of variability—not just the standard maximum screen resolutions. Table 14.1, which shows screen resolutions of various devices, and Table 14.2, which shows the color depth settings of different displays, should help your testing.

In addition to the displays mentioned in Table 14.1 and Table 14.2, there are standalone tools—such as BrowserCam,[11] an online subscription service—which provide screenshots depicting the way your content will appear in a wide range of screen resolutions and browsers.

Table 14.1. Typical screen resolutions and displays (in pixels)

Computer displays	640x480, 800x600, 1024x760, 1280x1024, 1440 x 900 (iMac G5 17" display), 1680 x 1050 (iMac 20" G5 display)
WebTV/MSN TV	544 x 383
PDA, Pocket PC with Windows Mobile, smart-phones	240x160: Palm; 320x240: Palm, Pocket PC with Windows Mobile pre-2003, v2; 640x480: Windows Mobile pre-2003, v2; 320x320: Palm OS smartphone [a]

[a] Lisa Gade, *palmOne Treo 650 Palm OS Smartphone*, *Mobile Tech Review* (December 10, 2004) [http://www.mobiletechreview.com/Treo_650.htm].

---

[10] For more on Firefox's tools for web developers, see Chris Pederick's article, *Web Developer Extensions for FireFox and Mozilla* [http://www.chrispederick.com/work/firefox/webdeveloper/].
[11] http://browsercam.com/

Table 14.2. Typical display color depth settings

Computer displays	Newer displays: 24-bit, 32-bit, 65,000 colors, 16,777,216 colors; Old displays: 16-bit, 256 colors, 65,000 colors[a]
PDA, Pocket PC with Windows Mobile, smartphones	Pocket PC: 16-bit, 65,000 color screens; Old PDAs: 8-bit, grayscale [b]

[a] *Browser Statistics: What Is the Trend in Browser Usage, Operating Systems and Screen Resolution?* W3Schools (January 2005) [http://www.w3schools.com/browsers/browsers_stats.asp].
[b] *What is a Pocket PC (PPC)? What models are out there?* Mobile Tech Review (no date) [http://www.mobiletechreview.com/ppc.htm].

☑ **Check for adequate color contrast.**

A good way to check color contrast is to change your browser display to grayscale, or print the web page in black and white. A tool that can be very helpful for checking your design's color contrasts is Vischeck,[12] which simulates colorblind vision, allowing you to see your pages as a colorblind user might.

☑ **Test the functionality of external and embedded scripts and functions.**

Some scripts and functions might work fine in one browser, though they may not work correctly, if at all, in other browsers or devices. Minor tweaking can resolve many cross-browser, cross-platform functionality issues. If older browsers or alternative and adaptive technologies don't support some functions, you may wish to provide alternative methods to allow those users to access those capabilities some other way.

☑ **Test all links, including navigation.**

Ensure that all links work properly, and point to the correct location. Link checking software can check for valid, broken, and redirected links. Some HTML editors, such as Macromedia Dreamweaver[13] and HomeSite,[14] offer link checking capabilities. Free tools are also available—try Xenu's Link-Sleuth[15] and W3C Link Checker.[16] See WebsiteTips.com's section, "Link Checkers, Maintenance"[17] for more. Note, though, that link checkers aren't

---

[12] http://www.vischeck.com/
[13] http://www.macromedia.com/software/dreamweaver/
[14] http://www.macromedia.com/software/homesite/
[15] http://home.snafu.de/tilman/xenulink.html
[16] http://validator.w3.org/checklink
[17] http://websitetips.com/tools/checklinks/

intuitive enough to check whether links direct to the correct location—be sure to check for this manually.

Check error pages.

Intentionally enter incorrect URLs into the browser's address bar to check that the appropriate error pages (404 errors, etc.) are in place.

Make sure that the error pages include helpful information and links that help users find what they seek. Keep in mind that, sometimes, visitors will incorrectly guess a domain name or slightly misspell a URL. Help those visitors by accepting common misspellings, typos, incorrect case sensitivity, different terminology for the same items, and predictable domain name errors: provide suggestions to redirect users to the proper page.[18]

Test all downloads.

Check to ensure that all your download links point to the correct files, and that the download files exist.

Test the search feature.

Ensure that the search feature functions correctly, and that search results are accurate and helpful.

Solid Security

Clear your Cache!

IMPORTANT

Be sure to clear the browser cache, including cookies, before each test.

Checklist 14.4

Check that digital certificates and SSL URLs work correctly.

Your SSL URLs should begin with `https://`. Also, when a visitor accesses a web page protected by SSL, most browsers will show a "lock" icon at the bottom of the browser, like that being shown by IE 6 for Windows in Figure 14.1.

---

[18] Matthew Linderman with Jason Fried, *Defensive Design for the Web: How to Improve Error Messages, Help, Forms, and Other Crisis Points* (Indianapolis: New Riders, 2004), 99, 224.

Figure 14.1. The "lock" icon displaying at the bottom of the browser window

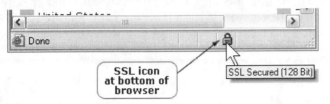

SSL is commonly used to encrypt online transactions and other sensitive data, as well as intranets and extranets. Verisign[19] and Thawte[20] are two popular companies that issue SSL certificates.

☑ **Check that all pages requiring SSL access are accessible only via SSL.**

☑ **Test the security of restricted areas.**

Users might share or try to guess the URLs of content and downloads in protected areas of your site. Restricted content URLs might appear within publicly available referrer logs. People might even share usernames and passwords without authorization or permission. As such, it's critical that you anticipate the kinds of security breaches that might take place, and test methods for their prevention.

 Tip

Hack your Site: the Ultimate Security Test

Download popular hacking tools to use in testing, to see if your protected areas can easily be comprised. Those managing larger-scale web sites might even consider outsourcing or hiring a hacking expert for testing purposes.

Ensuring security and data integrity—especially in terms of your confidential data, including customer credit card information—is critical for promoting and maintaining trust among your site's visitors. Don't assume that your web site's security is always okay. Test regularly to make sure it remains secure.

---

[19] http://verisign.com/
[20] http://thawte.com/

☑ **Test forms and form controls.**

Check to ensure that forms are submitted correctly, and that they're only submitted when the correct information is entered and required fields have been completed. Review form error messages to ensure that they are helpful and informative within the context of the form itself.

☑ **Test online shopping facilities.**

If your web site includes a shopping cart or similar functionality, thoroughly test back-end operations to ensure that all transactions are secure, and everything runs smoothly.

Accessibility Testing

If you plan to make your site accessible, and include accessibility testing in every phase of your project, chances are good that by the time your site is ready to launch, it will meet the W3C's WCAG Guidelines, as well as any other accessibility guidelines that it must address.

Conducting a Preliminary Review

The W3C recommends a two-phase process for testing a site's accessibility. First, developers should conduct a preliminary review of the site that includes testing a few pages to get an idea of the site's accessibility. Then, they should undertake a thorough, comprehensive review that includes an evaluation of every web page (or representative pages on larger web sites) with a variety of tools and users who have disabilities.[21] The checklist below is a guide for conducting a preliminary accessibility review.

Checklist 14.5

☑ **Select a random sampling of pages to test.**

You should test every page of a small web site. For larger web sites, select a random sampling of pages that includes your homepage, at least one or two pages from each section, and especially important or popular pages, such as the contact page and the sitemap.

---

[21] W3C, *Evaluating Web Sites for Accessibility*, W3C Web Accessibility Initiative (November 14, 2002) [http://www.w3.org/WAI/eval/].

☑ **Use a graphical browser to test sample pages.**

☑ **Use a voice *or* text-only browser to test sample pages.**

A text-only browser, such as the free Lynx text-only browser, can provide valuable insight into your web site's accessibility.

☑ **Use two evaluation tools.**

☑ **Manually examine representative pages using the checkpoints from WCAG 1.0, your government accessibility guidelines, or other requirements.**

☑ **Summarize the results.**

If your results summary indicates a number of accessibility issues, you might wish to make site-wide changes before you conduct a comprehensive review. Conduct another preliminary test after you implement these changes.

Conducting a Comprehensive Review

A comprehensive review is much more thorough and detailed than a preliminary review. Here's a checklist that will help you ensure you don't miss a thing!

Checklist 14.6

☑ **Identify, determine, and document site-wide conformance requirements and levels.**

You may include WCAG 1.0 Level 1, local government requirements, and company guidelines in your documentation, for example.

☑ **Test the site's accessibility conformance.**

Test every single page of smaller web sites. For larger web sites, test a representative sample that includes the homepage and all especially important or popular pages, pages from each section, pages for each different layout, and pages generated from databases.

☑ **Use *at least* two different accessibility evaluation tools.**

☑ Manually examine representative pages using the checkpoints from WCAG 1.0, your government accessibility guidelines, or other recommendations.

☑ Use a graphical browser to test sample pages.

☑ Use a text-only browser and a voice browser to test pages.

☑ Ensure that interface elements are operable with multiple input devices.

For example, test all interface elements with a mouse, with keyboard only, and with adaptive technologies. If you use JavaScript to create navigation rollover effects, ensure that links work without JavaScript, provide HTML text links, or implement both.

☑ Proofread all content.

Read over each page of the site to check that all the text is clear, simple, and appropriate for your web site's target audience, as well as those segments of the market that have cognitive or learning disabilities.

Make sure that your text is clear, simple, and written for the Web, then boost its accessibility by allowing for those with disabilities.

Tip

How Complex is your Writing?

Clear Language and Design (CLAD) offer a great Reading Effectiveness Tool[22] that's designed to assess the literacy skills that users will require in order to understand your text.

For helpful insight on cognitive and learning disabilities, see Roger Hudson, Russ Weakley and Peter Firminger's article, *An Accessibility Frontier: Cognitive Disabilities and Learning Difficulties*.[23]

---

[22] http://www.eastendliteracy.on.ca/ClearLanguageAndDesign/readingeffectivenesstool/
[23] http://www.usability.com.au/resources/cognitive.cfm

✅ **Conduct usability testing with a diversity of participants.**

If possible, conduct usability testing with people who have a variety of disabilities, technical expertise, and varying levels of familiarity with your web site. Use a variety of adaptive technologies, if possible.

There's no better way to assess your site's accessibility than to have disabled users test the site. It should be noted, for example, that a sighted person will not use a screen reader, such as JAWS, in the same way as a blind person who uses the tool daily.

Testing with a Graphical Browser

You can do a fair amount of accessibility testing with your browser. Opera is especially conducive to accessibility testing, since the browser makes it quite simple to turn off images, animations, style sheets, JavaScript, frames, and so on. Ian Lloyd has written a great tutorial about using Opera for testing a site's accessibility.[24]

There are also helpful accessibility testing extensions, sidebar panels, and toolbars for other graphical browsers, including Mozilla, Firefox, and Internet Explorer. As well as visiting your favorite browser's web site, see Derek Featherstone's *Testing Tools for Developing Accessible Web Sites*[25]—a helpful list of annotated browser links.

Checklist 14.7

✅ **View pages without images.**

As long as you've included the `alt` attribute for each image (for use by browsers that don't support images, or visitors who are browsing with images turned off), the browser will hide decorative images that have blank `alt` attributes. However, if you don't include `alt` attributes, browsers will not hide the images, and screen readers will read the word "Image," as indicated in Figure 14.2.

---

[24] http://www.accessify.com/features/tutorials/opera-accessibility/
[25] http://www.wats.ca/show.php?contentid=46

Figure 14.2. Viewing images with blank `alt` attributes in Opera 7 for Windows

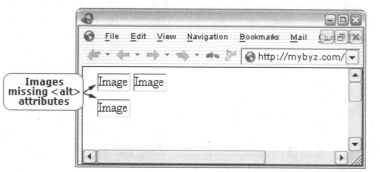

☑ **View pages without style sheets.**

☑ **Check that your pages allow users to vary the font sizes displayed.**

☑ **View tabular data with tables disabled or in a browser that doesn't offer table support.**

This process will indicate how usable your tabular data might be for visitors using screen readers, text-only browsers such as Lynx, and older PDAs.

☑ **View the web site with new technologies turned off.**

These "new technologies" include JavaScript, Java, sound capabilities, and plugins. Your page should remain functional and accessible when these technologies are unavailable.

Testing with a Voice or Text-only Browser

If you don't have handy access to a voice browser, you can use Lynx, a free text-only browser, or Delorie's online Lynx Viewer, for preliminary testing. For comprehensive testing, the W3C recommends testing with a text-only browser and a voice browser.[26]

---

[26] W3C, *Evaluating Web Sites for Accessibility*, Web Accessibility Initiative, W3C (November 14, 2002) [http://www.w3.org/WAI/eval/].

☑ **Check that web site navigation is available and works properly.**

If your web site uses images—including image maps—for navigation purposes, text hyperlinks should appear in their places (via `alt` attribute text, and possibly also in the `title` attribute text, if needed). If you use Flash or Java applets for navigation, your site should include alternative text navigation links to help ensure accessibility.

 Tip

Helping *Everyone* get Around

Keep in mind that this approach also helps search engine bots to crawl and index your web site. For more on optimizing your web site for search engine crawlers, see Chapter 11.

☑ **Check all hyperlinks.**

☑ **Check that decorative images don't appear in text-only browsers and aren't read by voice browsers.**

As we discussed above, all decorative images, such as bullets and design-related images, should have blank `alt` attributes so that text-only browsers and voice browsers ignore them.

☑ **Check that the information is presented in a way that's comprehensible when read serially.**

Lynx allows you to simulate serial access, so that you can make sure the information you've presented is understandable to users of voice and text-only browsers.[27]

☑ **Test form controls.**

Figure 14.3 depicts the testing of an accessibility-friendly form with Lynx 2.85.

---

[27] Joe Clark, *Building Accessible Websites* (Indianapolis: New Riders Publishing, 2003), 236.

Figure 14.3. Testing a form in Lynx

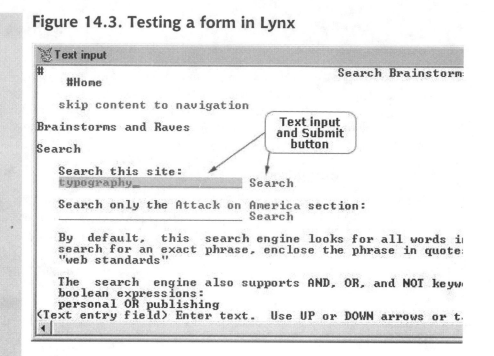

Usability Testing

If you find yourself short on money, time, or both, you might be tempted to consider skipping the usability testing phase. Rather than skipping this process altogether, it's far better to test on an abbreviated, informal scale. It's better to conduct a number of small, fast tests during development, rather than one big test at the end—especially if that final usability test is to be scheduled just before the site's launch.

The main goal of usability testing is to make sure your final-version, live web site is user-friendly and works well for your visitors. Three main dimensions of usability testing are effectiveness (testing to see if the user can accomplish desired tasks), efficiency (testing to see how much effort is involved in accomplishing the desired tasks), and satisfaction (testing to see if the user has a satisfactory experience and will return).[28] Use the following checklist as a guide to determining and conducting your usability tests.

---

[28] Dey Alexander, *Quick Wins with Usability Testing* (presentation, Web Workshop Series at Monash University, Melbourne, 2002), slide 3.

☑ **List test objectives and concerns.**

Be specific, making note of tasks and areas of the web site that might be of concern—for instance, forms that might be difficult to complete or use, or the methods by which users are expected to find certain products. Be sure to specify these age groups and computer skill levels that you wish to test.

To help determine your objectives and concerns, check with your clients, management, designers, developers, and others involved in the project.

☑ **Choose test approaches.**

Numerous approaches have been developed to testing various aspects of sites' usability. In planning your usability tests, it's important that you research and consider the available approaches in light of the resources and time you have available.

For example, you may choose to use personas or card sorting to help test your web site's information architecture—one single, but critical aspect of your site's usability. By creating personas, you can document the steps typical visitors would take to accomplish particular objectives, then test those steps—looking specifically at the information architecture, navigation, and forms, for example, that that persona might use to achieve that goal.

Card sorting can be a helpful way to understand how your web site visitors will likely understand and explore the information on your site.

Conducting a Card Sorting Test

 Tip

To conduct a card sorting test, give users index cards on which are written the titles of pieces of content, features, or categories. Include brief descriptions on each card, but don't hint at any information structure or classification. If you plan to add more content to your web site in future phases, it can help to add those specific elements to the cards if you can.

Be sure to brief your test users, explaining that there are no right or wrong answers. Ask them to read each card carefully and group them into piles that make sense to them. If the users aren't sure about a card, they can set it aside and come back to it whenever they wish. When they finish, ask them to label each pile.

Compare the results with your web site's information architecture as one way to determine whether or not further tweaks or changes are required.

☑ **Recruit users for testing based on your target market.**

Test users should represent your target audience profiles. For example, if your typical users aren't very technology-savvy, but you test with technology-savvy users, your test results won't uncover potential technology-related problems, such as confusion with drop-down menus or multiple browser windows.

A test group of five users is considered large enough to provide information that will help improve your site's usability.

☑ **Prepare an NDA (non-disclosure agreement) ready for users to sign prior to starting your tests.**

☑ **Determine testing location(s).**

Jakob Nielsen and other usability experts talk about conducting testing in usability labs. Indeed, labs can be helpful when you're testing a highly sensitive and secure web site, you have significant hardware components or specific hardware that must be used for testing, you anticipate long testing sessions (more than a couple of hours or so), and you have a project for which you'd like a team of observers to watch the tests.[29]

Alternatively, there can be advantages to "field" testing—testing the site in an office or home setting, using testers' own computers at these locations. This approach eliminates the costs of a usability lab while allowing you to observe how your web site will work for typical visitors. In addition, testers may be more comfortable and relaxed using their own computers. However, Jakob Nielsen reports that field studies tend to be expensive, and it can be challenging to get permission to conduct them at company locations.[30]

Consider also the possibility of conducting remote testing. For example, you could be at your office and use the telephone to verbally communicate instructions, obtain user feedback, and engage in discussion. Unless you

---

[29] Julia Houck-Whitaker, *Remote Testing versus Lab Testing*, Bolt | Peters, Inc., (February 3, 2005) [http://boltpeters.com/articles/versus.html].
[30] Elizabeth Neal, *Why You Don't Need a Usability Lab*, SitePoint (October 8, 2004) [http://www.sitepoint.com/article/dont-need-usability-lab].

have online video cameras set up strategically for testers' computers, though, you'll miss the important observation part of your testing. You'll need to encourage them to "think out loud," and remember to phrase your responses and questions to remain as neutral as possible. Remote testing can be quite effective for large web sites, those with ecommerce capabilities, web applications, and intranets.[31]

Videotape your Tests

Tip

Videotaping tests can be helpful, as the videos can facilitate later review, allowing you to see details that you may not have noticed during testing, and to show the tests to others on the project team. Time-stamping the videos will make it easier to reference key findings later.

Top Testing References

Tip

For more on testing approaches, see Janice Fraser's *The Culture of Usability: How to Spend Less and Get More from Your Usability-Testing Program*,[32] and Lane Becker's *90% of All Usability Testing is Useless*.[33]

☑ **Create a relaxed atmosphere for testers.**

Rather than making people think they're in a lab being assessed, decorate your test area as if it were a typical office setting or perhaps a living room. The SitePoint article, *Why You Don't Need a Usability Lab*,[34] has more on this.

☑ **Establish realistic tasks for users to perform and identify what, specifically, you will measure.**

For example, to test a web site that offered numerous articles categorized by topic, you could set tasks that require users to find specific articles or topics. From these tests you could collect data on the time the test subjects needed for each task, whether or not the navigation was helpful, whether the local search was used, and if the results were accurate and helpful.

---

[31] Houck-Whitaker, Velda Bartek, and Deane Cheatham, *Experience Remote Usability Testing, Part 1* IBM developerWorks (January 1, 2003)
[http://www-106.ibm.com/developerworks/web/library/wa-rmusts1/].
[32] http://www.ddj.com/dept/architect/184411669
[33] http://www.adaptivepath.com/publications/essays/archives/000328.php
[34] http://www.sitepoint.com/article/dont-need-usability-lab

☑ **Provide simple, clear instructions only.**

For accurate test results, do *not* provide any hints.

☑ **Allow users to perform their own tasks in addition to your pre-defined tasks.**

Users will often come up with tasks you haven't thought of, and by pursuing these tasks, can uncover important subtleties and problems with a site.[35]

☑ **Create a post-test questionnaire.**

Consider what, in particular, you'd like feedback on, and create a questionnaire that addresses those issues. Also, include areas for comments and suggestions. You may choose to make a questionnaire with a 1–5 ranking system (1 being poor and 5 being excellent), and that asks users to rate the following:

❑ their overall satisfaction with the web site

❑ their overall satisfaction with the design and layout

❑ the ease with which specific tasks were completed

❑ the ease with which specific information was found

❑ whether navigation labels, page titles, headings, and other terms were easy to understand and accurate

❑ whether icons and other images were helpful and easy to understand

❑ whether downloadable items downloaded quickly and satisfactorily

❑ whether password-protected areas were easy to log into and use

❑ whether errors occurred, and, if they did, whether appropriate and helpful error messages were encountered

❑ whether product information was sufficient, or there was too little or too much information

---

[35] Carolyn Snyder, *Paper Prototyping: The Fast and Easy Way to Design and Refine User Interfaces* (Amsterdam: Morgan Kaufmann Publishers, 2003), 330.

- ❏ the ease with which they completed ecommerce transactions

- ❏ whether or not the user would return to the web site

- ❏ whether or not the user would recommend the web site to others

- ❏ suggested improvements

Using a ranking system with areas for comments gives you valuable data. You can analyze the ranked responses, and use the comments and explanations for further helpful insight.

☑ **Analyze test results.**

You may decide that it is necessary to meet with your entire web site project team following each testing session to discuss what worked, what didn't, and what the possible solutions may be.

Concentrate first on high-level functionality issues, such as global navigation, links, and page layout; then focus on specific areas and recommendations.[36]

You may also wish to create a report on the results and recommendations to present to the designers and developers and, if applicable, to clients.

Summary

This chapter emphasized the importance of checking your work and testing the site throughout every phase of its development and long-term maintenance. There were checklists to help you test your designs, content, and markup; procedures for cross-browser, cross-platform testing; and discussions on testing labels, functionality, security, accessibility, and usability.

---

[36] Kelly Goto and Emily Cotler, *Web ReDesign 2.0: Workflow that Works* (Indianapolis: New Riders / Berkeley: Peachpit Press, 2005), 230.

15 Preparing for Launch

The time has come. All that hard work of researching, planning, designing and developing your web site has finally paid off, and Launch Day is drawing near. By this stage, you've probably tested and retested your web site to ensure that it works properly. You've likely read your content over and over in an effort to catch any typing errors.

It's time for your development site to go live ... but your work here is not yet complete! Part of this transition process includes a web site handover in which project documentation is checked and finalized, a handover package is created, training is provided to the staff who will manage the site, and your project documentation and files are archived.

This chapter's checklists will guide you through preparing for your site's launch and completing the handover phase.

Conducting Final Checks

Conduct a final review of your web site, including a check of all templates and markup, layouts, content, functionality, and server-side requirements. The following checklists will aid you as you carry out your final review.

Checking Templates and Markup

Your final web page templates will probably be used to create new web pages after the launch, so include them in your handover package.

Checklist 15.1

☑ **Ensure that your web page templates adhere to your web site style guide.**

☑ **Provide clear instructions for the template's use and implementation.**

Include these instructions in comment text, as well as your web site style guide.

☑ **Ensure template markup is semantic, structural, and valid.**

☑ **Ensure that all style sheets are validated.**

note

Check All Validation Errors

Note that some CSS validation errors could impact browsers' rendering of your pages, so be sure to conduct cross-browser, cross-platform testing and make any required corrections to your CSS.

☑ **Conduct a final web site optimization check.**

Check the markup to ensure that there's no excess whitespace or carriage returns. Check that your web site uses external style sheets whenever possible, rather than embedded or inline styles. Check that your images are cropped appropriately, and that thumbnails are available when needed. Be sure to check the file sizes of your web pages, images, PDF files, and other files to ensure they're as small as possible without incurring any noticeable quality degradation.

☑ **Conduct a final web site search engine optimization check.**

For example, you might check for appropriate keyphrases within `title` element text, hyperlink text, and body copy. For your final SEO check, use the checklists in Chapter 12.

Checking Layouts

 Check overall page layouts and formatting for consistency.

Check that your page layouts are based on the appropriate final version of your HTML/XHTML template.

You've probably worked with several iterations of your web site during the design, development, and soft launch processes, so make sure each web page uses your final version HTML and XHTML templates, rather than earlier iterations. Be sure to check links to final versions of your external style sheets, and final versions of external JavaScript, if applicable.

Check that images are formatted and optimized correctly.

Check that lists and tables are formatted correctly.

Finalizing Content

Ensure that all content templates are complete, and provide detailed operational instructions.

You may be providing templates for images, PDFs, Flash, video or other multimedia files. Ensure that each template is complete and works correctly, and provide detailed instructions for its operation and usage. For example, you may wish to provide instructions on how to convert documents to optimized PDF format.

Nominate outsiders to review on-site content.

Fresh Eyes are Best!

It's helpful—and recommended—that you have different sets of "eyes" look over your content to check spelling, grammatical errors, and the site's general adherence to your style guide. Sometimes, we make typos without even realizing it—even in navigation graphics and company logos. Each person is prone to discovering different things, so if possible have several people review the content.

☑ **Check the accuracy of your web page titles.**

☑ **Proofread content for correct spelling and grammar.**

☑ **Ensure that written text adheres to your web site style guide.**

☑ **Ensure that required legal information is included and accurate.**

Check your copyright information, as well as links to your web site's privacy policy and terms of use pages.

Larger companies might have an in-house legal department that must check the validity of the site's legal content, and signs off on it. It might be the web site project manager's responsibility to conduct a final check and give his or her approval that the legal information appears according to company policies.

For smaller web site projects, the copywriter, web site editor, or developer might conduct the final check to ensure that all the legal information is accurate and follows the web site style guide's legal information specifications.

Checking Functionality

Checklist 15.4

☑ **Check all internal and external links.**

Check that global navigational links, local/section navigational links, internal page navigation links, and text content hyperlinks point to the correct locations, and that none are broken.

Using Automated Link Checking Software

To help you check links for an entire web site, you might consider an automated link checking program, such as Xenu's Link Sleuth (free),[1] REL Software's Web Link Validator,[2] or a link checking utility within your HTML editor, such as Macromedia Dreamweaver or HomeSite.[3]

---

[1] http://home.snafu.de/tilman/xenulink.html
[2] http://www.relsoftware.com/wlv/
[3] http://www.macromedia.com/

The W3C Link Checker[4] will check smaller web sites online, but you can download and customize it to check the links on larger web sites. In addition, web site quality assurance programs typically include link-checking utilities. For more tools, see also WebsiteTips.com's "Tools" section.[5]

Note that link checking software and utilities cannot check whether or not your links go to the correct location. Humans still need to intervene in this aspect of web site link checking!

☑ **Check the functionality of all forms and form elements.**

☑ **Test all scripting functions.**

☑ **Check the accessibility of plug-in content using the specified plug-ins.**

For example, if you provide documents in PDF format that require the use of Acrobat Reader, open each PDF document from the web site to ensure that it opens properly and is intact.

Checking Server-side Requirements

Checklist 15.5

☑ **Ensure that domain names point to the correct server.**

☑ **Ensure that web site statistics logging software is working properly.**

In addition to testing statistics software on your development web site, test it during your web site's soft launch to ensure it's working properly on the site's live server.

☑ **Ensure that periodic back-ups are set up and running properly.**

Ideally, files should be backed up and archived each night—especially for larger web sites—and those backups should be stored offsite. At a minimum, back up and archive your entire web site before you upload any changes.

---

[4] http://validator.w3.org/docs/checklink.html
[5] http://websitetips.com/tools/

For smaller web sites, or those that aren't updated as frequently, weekly backups and archiving might be sufficient.

Be sure to test the retrieval of backed up files to ensure your back-up system works properly. This will also make you familiar with the process of restoring the site from backups, and ensure that you know how much time to allow for such procedures.

Conducting a Soft Launch

A soft launch involves uploading your web site and all its supporting files to the live server in order to retest the site in its live environment. This step occurs before the official hard launch, when the web site becomes publicly available and, most likely, is widely promoted. Use the checklist below to help ensure the success of your web site's soft launch.

Checklist 15.6

☑ **Freeze web site production and modifications.**

It's critical to halt all modifications to the web site at a specific time—this helps keep your project on schedule and prevents last-minute scope creep. Once the web site is frozen, changes, modifications, and updates must wait until after the launch takes place.

☑ **Allow one to four weeks for the soft launch testing phase.**

Small web sites might need only a week for the soft launch testing phase, while larger, complex web sites may need several weeks or more. Don't cut corners on time allotted for the soft launch, though: it's important to allow plenty of time to ensure that everything at your new web site works properly, and functions optimally.

☑ **Move all necessary directories, files and databases from the development server to the live server.**

☑ **Verify functionality after the migration is complete.**

☑ **Ensure visual display elements remain intact after migration.**

☑ **Invite a selected group of users to trial the web site privately and provide feedback.**

Password-protecting your Soft-launch Site

note

You might need to password-protect your soft launch web site testing area if you don't want the general public or search engines to find it before it's ready. In most cases, using a URL other than the default for your homepage may be sufficient "protection."

☑ **Fix bugs and resolve issues that require immediate attention.**

☑ **Ensure a solid plan is in place to rectify unresolved bugs and issues, and make post-launch web site fixes and immediate content updates.**

☑ **Provide web site maintenance training.**

As we discussed earlier, often those who build and launch the web site are not the ones who maintain it. In addition to educating staff who will maintain the site, site maintenance training will help sustain the web site's original look and feel, and cohesiveness.

Launching the Web Site

Checklist 15.7

☑ **Coordinate the web site launch with related events.**

If you're conducting a marketing campaign that includes mailing announcements, and ad placements that are scheduled to begin on certain dates, you need to stay in touch with those involved to let them know the progress of the web site's launch. If your web site is launching on schedule, the announcements and ads can also appear on schedule; however, if there is a delay in the process, you might need to adjust the release of announcements and ads, and, possibly, make associated changes to their content.

☑ **Launch during off-peak hours.**

Launching your web site in off-peak hours will allow you to check and correct any problems that might occur during your launch phase, without exposing those errors to a large number of site visitors.

Don't Launch on Friday!

Don't launch on a Friday evening unless you have staff available to work through the weekend. Otherwise, you won't have people around to fix problems until the following Monday!

☑ **For larger web sites, plan to launch sections in phases, and launch the homepage last.**

Completing your Web Site Handover

In many web development projects, one team is responsible for building and launching the web site, and another team is responsible for the site's maintenance. Many organizations outsource the tasks of building and launching, and plan to handle web site maintenance in-house. Small businesses might outsource the building and launching, then wish to make simple content changes themselves, but continue to have the development company handle any images, section additions, and larger changes.

Regardless of the approach you've taken, it's important to organize and finalize all your documentation, and put together a handover package that contains everything—instructions, files, documentation, and so on—that the site owners will need to run the site. In addition, web site maintenance training is an important part of a web site handover phase, ensuring the smooth running of the web site into the future. Use the checklists below as a guide to completing your handover phase.

Checking and Finalizing Project Documentation

Checklist 15.8

☑ **Finalize your site administration information, such as server login information and hosting control panel login details.**

☑ **Finalize your web site style guide.**

Before handover, check that your web site style guide is current with the final, launched version of your web site. Include color swatches, font specifications, style sheets, HTML formatting, all web site-related templates, a listing of each design-related image and its use and location, a printout of the directory structure, and the policy regarding naming conventions. As you'll recall, web site style guides were covered in detail in Chapter 1.

☑ **Finalize your web site maintenance document.**

The maintenance document needs to describe which parts of the web site are to be updated and when, the tools to use (e.g., an HTML editor, a CMS, Photoshop, etc.), who will handle the maintenance, and what those staff members' roles will be. If the site relies on databases, have the programmers include diagrams (i.e., **Entity Relationship** (ER) diagrams that identify entity types, relationship types, and attributes) or descriptions of how the database tables fit together with the web site.[6]

☑ **Finalize your web site testing plan and Quality Assurance document.**

This document should outline the processes of checking and testing broken links, checking functionality, performance, spelling, content accuracy, and the site's overall adherence to the style guide. It should also include information about tools that are to be used for checking and testing, a schedule and guidelines for testing, and related helpful information as discussed in Chapter 14.[7]

☑ **Finalize all other related documents and instructions.**

☑ **Ensure that the CD containing the handover package works.**

CDs can fail, and CD burning fails occasionally, too, so it's important to test each CD that you make, preferably on a different computer from the one that was used to burn the CDs.

Creating a Handover Package

A handover package should include everything that's needed to manage the web site, such as all the source files, materials, tools and instructions, and documentation for the web site project. As you pull together the materials for the handover package, consider what would be necessary—and helpful—to include for those

---

[6] Thomas J. Shelford and Gregory A. Remillard, *Real Web Project Management: Case Studies and Best Practices from the Trenches* (Boston: Addison-Wesley, 2003), 208; Douglas K. Van Duyne, James A. Landay, and Jason I. Hong, *The Design of Sites: Patterns, Principles, and Processes for Crafting a Customer-centered Web Experience* (Boston: Addison-Wesley, 2003), 102.
[7] Van Duyne, Landay, and Hong, 102.

maintaining the web site. The material in the handover package should provide the site owners with the ability to maintain the site self-sufficiently, with minimal hassles.

Although I recommend that you create a CD that contains all of these materials, including scans of signed contracts and other papers, you may also have some print materials that are impractical to scan, such as software instruction manuals that aren't available in electronic formats. You may wish to present your handover package in a binder that holds the CD(s) and print materials.

Naturally, some of us are more organized than others. But if you can try to organize your files and paperwork throughout the project's planning and development phases, putting together the handover package will be relatively easy. If you're working with a team of people, be sure that each person knows ahead of time what specific information they will need to contribute to the handover package. Toward the end of the project's final testing phase, you might need to review with the team the finer details of files that the package will include.

Your Own Handover Package

Even if you're a one-person operation, it's still incredibly helpful to create a handover package for yourself. Having your materials organized and ready for quick access is far more efficient when it comes to updating and maintaining your web site.

Use the checklist below to guide you as you create your handover package.

Checklist 15.9

Include copies of all original graphics program files, including custom preset files, Photoshop actions, and other automation tools.

If your graphics program files include layers, production notes, or similar components, keep them intact. In addition, if your image templates use Photoshop actions or other automation technology, be sure to include them. If any of your templates require a specific graphics program custom presets (i.e., Photoshop gradients, textures, patterns, or other custom presets), include the custom files with your templates, along with documentation of the program's compatibilities, instructions on where to place each file on a local computer (i.e., place Photoshop gradient files within `C:\Program Files\Adobe\Adobe Photoshop CS2\Presets\Gradients\` for Windows computers), and an explanation of how they can be accessed with the appropriate graphics program.

☑ Include copies of all photos and illustrations, and their related copyright and usage rights information.

☑ Include copies of all fonts and their related usage permissions or licensing information (or purchase information, if needed).

☑ Include copies of all HTML templates, pages, and corresponding style sheets.

☑ Include a detailed administrative sitemap that encompasses all of the site's pages, images, and related documents.

Your web site's online sitemap will not and should not display the level of detail that's included in this administrative sitemap. The administrative sitemap should indicate the flow of the site from page to page, including online forms and user confirmations. For ecommerce, the sitemap could be expanded to include the product fulfillment process, too.

☑ Include copies of all database files.

☑ Include instructions, licensing, and tools (or purchasing information, if needed) for content management systems, editing tools, and other software.

☑ Include administrative login information.

☑ Include server login and authorization information.

Server login information typically includes the host's address, account usernames and passwords, and remote folder information. It's also important to list file types that require transfer in ASCII format (i.e., text files) and binary format (i.e., compressed files, images, software, games, music, movies, and so on).

☑ Include a copy of the web site's root directory and all related files.

☑ Include the web site maintenance document.

☑ **Include your web site testing and Quality Assurance document.**

☑ **Include the final web site style guide.**

☑ **Include electronic versions of print materials.**

In addition to signed contracts and other signed papers, you might have brochures, letterhead, and other print materials that you used for reference as you planned and designed the web site. Scan them and include them on the CD-ROM.

On the other hand, print materials that have many pages, such as software manuals, might be available in electronic format from the software vendors. If not, or if their size makes their scanning impractical, include them as part of the print documentation in your handover package.

☑ **Include a table of contents.**

☑ **Include a list of the names, contact information, and responsibilities of those involved in the web site's production.**

☑ **Include a list of the names, contact information, and responsibilities of those who will be involved in the web site's maintenance.**

Archiving Project Documentation and Files

When you're ready to wrap up the project, it's important to archive documents, files, notes, and a copy of the handover package for safe storage and future reference or use. Use the checklist below to help determine what should be archived.

Checklist 15.10

 Archive a copy of the web site project proposal.

 Archive a copy of the web site project plan or creative brief, as applicable.

☑ Archive competitive analysis reports, if conducted.

☑ Archive the signed web site project contract.

☑ Archive budget approvals, if separate from a signed web site project contract.

☑ Archive copies of additional charges, invoices, and payments received.

☑ Archive copies of all emails related to this project, especially those that document change requests and approved changes.

☑ Archive usability testing reports and all related documentation and notes.

☑ Archive notes, sketches, and files regarding information architecture and visual design.

☑ Archive any other notes or helpful information related to the project.

☑ Archive contact information for all those involved in the project, including vendors who provided photos, software, hardware, and other supplies for the project.

☑ Archive a copy of the handover package.

The Paperless Archive

Tip

In archiving web site projects, my office takes an almost paperless approach. I have on my computer a digital folder for each project. The folder contains scans of signed contracts and other papers, all the files for the project, the fonts used, important emails, notes and other documentation, and any other information that's related to the project. When a project is completed, I add all the files to a web site project archive folder for safe keeping. In addition, I burn CD-ROM copies for separate archival storage, and I also archive the original signed contracts and other necessary papers in physical project folders. Over the years, this has repeatedly proven to be a terrific approach for keeping all my projects well organized. Sure, it makes for handy access whenever I need to revisit the information from past projects, but having multiple copies of files has been a life-saver on the rare occasions when a hard drive crashes or a particular CD-ROM won't work.

Summary

This chapter dealt with the project's finalization, including the completion of templates, layouts, content, and web site functionality. Next, we discussed how to launch your web site, before we addressed the question of how to complete the site's handover, including the creation of a handover package.

We're almost there! The next and final chapter of this book covers what you need to do after the web site has launched.

16 Post-launch Follow-up

When a web site launches, there's reason to celebrate: launching a web site is quite an accomplishment! You won't have any time for hangovers, though, because you'll have two big jobs to do. First, you'll need to let the world know about the existence of your web site; then, you'll need to watch over it.

Many new web sites quickly go stale, as little or no maintenance has been planned. It's very important to keep the momentum going after your web site launches. You'll need to review and formalize your site's maintenance responsibilities, take care of the initial post-launch tasks, review your site files and documentation, and make your presence known.

This chapter provides checklists to help guide you through the site's important post-launch phase.

Conducting a Post-launch Review

Conduct a post-launch review of your web site project. A post-launch meeting can be an excellent opportunity to review the project overall, and to learn from what took place during the site's development and launch phases. Discuss what went right and wrong, and explore possible ways to avoid similar problems in the future.

Use this review to examine and update the web site maintenance responsibilities in writing; sometimes, the resulting document is called a service-level agreement (SLA).

Plan Post-launch Activities During Project Planning

Everything that's mentioned here should have been planned and determined during the project's initial planning stages, and should have been identified in your web site contract. Needs and circumstances can change, though, so it's important to review where things stand—including responsibilities for maintaining your web site—after the site's launch.

Checklist 16.1

☑ **Refine and instigate the levels of support and training that will be provided, and their timeframes.**

It's a good idea to identify within your contract a set number of hours that will be dedicated to support and training, and the fees that will be charged for any support beyond that. If ongoing support might be needed, set that up in advance, in a separate contract that clarifies the fees involved, and outlines what is and isn't included. Being as clear as possible in these documents helps to avoid potential misunderstandings.

☑ **Determine who will be responsible for updating the site's content.**

☑ **Determine who will be responsible for fixing web site bugs.**

For example, programmers might be responsible for fixing program-related bugs. The site's developers might be responsible for fixing markup-related problems, and general administrative assistants might correct typographical and other content errors.

☑ **Determine who will respond to web site-related email.**

☑ **Determine how frequently web site-related email and queries will be answered.**

☑ **Review and implement plans to deal with potential problems.**

Anticipate, and formulate plans to address, issues such as server downtime or other server problems, security issues, database hiccups, lost passwords, broken links, out-of-date content, duplicate content, typos and other text content errors, slow pages, accessibility problems, functionality errors, or the creation of web pages that are inconsistent with the web site style guide.

☑ **Review and instigate methods to deal with post-launch usability issues.**

☑ **Organize your resources and ensure that they are sufficient to cover your web site maintenance schedule.**

For example, to manage updates and maintenance, you might create a simple spreadsheet that lists your web site's main sections as well as individual pages or other content. The spreadsheet can show the update schedule for each page, helpful notes, and who will be responsible for each update.

☑ **Determine who is responsible for monitoring the performance of the web site and resolving server issues.**

Completing Initial Post-launch Tasks

Checklist 16.2

☑ **Implement the initial scheduled updates, and plan for upcoming updates.**

☑ **Schedule and instigate unresolved post-launch fixes.**

Your final web site testing might have revealed some bugs whose resolution was left until after the site's launch. Now's the time to fix them.

☑ **Obtain user feedback and usability test results.**

User feedback is invaluable to your web site's success and can be critical in shaping your approach to web site improvements.[1] As such, it's a good idea to provide a form or contact information on the site, so that users can provide feedback directly.

---

[1] Kelly Goto and Emily Cotler, *Web ReDesign 2.0: Workflow that Works* (Indianapolis: New Riders / Berkeley: Peachpit Press, 2005), 198–9.

☑ **Implement plans to integrate quality assurance (QA) procedures with maintenance and updates.**

Once you've scheduled updates to the site, it's important to work out procedures that will ensure the quality of that work, both in terms of its technical functionality and the content enhancements that the updates provide. Consider content (spelling, grammar, consistency of terms, presence of legal information as needed, page titles, headings, navigation labels, etc.); documentation; graphics and layout (image quality, optimization and file sizes, layout and alignment of elements, colors and color accuracy); cross-browser, cross-platform compatibility (including allowances for assistive devices and addressing accessibility issues); user preferences (consider font sizes, link colors and underlining, and browser window size); functionality (navigational elements and all links and forms); and any other interactivity.

☑ **Confirm periodic, offsite backups of your entire web site.**

Although ISPs should make frequent redundant backups of their servers—including your web site files—you should still run your own regular, off-site backups. In the event of a problem, it's often easier and faster to retrieve your own backups than it is to request them from your ISP. If backups aren't yet scheduled and running, run one immediately and schedule regular backups.

☑ **Implement your web site marketing and promotion campaigns.**

Part of your web site planning should have been preparing to meet the marketing and promotional needs of your site—preparing press releases and announcements, getting print materials ready to go, implementing your SEO and reciprocal links campaign, and setting up online and offline advertising in preparation of your launch date, for example.

☑ **Ensure that appropriate resources are available for web site maintenance.**

Be sure that each person involved with the site's maintenance can do his or her job efficiently and correctly: provide the appropriate tools, training, files, and documentation.

Orientating New Staff

Often, those who design and develop a web site don't maintain it. In such cases, those nominated for maintenance need to become familiar with the web site. The following checklist can be used to orient those who are new to the site.

Checklist 16.3

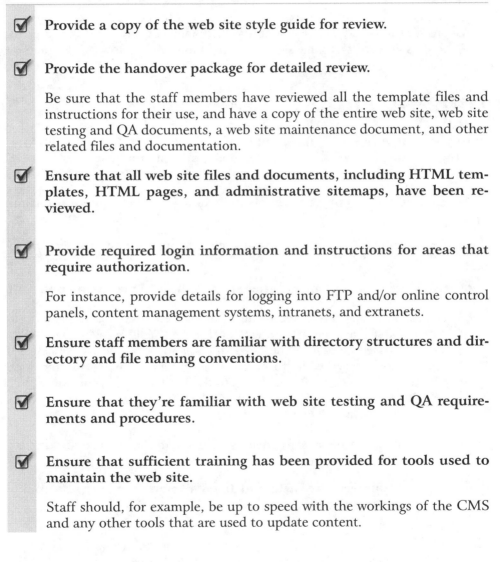

☑ **Provide a copy of the web site style guide for review.**

☑ **Provide the handover package for detailed review.**

Be sure that the staff members have reviewed all the template files and instructions for their use, and have a copy of the entire web site, web site testing and QA documents, a web site maintenance document, and other related files and documentation.

☑ **Ensure that all web site files and documents, including HTML templates, HTML pages, and administrative sitemaps, have been reviewed.**

☑ **Provide required login information and instructions for areas that require authorization.**

For instance, provide details for logging into FTP and/or online control panels, content management systems, intranets, and extranets.

☑ **Ensure staff members are familiar with directory structures and directory and file naming conventions.**

☑ **Ensure that they're familiar with web site testing and QA requirements and procedures.**

☑ **Ensure that sufficient training has been provided for tools used to maintain the web site.**

Staff should, for example, be up to speed with the workings of the CMS and any other tools that are used to update content.

☑ **Ensure that sufficient training has been provided to handle ecommerce requests.**

If your site uses ecommerce software, train those who are responsible for product updates to use the software. If you're handling product fulfillment in-house, train the appropriate staff so that you can ship products in a timely manner. If you're outsourcing product fulfillment, make sure someone on your staff regularly checks on product fulfillment status to ensure the timely management and fulfillment of orders. Make sure customers receive shipping status emails and other follow-up contacts as needed.

Getting Attention

Now that your web site is online, you need to let the world know that it exists. Use the checklist below as a guide to help take your site to the masses!

Checklist 16.4

☑ **Update existing print materials to include your web site information.**

☑ **Create new print materials that include your web site information.**

☑ **Consider and implement other advertising and marketing options.**

For example, consider advertising at other web sites that cater to your target market, as well as through the Internet Yellow Pages, nationally- and city-based guides, online newspapers, and other local businesses. It might also be worthwhile to purchase an enhanced listing in your local Yellow Pages directory. For example, in the United States, consider SBC's SMARTpages.com or Verizon's SuperPages.com, since many other online directories use their information.[2]

In addition, consider placing advertisements in magazines and newspapers, and on television and radio.

☑ **Include your web site URL(s) in an email signature at the bottom of every email you send.**

---

[2] Ralph F. Wilson, *How to Promote Your Local Business on The Internet* (Rocklin: Wilson Internet Services, January 26, 2005), 25. Also available online [http://www.wilsonweb.com/ebooks/local.htm].

☑ **Use search engines and directories to bring in traffic.**

As well as registering your web site (via free submissions), you might consider paid placement listings, paid inclusions/submissions, content promotion, banner ads, and programs such as Google AdWords. [3] Keep in mind that it's critically important to provide keyphrase-rich content, optimize your web site for search engines, and provide valuable content and good service.

☑ **Launch and maintain a reciprocal links campaign to help with online networking and boost search engine rankings.**

Incoming links to your site can boost your search ranking. Web sites that boast a higher search ranking than your own can give your site's search rank a greater boost than can lower-ranked sites.

Resources: Paving the Way for Reciprocal Links

Tip

Consider creating a Resources or Helpful Links section on your site. Include links to valuable online resources—as well as benefiting site visitors, this can help encourage other web sites to link to yours. You can contact other site owners, let them know that you've linked to their site, and ask for a reciprocal link. Keep in mind that not all web sites will link to yours just because you link to them.

When your web site visitors click on those links to visit other web sites, your URL will show in those sites' referrer logs, which is another way for other web sites to find yours. I can't count the number of interesting web sites I've learned about from my referrer logs over the years. And I've linked to many of them as a result.

Consider hiring an expert if you don't wish to handle your reciprocal links campaign yourself. Many SEO (search engine optimization) firms offer services that will help you obtain links to your web site. Ask friends and colleagues for recommendations to good services, and check references before you hire anyone (unfortunately there are plenty of people who make false promises where SEO is concerned!).

Are you in a hurry to establish your link campaign? Consider purchasing text links. In addition, you can boost link popularity quickly by purchasing

[3] Danny Sullivan, *Buying Your Way In: Search Engine Advertising Chart*, Search Engine Watch (November 22, 2004) [http://searchenginewatch.com/webmasters/article.php/2167941].

well-placed, targeted links to your web site through services such as LinkAdage,[4] or buying a Yahoo! Express listing in the Yahoo! Directory.[5]

Managing Maintenance

You've created your web site, and you've implemented your marketing strategies to let the world know about it—great! Remember, though, that it's critically important to give your web site visitors good reasons to come back to your site in future. Visitors will return to your site if its quality is maintained, and content is kept fresh. Following a schedule that tells you which areas need attention—and when—will help you to stay on top of the maintenance challenge.

Checklist 16.5

☑ **Ensure that staff involved with web site maintenance possess adequate skills.**

Maintenance staff need, at the very least, a basic knowledge of HTML, basic to advanced skills in graphics and optimizing images for the Web, basic to advanced skills in programming the flavor of scripting used on your web site, and the ability to use the variety of tools required by your web site, such as an FTP program, HTML editor, CMS, and copywriting and editing tools.

☑ **Ensure that all maintenance staff members have a copy of the handover package and web site style guide.**

Your web site's cohesiveness, branding, and professionalism strongly depend on the continuing maintenance of its original look and feel. Maintenance staff must follow the web site style guide very closely, otherwise the site is likely to degrade over time.

☑ **Ensure that procedures for version control, backups, and site rollback are operational.**

Back Up any File Before you Change It

WARNING

Always save a backup copy of a file's original before you update or change it, and before you upload a change or update to the web site. If more than one person is involved in updating the web site, version control is even more important if you are to prevent team members

---

[4] http://www.linkadage.com/
[5] https://ecom.yahoo.com/dir/express/intro

from accidentally overwriting files. It's critically important that you have the ability to go to a backup copy, or roll back to a previous version, of any file. Losing or accidentally overwriting an important file can be avoided if you have good version control in place, regardless of whether one person, or a team of people, maintains the site.

Web content management systems frequently provide version control among their helpful content management features. Software such as Macromedia Contribute[6] can also provide version control, permissions control, editing control, and other helpful collaborative content management features.

Implement a method to update outdated content.

An important part of keeping your content fresh and current is to remove time-oriented information immediately it becomes outdated. Providing current and accurate information to your web site visitors supports your credibility and professionalism.

For example, if you have a section on your homepage for announcements or latest news, be sure to date each item, and make sure that you plan to remove that time-oriented content as soon as it becomes outdated. Ideally, replace it with new announcements.

If removing outdated content entails removing a web page, be sure to re-place it with a page that indicates that the page is no longer available, and provides a link back to relevant parts of the web site. However, it's common practice to leave the web page online, but provide with it an obvious note that its content is outdated. You might also include links to any newer, related content that's available. Figure 16.1 shows an example of such a note in action on Websitetips.com.

You can manage time-sensitive content manually, automate it with scripting, or use a combination of these approaches to keep content current. If you automate the updating process, be sure to check that updates and changes are handled correctly, and on schedule, and that each contains accurate information.

Check each content addition or change for correct spelling, grammar, consistency of terms, and other content requirements specified in your web site style guide.

---

[6] http://www.macromedia.com/software/contribute/

Figure 16.1. Displaying a note alongside outdated web content

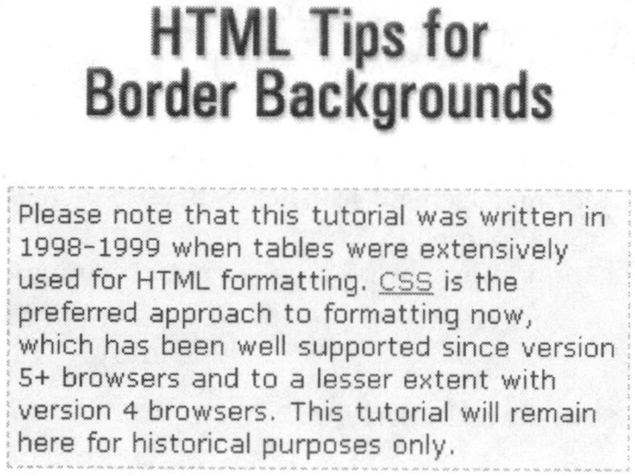

HTML Tips for
Border Backgrounds

Please note that this tutorial was written in 1998-1999 when tables were extensively used for HTML formatting. CSS is the preferred approach to formatting now, which has been well supported since version 5+ browsers and to a lesser extent with version 4 browsers. This tutorial will remain here for historical purposes only.

☑ **Ensure that new pages are created with the correct web page templates, as specified in the web site style guide.**

☑ **Validate the markup for new or changed pages,**

You might use a CMS that formats the site's HTML for you, but don't assume it will always do so properly—especially if you make deletions, changes, or replace content as you type within the CMS. Running each new or changed web page through a W3C-based validator will help you ensure that the site contains only valid markup.

It's also a good idea to check the markup visually, just to make sure that it's as lean and clean as possible. CMS tools often create "tag soup," which bloats page file sizes and causes rendering issues. Yet the soup validates! A visual check is always helpful.

☑ **Ensure that new pages are linked from the appropriate navigational sections and pages.**

For example, if you add a page for a new product, you might add links to that page from the Products page of your web site, your Products local/section navigation, the What's New section of your home page, and from your web site's sitemap.

Tip 💡 ### Check the Automatic Creation of Links to New Content

If you have a CMS, it probably offers the functionality to generate these links for you automatically. However, it's still a good idea to check for their correct addition to the appropriate pages.

☑ **Update your administrative sitemap to include new web pages.**

An administrative sitemap should make reference to all web pages, images, and related web site documents. If you update it whenever you update the site, you'll keep an ongoing, current, and detailed content audit of your entire site.

☑ **Ensure that new images are optimized and adhere to the web site style guide.**

Treating images consistently is an important part of maintaining your web site's visual coherence and professionalism. Using image templates and providing instructions and examples within your web site style guide can certainly help, but also make sure you optimize images to reduce file sizes without compromising image quality.

☑ **Inspect the licensing agreements and copyright terms of images obtained from third parties.**

Some image licenses allow the images to be used on personal web sites only; some charge different fees for personal and commercial use; some charge different fees for web and print use; some don't allow the images to be altered; some include other specific terms.

note ### Keep Image Licenses On File

Ensure that you keep a copy of each image license with your web site documentation.

☑ **Review, validate and approve all site updates and changes before they're published to the Web.**

Reviewing, validating, and approving each web site update will help you to prevent errors from appearing on your web site—an important part of promoting your credibility and maintaining a professional web site.

☑ **Review server logs regularly to catch and resolve errors and other issues.**

Server logs typically show broken links, form submission failures, server overload, and more. You can use this information to help catch and resolve errors and problems.

☑ **Review bug tracking reports regularly to catch and fix bugs.**

Imagine that a customer tries to place an order, but the form fails to process. What happens if a visitor tries to log in to a password-protected area but can't—even though the login information he or she used is correct? You need to know right away, so that you can resolve such problems quickly.

☑ **Run periodic web site accessibility tests to ensure that your web site remains accessible and continues to adhere to accessibility requirements and guidelines.**

Anyone who makes changes or additions to the site should be required to test that the altered or added content meets the site's accessibility requirements. But it's also important to run periodic checks on your entire site, to ensure that it remains accessible. This is particularly important if your site is legally required to meet or exceed specific accessibility requirements, such as the W3C's WCAG (Web Content Accessibility Guidelines).

☑ **Run periodic web site QA tests to maintain the site's quality and functionality.**

For example, you might run a link-checking utility regularly to eradicate broken hyperlinks, perform site-wide validation checks for all markup and CSS, and so on. If you have a large web site that changes frequently, you might need to run such tests once a week, but for many sites, monthly tests may be sufficient. Whatever the frequency of your QA tests, make sure they happen regularly—don't wait for a vocal site visitor to complain about an error, as you may already have let down 99 not-so-vocal visitors.

Undertaking Daily Duties

Some aspects of web site maintenance need to be checked on a daily basis if you are to ensure that your site continues to function optimally. Use this checklist as a guide.

☑ **Check and respond to web site-related email promptly.**

☑ **Check and review web site feedback forms, and follow up as needed.**

☑ **Ensure that your web site is online, fully functional and secure.**

Site Monitoring Tools Can Help!

Tip

A wide range of web site monitoring tools are available that can check automatically that your web site is online, that every page component is online, that ecommerce transaction capabilities are fully functional, that secure areas of the site remain secure, that cookies are working properly, and so on. They can check for any problems, and notify you of any problems by telephone, pager, SMS, or email. Search for "web site monitoring tool" at your preferred search engine and you'll find plenty from which to choose.

☑ **Check the fulfillment of ecommerce orders.**

Larger web sites with higher traffic volumes might have an automated order fulfillment process. But many other web sites process orders manually, so it's important to process them quickly, to best serve your customers. Remember, though, that automation isn't just for larger web sites with big budgets.

☑ **Check for and correct any broken internal and external hyperlinks.**

☑ **Review your server logs.**

Conducting Monthly Minding

☑ **Compare your goals for the site with its current status to evaluate whether or not you're on track.**

If you defined clear, measurable goals when you planned your site, you'll find it easy to evaluate your site's success (or otherwise!). Your measurable goals might include attracting a specific number of visitors to your web site, obtaining certain search engine positions for specific keyphrases, having a certain number of web sites link to yours, product sales, and so on. If you're not meeting your goals, you might need to consider making changes to the site, re-evaluating your marketing strategies, and stepping up or refocusing your advertising.

☑ **Look for overall trends in your server logs.**

For example, check the browsers visitors are using and watch for changes as they migrate between certain offerings. Keep an eye on your most popular pages, and on trends around the site's top entry and exit pages.

☑ **Check your site's status with search engines and directories.**

After you submit your site to search directories such as DMOZ and Yahoo!, it's important to follow up to make sure the site appears in their listings. It's also important to check on your search rankings with search engines such as Google. As we saw in Chapter 12, if you submit your web site to the major directories, and it's listed, Google and other search crawlers will most likely list your web site.[7]

☑ **Review your marketing and advertising campaigns and web site metrics to evaluate their successes, problems, and status.**

☑ **Plan the next iteration of your web site.**

Over time, you'll receive user feedback, you might collect data from periodic usability tests, and you should have compiled data from bug reports and server logs. In addition, you might have new ideas for ways to improve your web site. Plan how and when to make those changes, and always use the testing area to work out any updates, conduct usability testing, and run technical tests prior to applying the changes to your live site.

Performing Periodic Processes

Checklist 16.8

☑ **Check for and correct any broken internal and external hyperlinks.**

---

[7] Danny Sullivan, *Submitting To Crawlers: Google, Yahoo, Ask/Teoma & Microsoft's MSN*, Search Engine Watch (July 5, 2004) [http://searchenginewatch.com/webmasters/article.php/2167871].

☑ **Run site-wide validation tests.**

An important part of maintaining your web site's quality and functionality is the task of keeping your site markup error-free. Invalid markup can cause entire web pages or parts of web pages to not render or function properly in some browsers.

☑ **Run site-wide accessibility tests for sites that, by law, must adhere to accessibility guidelines.**

Although anyone who's making changes or additions to your web site should be required to run accessibility tests prior to uploading their alterations, it's still important to run site-wide accessibility tests to ensure that the site's accessibility is maintained. This is especially important if the site is legally obligated to meet or exceed government accessibility requirements.

☑ **Check that directory structures, directory names, and filenames continue to adhere to your web site style guide.**

☑ **Test your web site's local search function to make sure search results continue to be current and accurate.**

Site visitors will be frustrated if your local search provides links to pages that no longer exist, or to pages whose information has been changed or removed. Of course, if you have new content, you should present it to your web site visitors through your local search feature.

☑ **Check that your shipping policies, options, and prices are still current and accurate.**

Shippers tend to change their rates periodically, and you'll likely need to reflect these changes within your shipping information. In addition, you might change or add shipping carriers and features.

☑ **Check on software updates, licensing, and registrations.**

Some software will check for updates automatically, and vendors often send emails about product updates. However, if you've opted out of these notifications, it's especially important to check for updates. Some software is licensed on a time-dated subscription (e.g., an annual or two-year subscription), so it's important to check the expiration dates periodically, and keep your subscriptions current. You might find it handy to create a spreadsheet to keep track of software licenses, versions, and subscription expiration dates; this could also help you plan annual budgets.

Check and test that all forms and error messages function properly.

Server software updates can influence the functionality of your forms, so it's a good idea to check for them regularly. Some site monitoring tools can check server software versions automatically, so if you use such tools, be sure to review their documentation for this feature.

Perform content audits.

A web site content audit can provide you with a far-reaching view of your site's content, and help re-familiarize you with the content inventory. It will also let you identify content to remove, update, or edit, and show you where information is lacking and could be improved.

A content audit can also help you to determine whether you need better content management processes, or specific tools to help streamline your site's content maintenance.

 Tip

Check for Orphaned Pages

If you use link-checking software (which we discussed above), see if it offers the ability to check for orphaned pages, that is, pages that have no incoming links and therefore cannot be found easily. This can help you to identify content that's no longer required (or, conversely, content that's still valid but needs incoming links to be of any use).

Conducting Annual Activities

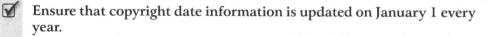

Checklist 16.9

Renew your domain name registrations.

Ensure that copyright date information is updated on January 1 every year.

If you use automated scripting to change the date, be sure to check that the dates change appropriately. You can also use an "include" file that allows you to make a site-wide change to the copyright information through just one file.

☑ **Ensure that your legal documentation, including your privacy policy, web site terms of use, and copyright terms, is current.**

☑ **Review web site hosting prices and features to ensure that you're still getting the best value for money.**

Collecting Data

To help improve your web site, collect as much data as you can about it, in both **qualitative** and **quantitative** forms. Data can be collected from a number of sources, including your web site's statistics logs, sales reports, and user questionnaires.

Collecting and Using Quantitative Data

Quantitative data is presented in the form of numbers, percentages, or statistics. It's typically collected from closed-ended questions in which users must choose from a limited set of possible answers.[8] Knowing how to analyze this data is what creates its value. The checklist below is designed to give you ideas about the data you might wish to collect and track for your quantitative evaluation.

Checklist 16.10

☑ **Collect data about user demographics and the reasons users visit your web site.**

For example, you could collect demographic information and feedback about reasons why users visit your site through a short online questionnaire. If you collect the same information from your off-line visitors, you can then compare the results.[9]

☑ **Collect data about the sources of your web site traffic.**

For example, online sources of traffic can include other web sites, search engines and directories, online advertising links, and referrals from email discussion lists, online forums, and newsgroups.

---

[8] P. J. Taylor, *A Brief Guide to Quantitative Data Collection at GaWC, 1997–2001* (2002), Globalization and World Cities [http://www.lboro.ac.uk/gawc/guide.html].
[9] Ashley Friedlein, *Web Project Management: Delivering Successful Commercial Websites* (San Francisco: Morgan Kaufmann Publishers, 2001), 244–46.

☑ **Collect data about which search engines and directories provide the most traffic to your site.**

☑ **Collect data about which keywords and keyphrases generate the most search engine referrals, and which aren't working well.**

☑ **Collect data about PPC (pay-per-click) results to help refine and improve your PPC campaign.**

☑ **Collect data about your web site's traffic, including the most popular and least popular web pages.**

☑ **For ecommerce sites, collect data on shopping cart abandonment and the reasons for it.**

If you can learn about why and where your visitors abandon their orders, you can improve your web site, increase conversion rates, and build your return customer base too.

Shoppers don't always abandon a cart for a negative reason; however, if visitors abandon their cart because of a problem with your site, you need to know about it. Common problems include navigation issues, frustration with the number of steps in the purchase process, unexpected shipping or handling charges, broken online order forms, or the discovery of a better price elsewhere.

☑ **For ecommerce sites, collect data on order sizes to see if an upsell or cross-sell marketing strategy is working.**

Cross-selling—suggesting items that are related or complementary to a product shoppers already have in their cart—is growing increasingly common in the world of ecommerce. Upselling, or the recommendation of related items that are more expensive than the item in the shopper's cart, is another popular technique used by many ecommerce sites.

☑ **Collect data about your web site's local search to learn more about what users are seeking and to assess potential navigation problems.**

If you find that many users search for similar keywords or keyphrases, review the pages from which they're searching for those terms. It could be that some aspect of your navigation needs improvement.

On the other hand, you can use this information to help provide visitors with content that's more relevant to their needs. If you find that they're searching for content that's not currently available on your site, consider adding new content to meet those needs.

☑ **Collect data from bug reports and server logs to learn about and fix web site problems.**

☑ **Collect data about problems found on the web site, and apply appropriate fixes.**

Look for broken links, spelling or grammatical errors, typographical errors, outdated content, browser rendering issues or confusion, and forms or other interactive elements that aren't working properly.

Collecting and Using Qualitative Data

Qualitative data is descriptive in nature, typically arising from open-ended questions with answers that are not limited by a set of choices or a scale. Examples of qualitative data include descriptive answers to questions about how to improve your web site or what the user liked best. Common ways to collect qualitative data include interviews, focus groups, observation, and questionnaires.

It's often possible to use a combination of off- and online techniques to gather feedback and data about your web site for qualitative analysis. It might be better to outsource your qualitative data evaluation tasks to a market research company, as they may take a more objective view and should be highly skilled with tackling these valuable information gathering and evaluation techniques.[10]

---

[10] Friedlein, 247–48.

☑ **Collect information about your brand, such as brand recognition, perception, and relationship information.**

You can use this information to help target your web site's advertising campaigns, and to help you determine the exposure that you need to achieve to boost your brand recognition and reputation. For example, McDonald's golden arches and gold and red color schemes are typically well-recognized throughout the world by people within that organization's target audience. If you visit the company's web site,[11] you'll find that they continue this branding throughout their online collateral—it's not reserved for their physical store locations.

☑ **Collect user feedback via email, questionnaires, focus groups, and reviews and ratings of your web site to help improve your web site.**

☑ **Collect data for use with customer relations management (CRM) processes and tools.**

This data can help you determine changes that you can make to your web site to meet changing customer preferences, and satisfy customers on an ongoing basis. Metrics could include the number of customer service requests, turnaround time for responses, speed of problem resolution, customer retention, and average order size. Your web site can help to reinforce relationships with your customers.

☑ **Collect information about your web site's competitive advantage.**

Maintaining an advantage over your competitors can help your web site (and your business!) to thrive. Researching and collecting data about your competitors' web sites can help you maintain your web site's competitive advantage. Collecting data on search engine rankings, your web site's ease of use, and how well you're providing the information and services your customers seek can help you to evaluate and improve your web site's competitive advantage.

☑ **Collect data about which web site features your visitors like most and least, and why.**

---

[11] http://mcdonalds.com/

Summary

The final chapter of this book covered checklists to help you maintain your web site after its launch. Checklists to help you conduct a post-launch review, carry out initial post-launch tasks, orient new staff members, and announce the existence of your web site were discussed. We also stepped through comprehensive checklists that showed how to maintain your web site after the launch. Finally, we explored checklists that highlighted some of the data that could be collected and used to improve your web site.

Appendix A: Ecommerce Checklists

Assessing Ecommerce Content Usage and Management Needs

Use the checklist below to help clarify your ecommerce content usage and management needs.

☑ **Accept and manage online payments.**

☑ **Accept and manage online credit card payments in real time.**

☑ **Automate order processing.**

If you anticipate a high volume of orders, consider a shopping cart program that can automate order processing for you.

If you're selling products infrequently and are able to monitor your web site closely enough to process orders manually, a simple form-based approach may be all you need.

☑ **Calculate and manage sales tax.**

☑ **Calculate and manage shipping costs, including international calculations.**

☑ **Manage order processing, shipping, or both.**

☑ **Send order confirmations or other related correspondence.**

☑ **Manage order tracking.**

☑ **Process and manage returns.**

☑ **Integrate ecommerce finances with existing book-keeping systems.**

☑ **Manage photos for each product or service.**

☑ **Manage data for products or services in a database.**

☑ **Manage customer information or related ecommerce information in a database.**

☑ **Manage and administer downloadable products that may be accessed only after purchase.**

For example, customers might purchase software, photos, music, ebooks, articles, or other products, after which they'd be able to download them via a secure, password-protected area.

Features to Seek in a Shopping Cart Program

Use the following checklist to assess whether a shopping cart program meets the ecommerce content usage and management needs you identified using the checklist above, and provides any additional features you require.

Checklist A.2

☑ **Automated, customizable sales tax calculation facilities.**

Examples include sales tax according to the customer's state, county, and country, and customized sales tax according to your specifications.

☑ **Automated, customizable shipping cost calculation facilities.**

Shipping options you might want to consider include overnight delivery, ground delivery, and choice of specific carriers; shipping by location, including international shipping; shipping by weight, quantity, or dollar amount; and a shipping calculator that allows customers to estimate shipping cost options.

☑ **Automated, customizable choice of payment methods, and the acceptance of online payments.**

Payment options should include the ability to pay online by credit card, PayPal, check, and other online options; pay by fax; pay by phone; pay by postal mail; or pay by COD (cash on delivery).

☑ **Integration with online credit card payments, including real-time credit card payment verification.**

☑ **Integration with your existing book-keeping systems.**

☑ **Seamless PayPal integration.**

☑ **Automated, personalized email order confirmations, shipping status and confirmations, and other automated order-related correspondence.**

☑ **Automated production of personalized, printable receipts.**

☑ **Automated customer follow-up and tracking.**

☑ **Display of a shopping cart order confirmation page prior to purchase finalization.**

☑ **"Remove" feature for customers to remove one, several, or all items from the shopping cart.**

☑ **Shopping cart summary to show products in customer's cart as the customer continues to shop.**

☑ **Option to change the quantities of each product ordered on the confirmation page, and recalculate costs accordingly.**

☑ **Option to show prices with and without local taxes.**

Examples include GST, VAT, county or state tax.

☑ **Customizable product search.**

For example, include the ability to search for products by price, description, popularity, availability.

☑ **Flexibility to use the software with your existing products database.**

If they aren't compatible, make sure there are easy-to-use tools to let you port your existing data quickly to the new system without any loss. Remember to run backups before you perform any conversions!

Buyer Beware!

If the new system you're considering is proprietary and incompatible with common database formats, seriously consider another system!

☑ **Standards-based integration and customization to blend with your web site design.**

☑ **Customizable product display in your online store.**

☑ **Customizable directory names.**

☑ **Customizable, search engine-friendly, human-friendly filenames and URLs.**

☑ **Ease in adding or changing product attributes, including pricing, photos, descriptions, and other details.**

☑ **Ability to remove products from the store temporarily.**

Customizable pricing.

You may wish to display sale pricing by quantity, date, item, code, and discount pricing, such as by using a code or coupon.

Customizable minimum and maximum quantities or units, and the ability to hide this feature if it's not applicable.

Automated product inventory tracking.

You might want to have the ability to hide products automatically based on your inventory. You might also want to set customized automatic messages, such as "Only 3 left in stock," and the ability to provide information about when out-of-stock items will be back in stock.

Ability to import and export all data and reports.

Limitless number of items or products.

Manual order processing.

This feature is especially necessary for orders received by phone, fax, or postal mail.

Customizable product download details.

You might need time-sensitive options, personalized download facilities, a premium support area, bundling options, download monitoring and tracking facilities to prevent abuse, definable file-type options, and support for multiple versions of a product.

Index

Symbols

&, XHTML, 162

A

accessibility testing, 268–273
  browsers, 272–273
  forms, 273
  JavaScript, 272
  navigation, 273
  plugins, 272
  tables, 272
accessible web sites, 173–197
alignment, design, 240
alt attribute, XHTML, 161–162
ampersand, XHTML, 162
anchor pseudo-class rules, CSS, 164
animations, 187
archiving, 292–294

B

backing-up
  automated processes, 43
  checking, 285–286
  maintenance, 302–303
  post-launch follow-up, 298
banning by search engines, SEO, 228–229
best practices/standards
  coding, 147–171
  CSS, 163–170
  learning from, 9
  markup, 148–159
  XHTML, 159–163
bookmarking, web site usability, 67–68
borders, CSS, 163–164
brainstorming, design, 250–253

brand protection
  domain names, 21–22
branding, consistency, 26
broken content, internal page navigation, 139
browsers
  accessibility testing, 271–273
  problems, CSS, 166–167
  testing, 261–263
  web site usability, 70–72, 126–127
budgets/budgeting, 21–32
bug tracking/fixing
  post-launch follow-up, 296
  testing, 259–260

C

cache clearing, testing, 266
calendar, keyphrases, SEO, 236
Cascading Style Sheets (CSS)
  anchor pseudo-class rules, 164
  best practices/standards, 163–170
  browser problems, 166–167
  optimizing, 205–211
  SEO, 226
case studies, learning from, 6
CGI (*see* Common Gateway Interface)
changing over time, 4–5
checking
  (*see also* errors; launch preparation)
  automated software, 284–285
  fresh eyes, 283
  functionality, 284–285
  legal issues, 284
  licensing, 309–310
  links, 236, 284–285
  optimizing, 282
  orphaned pages, 310
  PDF files, 285
  search features, 309

Books for Web Developers
from SitePoint

Visit http://www.sitepoint.com/books/
for sample chapters or to order!

BUILD YOUR OWN
WEB SITE
THE RIGHT WAY
USING
HTML & CSS
BY IAN LLOYD

HTML UTOPIA:
DESIGNING
WITHOUT
TABLES
USING CSS

BY RACHEL ANDREW
& DAN SHAFER

THE ULTIMATE BEGINNER'S GUIDE TO CSS

THE CSS ANTHOLOGY

101 ESSENTIAL TIPS, TRICKS & HACKS

BY RACHEL ANDREW

THE MOST COMPLETE QUESTION AND ANSWER BOOK ON CSS

DHTML UTOPIA:
MODERN
WEB DESIGN
USING
JAVASCRIPT & DOM

BY STUART LANGRIDGE

PRACTICAL UNOBTRUSIVE JAVASCRIPT TECHNIQUES

THE
JAVASCRIPT
ANTHOLOGY

101 ESSENTIAL TIPS, TRICKS & HACKS

BY JAMES EDWARDS
& CAMERON ADAMS

THE MOST COMPLETE QUESTION AND ANSWER BOOK ON JAVASCRIPT

BUILD YOUR OWN
AJAX WEB
APPLICATIONS

BY MATTHEW EERNISSE

LEARN TO BUILD SLICK, INTERACTIVE WEB SITES

BUILD YOUR OWN
STANDARDS
COMPLIANT
WEBSITE
USING
DREAMWEAVER 8

BY RACHEL ANDREW

A PRACTICAL STEP-BY-STEP GUIDE TO MASTERING DREAMWEAVER 8

3rd Edition
Covers PHP5, MySQL4 and Mac OS X

Build Your Own

Database Driven Website
Using PHP & MySQL

By Kevin Yank

A Practical Step-by-Step Guide

NO NONSENSE
XML WEB DEVELOPMENT
WITH PHP
BY **THOMAS MYER**

MASTER PHP 5'S POWERFUL NEW XML FUNCTIONALITY

RUN YOUR OWN
WEB SERVER
USING
LINUX & APACHE

BY **STUART LANGRIDGE**
& TONY STEIDLER-DENNISON

GET STARTED WITH LINUX AND APACHE — THE EASY WAY!

Kits for Web Professionals
from SitePoint

Available exclusively from
http://www.sitepoint.com/

BUILD YOUR OWN
ASP.NET
WEBSITE
USING
C# & VB.NET
BY ZAK RUVALCABA

THE ULTIMATE ASP.NET BEGINNER'S GUIDE